France and Panama

American University Studies

Series IX
History

Vol. 50

PETER LANG
New York • Bern • Frankfurt am Main • Paris

James M. Skinner

France and Panama

The Unknown Years, 1894-1908

PETER LANG

New York • Bern • Frankfurt am Main • Paris

Library of Congress Cataloging-in-Publication Data

Skinner, James M.
   France and Panama : the unknown years, 1894-1908 /
James M. Skinner.
      p. cm. – (American university studies. Series IX,
History ; vol. 50)
    Bibliography: p.
    1. Compagnie nouvelle du canal de Panama –
History. I. Title. II. Series.
HE537.4.S65   1989   386',444 – dc19   88-23656
ISBN 0-8204-0822-0   CIP
ISSN 0740-0462

CIP-Titelaufnahme der Deutschen Bibliothek

Skinner, James M.:
France and Panama : the unknown years, 1894–
1908 / James M. Skinner. – New York; Bern;
Frankfurt am Main; Paris: Lang, 1988.
  (American University Studies: Ser. 9,
  History; Vol. 50)
  ISBN 0-8204-0822-0

NE: American University Studies / 09

Printed by Weihert-Druck GmbH, Darmstadt, West Germany

TABLE OF

CONTENTS

Acknowledgements

Whilst engaged on this work, I received a great deal of help, and I welcome this opportunity to make formal acknowledgement of it.

I am particularly grateful to Professor Jean Bouvier for suggesting the theme as an alternative to the well-worn furrow that is the de Lesseps endeavour that preceded it. I also owe a debt of gratitude to several of my colleagues at Brandon University. In particular, I wish to thank Professor Henri Francq and Mr. Terry Mitchell of the Arts and Science Library who were good enough to give of their valuable time to guide me through some of the more perplexing intricacies of French commercial terminology. Mrs. T.F. Gonzales also gave assistance with the translation of Spanish sources, and she and her staff ensured that I had a steady flow of material from many North American sources. From Dr. Hardee Allen and Mr. Edward Anthony of the Federal Records Center in Suitland, Maryland, I received a personal service which the researcher dreams about but seldom finds. My debts of gratitude to the staffs of the National Archives and the Library of Congress in Washington, the Bibliotheque Nationale, the Archives Nationales and the Credit Lyonnais in Paris will be obvious to all who have had the privilege of working there. I am also indebted to Dr. Charles Ameringer of Pennsylvania State University who placed his advice and vast knowledge of Panama at my disposal. Finally, I owe a very great deal to Dr. Maurice Larkin of Edinburgh University, Scotland. During the gestation period he was an unfailing source of kindness, help and encouragement.

This manuscript was patiently assembled by members of the Brandon University Arts Faculty typing pool who bore the experience with cheerfulness and optimism.

James M. Skinner,
Brandon, Manitoba
1988.

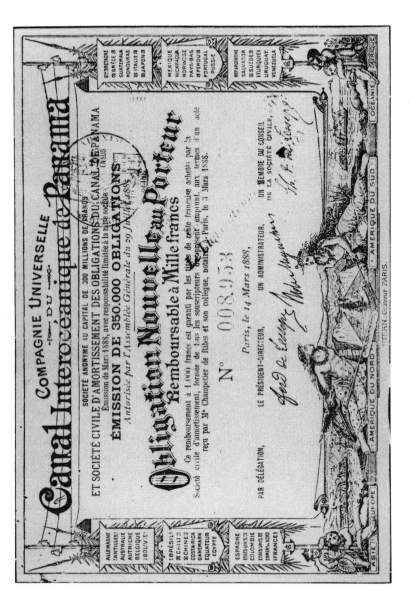

1888 lottery bond of the Compagnie Universelle

Introduction

It is said that bygone scandals, no less than major disasters, make the best subjects for popular history. The historian's scalpel has certainly been wielded with expert skill on Ferdinand de Lesseps's valiant but vain attempt to build a Panama Canal. Books issue from the presses at regular intervals recounting for yet another generation the catalogue of disasters that left the victor of Suez a broken, old man when once he had been a hero to his countrymen. For a time, Panama became synonymous with corruption in French lexigraphy. Yet, as one scholar of the events has observed:

> There remains a lacuna in everything that has so far been written ... that concerns the second company of Panama, the Company called New which, in 1894, replaced the first which had been liquidated by court order at the beginning of 1889. Its internal history has not yet been written.... [1]

One does not have to search far to discover explanations for the neglect of this second company – La Compagnie Nouvelle du Canal de Panama. For the popularizer, the cataclysmic failure of its predecessor and the drama attached thereto have an obvious fascination and a ready readership. Lodged in time between this, the vainly heroic French venture, and the triumphant achievement of the United States,

the New Panama Canal Company has inevitably languished
in the shadows, meriting no more than a few lines in most
narratives of transisthmian projects.² The professional historian has been faced with another, not unfamiliar problem
– lack of *prima facie* evidence for some vital developments
that occurred during the brief life of this little-known concern. This will be examined in more detail in a subsequent
part of the chapter. For the moment, suffice it to say that,
while few historical topics lend themselves to easy investigation, the task of charting the life span of the Compagnie
Nouvelle is rendered particularly difficult by the paucity and
discontinuity of primary material, most of which has become
available only within the past twenty-five years. It might
also be added that the task is made no easier by its disper-
sal in three, widely separated locations – Paris, Washington,
D.C. and the Canal Zone.

When the Compagnie Nouvelle du Canal de Panama has
attracted attention, it has been largely that of North American writers who have tended to regard it, perhaps not un-
fairly, as an insignificant prelude to the considerable achievement of the Americans. The majority of studies concerned
with the physical task of completing the canal emanating
from the United States has stressed the era that began when
the last Frenchman departed the Isthmus of Panama. Space
has been devoted to the second company only when incidents
or developments associated with it have led causally in that
direction, and, in particular, the Panamanian Revolution of
1903. Even in lengthier works which tackle the entire span
of transisthmian projects, from the days of Charles V of
Spain to the present, it has received but a cursory glance.
The tendency has been to wedge it, insignificantly, between
the colossal tragedy of the Compagnie Universelle and the
solid inevitability of the American enterprise. And yet, as
Dr. Allen Nevins suggested in his diplomatic study of the

period, this "remarkable adventure story in politics and high finance" does not deserve to languish in obscurity.[3]

If this little-known corporation is really more than a mere chronological footnote to French disaster and American success, the fact is worth investigation. If the task proves worthwhile, it cannot then be maintained that nothing of import occurred between 1888, when disaster struck de Lesseps, and May 1904 when the Stars and Stripes were first hoisted in the newly-created Canal Zone. The New Company will emerge as a vital link between the two events, maintaining continuity as well as continuing the work started by the French in order to bequeath a more substantial project to the United States.

The story of its brief, fourteen year existence might have been written exclusively from the standpoint of commercial, business history. It was felt that this approach would be unsatisfactory because the political ramifications of the concern were every bit as important as the financial. Because it played a crucial role in the economy of the host country, Colombia, its fortunes became entwined with the vicissitudes of the Colombian government. The time span covered in this study is one which saw France relinquish her last political-cum-economic foothold on the mainland of the North American continent. An epoch had begun with Jacques Cartier and the fishermen and fur traders of New France in the sixteenth century. It had reached its zenith on the eve of the Seven Years' War when French influence predominated from Northern Quebec to the Gulf of Mexico. Thereafter it swiftly declined, reaching a rather melancholy end on the Panamanian Isthmus. On the morning of May 5, 1904, the physical delivery of the canal works was made by a Compagnie Nouvelle representative, Renaudin, to Lieutenant Mark Brooke of the United States army. By then, French investment was pouring into what then appeared to be more attractive fields, politically and economically – Tsarist Russia, North Africa and Southeast Asia. Lack of interest in Central America and the Caribbean was well enough advanced to render France's remaining possessions there as picturesque, tourist backwaters. As the last vestiges of her prestige vanished from the mainland, the United States filled the void. Nowhere is America's sudden rise to world power status more dramatically manifested than in her canal politics. The older maritime powers, of which Britain was still the most important, had taken it for granted that the waterway, begun in 1881, would retain its same, privately-owned format, under the New Company. The assumption held that the owners would be a commercial enterprise, operating on the same principles as de Lesseps's other endeavor at Suez. It was also assumed that it would be 'neutralized' and 'unfortified' as stipulated by the Convention of Constantinople of October 19, 1888, to which the major powers had affixed their signatures.

This was not to be. The reason lay in the American government's decision to have complete control over an Isthmian canal, and the steps it took between 1898 and 1903 to achieve that end. One consequence was the permanent alteration of the balance of power in the Caribbean. Britain reluctantly accepted the new equilibrium as the new century dawned, partly because of the special relationship existing between herself and the U.S.A., and partly because she had more pressing commitments elsewhere. France made even less of an objection. Franco-American relations had gradually recovered from the nadir into which they had sunk at the time of the Maximilian venture in the mid-1860's, and they were extremely cordial by the turn of the century. Delcassé, for one, had no wish to see the trend reversed for, in common with most politicians of the era, he regarded the New Panama Canal Company not as an instrument by which the *génie des Français* could be redeemed, but rather as an embarrassing memento of past indiscretions for the Third Republic. As such, it should be abandoned or, at best, used as a counter in the game of international relations. If there was a possibility that France could enlist American support for her expansionist policies in Morocco and elsewhere, the chance ought to be seized. If it could be aided, further, by facilitating the U.S. claim to Panama, it was a small price to pay for the loss of prestige.

This ready acquiescence of French ministers in the canal diplomacy of a friendly government goes some way to explaining the inflexible attitude adopted by Presidents McKinley and Theodore Roosevelt in their dealings with the Company. From the outset, they held all the best cards, including the ace – the threat to build elsewhere. Further, secure in the knowledge that the French negotiators who came to Washington could not count on the unswerving support of their own government, they were able to dictate most of the terms. Having made an initial offer of forty million dollars for the property, the Americans refused to increase it by a cent, even though three years were to elapse between the time the offer was made and the deal was finally concluded. In the face of such intransigence, those with a vested interest in the Compagnie Nouvelle could only strive to ensure that the money from the U.S. Treasury would be preserved from the depredation of others.

In this regard, the threat came primarily from the Republic of Colombia. A number of determined men in Paris and Washington were insistent that that nation's claim on New Company assets would be denied. The methods they employed to thwart it had a consequence beyond their imagining. The United States was induced to intervene in (or, some would maintain, become a party to) a plot to 'save' the French investment and in a manner particularly offen-

sive to Colombian sentiment. The result was the creation
of a new, independent state in Central America from the
former Department of Panama. It is no exaggeration to say
that, but for the existence of the second Panama Canal Company, the future development of this part of Central America
would have been different. The American authorities would
have turned to the best alternative site in Nicaragua where,
in those days, its presence was more acceptable. There it
could have built a perfectly acceptable waterway, with only
slightly more effort in terms of time and money.

The impact of this insignificant corporation on the future of three nations, Colombia, Panama and the United
States is surely a phenomenon worth tracing from its origins. The issue of Panamanian independence, for example
had repercussions far beyond the strictly defined issue of its
separation from the federal state. Colombian resentment of
what it regarded as Yankee imperialism proved contagious.
The people of Panama, too, came to realize that the creation
of their tiny country had been but a means to an end, once
the first flush of enthusiasm for independence had subsided.
The territorial concessions which the founding fathers had
been induced to sign over to the United States in return for
a miserly financial return were appreciably greater than any
nation had a right to allow. What excited indignation even
more was the realization that those rights had been signed
away by an ex-employee of the de Lesseps company and a
stockholder in its successor. The economic interests of a foreign corporation had taken precedence over the aspirations
of the native population. It was a refrain that was to be
rehearsed many times thereafter in Latin American politics.
As late as 1977, anger at what had been done in 1903 was
still strong. On the question of Panamanian sovereignty over
the Canal Zone, the U.S. ambassador to Panama had this
to say:

> This is an issue – probably the only issue – which
> brings Panamanians together in a kind of national
> unanimity that is rare in history... Talk with Pana-
> manians. You'll find that whether they are rich or
> poor, city men or campesinas, university gradu-
> ates or day laborers, they are one in their dream
> of a Panama that is unified and sovereign, a coun-
> try that is no longer divided in half by a foreign
> enclave.[4]

If the foregoing gives the impression of a cool, calculat-
ing business enterprise working to a carefully conceived plan,
the picture is misleading. The Compagnie Nouvelle was born
out of chaos, lived a precarious life and expired amid controversy. It was designed as a last-ditch effort to save something of the huge investment that was de Lesseps's company
in which tens of thousands of Frenchmen of modest means
had staked their savings. A number of earnest attempts had
been to reactivate the canal project, abandoned in 1888, before the New Company saw the light of day. These earlier
efforts, appeals to financiers of repute to take the helm, had
failed because the misdemeanors of those associated with
the original concern had been laid bare in parliament and in
the courts during the previous three years. They had made
the very word 'Panama' synonymous with mismanagement,
blackmail and intrigue. The alternative was to abandon the
enterprise. It was seriously considered by the liquidation and
dropped, not so much because of the blow it would have dealt
French pride, but rather because of the sheer impossibility
of apportioning the assets among a legion of creditors, deserving and otherwise. A division at any time prior to 1894
would have meant an infinitesimal return on the original investment for the average creditor. Rather, the answer lay in
a pragmatic, if ignoble, scheme which was to be relentlessly

pursued by the liquidation in the critical months leading up to the New Company's incorporation in October, 1894.

The researcher, working in the tradition of Dansette, de la Batut and Marlio[5] has been apt to ignore the ultimate fate of those who profited unduly from the largesse of the original company. His attention has been focussed on the allegations made against these individuals, their sensational trials, the revelations and, in the majority of cases, their acquittal. The validity of this approach is strengthened by the amount of space devoted to the events of the de Lesseps era by the parliamentary inquiries and press of the day. The appeal of Boulangism, the growth of anti-semitism are linked to those occurrences. Thereafter, the villains and the duped fade from the canvas. The historian of the New Company, on the other hand, must regard the peculiar method of justice meted out to these miscreants, not their alleged crimes, as of prime importance. Their role in the story of Panama does not end when they step from the witness box or give their last deposition before a deputies' committee. They become, for the sake of this narrative, the so-called *pénalitaires*, and their sins are resurrected for a second time by the liquidator and the court-appointed *mandataire* or bondholder's spokesman. To analyze the full role played by these two men would be premature at this stage: but is necessary to emphasize that they were planning to revive the canal enterprise at the very moment when the ex-investors in the de Lesseps fiasco were sunk in gloom as a result of previous attempts. Both in court and in the press the gross errors of the past had been exposed in a highly dramatic manner. The confessions of Charles de Lesseps, of Rouvier and Baihaut, and the suicide (or possible murder!) of Baron de Reinach who had greased so many palms with canal money had seemingly dashed all hope that another spadeful of dirt would ever be removed by a French shovel.

It was as an alternative to this faint-hearted attitude that Gautron, the liquidator, and Lemarquis, the *mandataire*, hit upon a plan to finance a successor to the Compagnie Universelle. The particular ingenuity of their approach lay in the compromise or exit they offered these *pénalitaires*. Rather than make outright restitution of excess profits, they were to be allowed to invest their questionably-gotten gains in the new venture. It was, without a doubt, a face-saving investment, but one which offered a means of escape from further prosecution by a determined duo, as well as holding out a slim chance of future profit. Even so, there continued to be a small but vocal group of creditors who were convinced that a confidence trick had been performed in their name. They considered it monstrous that, the more deeply one had been implicated in the scandal of the old company, the greater would be one's stake in the new. Equally reprehensible, in their eyes, was the decision to allow representatives of the leading credit institutions who had profited from the *syndicats de garantie* of the de Lesseps years to occupy positions of responsibility on the board. Morally, their point had validity. The banks had, indeed, reaped handsome returns for no risk when they had dabbled in the financial dealings of the old company; and while it would be a mistake to regard the directors of the New Company as mere instruments of the will of these large, Parisian-based institutions from whom contributions had been wrung, the influence of such grey eminences as Henri Germain of the Crédit Lyonnais cannot be ignored. There is reason to suspect that New Company policy was influenced, at a crucial point in its brief history, by the dictates of the banking establishment whose power and prestige in the boardroom is incontestable. Nor can it be denied that these malefactors who had been driven to subscribe to the share capital of the new offspring in 1894 emerged with a modest profit fourteen years later.

Yet, those who criticized their influence failed to appreciate that public confidence in Panama was non existent, and was likely to remain so for a long time to come. It was expedient that those who were in a position to contribute should be forced to do so. The chilling fact revealed by the public appeal for funds for the Compagnie Nouvelle in September 1894 was that only six and a half thousand were willing to risk a second gamble on the outcome whereas a quarter of a million had rallied to the first.

Colombia's attitude towards her errant concessionary also helped to dictate policy. The contract on which the enterprise depended was due to expire only a few days after the New Company's formation. Had it been allowed to lapse, resumption of activity on the Isthmus might have been undertaken too late or at a price which would have bankrupted the project at the moment of its birth. This did not happen because of swift work on the part of the New Company, and the second generation of canal builders was hailed as prodigals with past sins forgotten. The Colombian attitude, as will be emphasized on subsequent occasions, was not motivated in the least by compassion. It owed much to the notion that the returning French would bring an inflow of money to a treasury parched as a consequence of civil war and general mismanagement. Equally, it was based on the supposition that, as a major shareholder, Colombia could look forward to a more regular source of revenue once traffic began to flow from sea to sea. Such enthusiasm was understandable. Bogota's isolation was as great politically as it was geographically in that era. Little of the breath of scandal that had astounded or amused French opinion had percolated as far as this remote corner of South America.[6] It was not difficult to be optimistic about the future when the physical means for success were at hand. The newcomers had inherited a concession, a plan, a railroad and a not inconsiderable quantity of excavation. Even if the task of completion was beyond it, the concession could always be sold to another corporation.

The determination of the United States to have a transisthmian waterway under its complete control for strategic reasons did nothing, at least initially, to upset these calculations. The Colombians believed that American *private* enterprise was probably more capable of 'dividing the land and uniting the waters' than the French with their paucity of resources and pennypinching ways. The spectre of intervention by a foreign power was hardly considered. True, there would be another delay until the canal was ready, but this was outweighed by the certainty that the concern would always be under the governmental control of Bogota.

It was not until serious discussion began between the Compagnie Nouvelle and Washington that the host country began to sense potential danger. The failure of a privately-financed concern to make progress in Nicaragua was one ominous portent. The other was the abrogation of the 1850 Clayton-Bulwer Treaty, and its replacement, in 1902, by the Hay-Pauncefote agreement. This meant that Great Britain would no longer have any part to play in decisions affecting canal diplomacy. Joint consultation which had been implicit in the earlier agreement ended. Furthermore, American foreign policy had undergone a swift transformation since the early days of the de Lesseps period on the Isthmus. From being an isolationist power, preoccupied with recovery from the ravages of the Civil War and with westwards expansion into her own, vast interior, the U.S. had developed a taste for empire in the last decade of the century. In most instances, interventionist policies were justified as crusades for the liberty of the oppressed. Yet, whatever the merits of that argument, when applied to Cuba, Puerto Rico or the Philippines, the outcome had appeared to be, more than anything else, a change of master for the liberated. Nor did the utterances of Theodore Roosevelt and like-minded Republicans indicate that America was a satiated power by the start of the twentieth century. Her strategic needs would best be served by a link between the two oceans in which she had the greatest interest. Colombia could only await developments and, on receiving confirmation of the New Company's decision to dispose of its property, feel disquiet. There were perspicacious citizens who concurred with the sentiments expressed in an editorial of Bogota's *El Correo Nacional* on March 17, 1903 that "Yankee control of the canal is a fact which we must accept as the unavoidable basis of all that is about to be projected."

But, if Colombia felt she had to bow to the inevitability of American control, there was surely good reason to justify her demand that the French be forced to donate a goodly proportion of their concession payment from the U.S. to her. The charter under which the Company operated specifically forbade transfer or sale to a foreign state. The price for breaking that clause, as more and more Colombians came to believe, ought to be paid by the concessionary. Had negotiations taken place exclusively in Paris and Bogota, there is a strong possibility that the French would have been driven to make some form of compensation, rather than lose the sale. It was the activities of two astute figures, William Nelson Cromwell and Philippe Bunau-Varilla that decided otherwise.

They were determined, each for his own reason, that there would be no alienation of any part of the forty million dollars coming to the Compagnie Nouvelle. Their device to ensure this dovetailed neatly with the aspirations of the anti-federalists in the Department of Panama and with the impatience of the Roosevelt administration. The Panamanians, for their part, felt that the future was being sacrificed to the greet, myopia or misguided patriotism of the despised *bo-gotanos*: the Republicans in Washington were eager to settle the canal issue before the electorate cast their vote for a new president. With Cromwell strengthening the resolve of Uncle Sam not to make any concessions, and Bunau-Varilla organizing a Panamanian revolution, the stage was set for the creation of a new state. It was triumph for daring, business acumen and gunboat diplomacy. The French got their concession monies undiminished; the United States had its Canal Zone, a thin strip of land ceded in perpetuity by the nascent state of Panama. Roosevelt was later to justify his conduct in these memorable words:

> To talk of Colombia as a responsible Power, to be dealt with as we would deal with Holland or Belgium or Switzerland or Denmark is a mere absurdity. The analogy is with a group of Sicilian or Calabrian bandits; with Villa and Carranza at this moment. You could no more make an agreement with the Colombian rulers than you could nail a currant jelly to the wall – and the failure to nail currant jelly to the wall is not due to the nail, it is due to the currant jelly.[7]

Whatever good faith Colombia ever placed in her powerful northern neighbour was destroyed by this attitude. And, if the New Company did not associate itself officially with these sentiments, it can hardly be denied that it was an accessory after the fact of Panamanian revolution.

*   *   *

Despite the value judgements expressed above, the writer did not undertake this study of a French corporation to point an accusing finger at the currently fashionable targets of business imperialism and ruthless capitalism. While the New Company was implicated in the 1903 revolution, the impartial observer of its history would be open to charges of prejudice if he did not recognize another, more salient, characteristic in the drama. This might be defined as the triumph of the human spirit over adversity. The businessmen and lawyers who guided its fortunes through its fourteen years of existence were faced with a succession of crises, any of which might have spelt total disaster. The sheer physical effort of launching the concern amid a welter of adverse publicity, the challenge posed by the alternative Nicaraguan route, the tergiversations of Colombian politicians and, at the last, the inflexible and rapacious mein of the French treasury when it levied a sizeable impost on the assets – all were met and surmounted because individuals refused to admit defeat. Through their efforts, the creditors of the Compagnie Universelle emerged with something regained when they had every reason to expect nothing from what has rightly described as "the greatest purely financial disaster since the Mississippi scheme nearly 200 years before."[8] History posing as morality is justly derided in our time; but there may well be a need to redress the balance in the writing of its economic and social aspects, as currently practised in the more radical circles of higher learning. If the saga of the New Company *has* a lesson to teach, it is provided by those industrious and resourceful representatives of the much-maligned *haute bourgeoisie* of the Third Republic who turned traumatic defeat into modest, respectable victory.

*   *   *

From the vantage point of the 1980's, it is easy to see that the Panama Canal, this "greatest liberty man has ever taken with nature" as Bryce described it, has proved its worth. After a sluggish beginning because of the contraction in international trade occasioned by the First World War, it rapidly became a major artery among the world's trade routes and, because of its geographical position, it was of unique importance in the economic development of the American continent. Since its opening, in 1914, more than four hundred thousand vessels have made the fifty mile transit, carrying two billion tons of cargo. Without it, Panama would have been a poor country; she is small, possesses few natural resources and has one of the lowest per capita values of export trade of all Latin American nations. Like most Central American states, she is heavily dependent on a single product; but, in her case, that has been the revenues produced by the canal. Nevertheless, this share has been a bone of contention for many years. The Hay-Bunau-Varilla Treaty gave the infant Republic a none too generous annuity of $250,000 per annum. It was not until 1956, with the signing of the Eisenhower-Remon Treaty that it was increased to $1,930,000 which, in real dollars, was less that the U.S.A. paid in 1914.

From a strategic viewpoint, World War Two demonstrated most impressively the strategic importance of the Panama Canal for the United States. As the only allied power able to fight simultaneously and continuously in Europe, North Africa and Asia, she found this link between Atlantic and Pacific theatres invaluable in terms of saving time, manpower and money. The Korean and Vietnam conflicts further underlined its strategic importance as a supply route between the front and the industrial heartland of the nation.

Since the expansion of the economics of Japan and her neighbours in South East Asia, a further boost has been given to the canal. In 1967, for example, a record 12,412 vessels made the journey, of which one third came from the Far East. The casual visitor cannot fail but be impressed by the number of ships flying the Japanese flag. However, the future of the Panama Canal is not totally assured. When planned, its capacity was more than adequate to handle the

largest vessel then afloat, a situation which remained unchanged, with a very few exceptions until the early 1950's.
Since then, the handling capacities of the locks for ships of up
to 50,000 tons has proved insufficient for an ever-increasing
number of supertankers and naval vessels such as aircraft
carriers. Today, more than six hundred ships are unable to
use the canal because of the dimension of the locks. Given
the trend towards super cargo carriers, the figure is likely
to grow substantially. A number of short-term improvements have been made: these include the widening of the
Gaillard Cut, and modifications to the three sets of locks.
Inevitably, though, there is increasing talk of obsolescence
among engineers. The concept of a sea-level waterway – the
de Lesseps dream fulfilled – has been gaining ground. The
proposed route would probably run through the sparsely-
inhabited jungle region of the Darien peninsula to the east
of the present site. For a time, there was talk of using nuclear
devices to excavate another path between the seas though
this has been strongly condemned by environmentalists. The
political situation in this sensitive part of Central America
also gives cause for concern; and there is little doubt that a
new canal would be under the jurisdiction of the host country.

Dominating the immediate future is the 1977 treaty signed
between President Carter and General Torrijos. This controversial piece of legislation will run until December 31, 1999
after which date the Republic of Panama will assume full
control of the Canal and the Canal Zone. What has particularly incensed right wing opinion in the United States is not
only the termination of American control of the waterway,
but the closure of U.S. military bases in the near future
and the undertaking by both sides that neither will make
plans for alternative waterway without consultation with the
other. To many it seems incredible, given her present con-

cerns in Central America, that the United States government should have signed away rights in a part of the hemisphere where the Monroe Doctrine's implementation has been much in evidence.

*   *   *

H.A.L. Fisher once chided social and economic historians that politics, not "laundry bills" were the stuff of great history. He could probably have agreed that balance sheets do not make for memorable history, either. But the most dedicated business historian cannot afford to neglect the political background against which the commercial drama of his choice unfolds. In the present instance, the decision to treat the topic from perspectives other than the strictly commercial had an added advantage in that it increased the size of relevant source material at the author's disposal very considerably.

Even so, there were gaps which it proved impossible to fill, despite an apparent *embarras de richesse* on file in Washington D.C., Suitland, Paris and the Canal Zone. When the sale of the canal was completed, maps, plans and voluminous records were transferred from Paris to the United States, as had been agreed in the contract. However, much important documentation was not surrendered, including personal correspondence of the directors and a detailed statement containing the complete list of New Company stockholders at the time of the liquidation, in 1908. An effort was made to unearth some missing items when a political storm erupted over the Panamanian revolution and the part played by Compagnie Nouvelle personnel. An unnamed investigator, working for the New York *World* reported on a futile expedition he had made to Paris before a House of Representative committee:

I have never known in my lengthy experience of
company matters, any public corporation, much
less one of such vast importance, having so completely disappeared and removed all traces of its
existence as the New Panama Canal Co....So thorough has been its obliteration that only the United
States government can now give information re-
specting the new company's transactions and the
identity of the individuals who created it to effec-
tuate this deal, and who, for reasons best known to
themselves, wiped it off the face of the earth when
the deal was carried through....I consulted French
lawyers, and they declared that there was no machinery, legal or otherwise, by which its records
could be brought to light.[9]

Fortunately, the picture is not completely blank, thanks
to successive liquidators of the Compagnie Universelle who
were kept informed of New Company operators. The major
guide to the records of both is in the Archives Nationales
in Paris. These contain forty-five boxes spanning the period 1876-1908 under the classification 7 AQ. When the
de Lesseps company collapsed, its records were given into
the custody of Brunet, the first liquidator, and thence to
Monchicourt, Gautron and Lemarquis who followed in that
order. From 1893 until his death in 1906, Gautron worked
closely with the *mandataire*, Lemarquis, and the latter assumed the liquidator's office in that year. Their intimate
connection with the Compagnie Nouvelle meant that they
received copies of correspondence with and reports from its
agents in Colombia, Panama and the United States. By
1904, the collection had become so voluminous that Gautron
requested and obtained court permission to destroy thousands of miscellaneous pieces dating from 1880 to 1894.[10]

Similar authorization was granted him two years later when, with the work of the liquidation office more than half completed, he was obliged to quit premises at 180 rue Lafayette for less commodious accommodation.[11] Lemarquis became responsible for the documentation from both companies after 1906. This was stored in his own property at St. Cloud where it remained until 1930 when it was deposited with the Archives Nationales at his request. By then, Lemarquis had become vice-president of the Société Générale and a major figure in French banking circles. The deposit was made with the proviso that none of the contents would be made public until 1950. At the time, Lemarquis confessed that he did not know what had happened to the bulk of material belonging to the New Company, and that most of what he had surrendered was in duplicate copy form. He assumed the originals must have been transferred to the United States by terms of the instrument of conveyance of April 23, 1904. As has already been indicated, this was not the case. Fortunately, much of what is to be found in 7 AQ is in the form of carbon copies of typewritten material, and so its authenticity can be more confidently assumed.

External comment on the various attempts to form a successor to the de Lesseps concern, together with ministerial correspondence on the New Company itself in to be found in F30 394-396. These three boxes are classified under "Projets divers de reconstitution," a somewhat misleading title because the material spans a period from 1890 to 1901 by which time, of course, the New Company was well established. Although there was a close relationship between the Compagnie Nouvelle and the Crédit Lyonnais which lasted until the former's dissolution, in 1908, nothing confidential is to be found in the archives of this major bank. However, much in the way of contemporary comment and opinion can be gleaned from its large collection of press cuttings, arranged in strict chronological order, and drawn mostly from financial newspapers and journals of the era.

The position regarding material in the United States is somewhat more satisfactory. Acting in conformity with the instrument of conveyance referred to earlier, an American commission arrived in Paris in the summer of 1904 and returned to Washington with plans, maps and other technical memorabilia, together with title deeds to lands on the Isthmus. Unfortunately, very little administrative correspondence was included in this consignment from the New Company's headquarters at 7 rue Louis-le-Grand, and, as in the case of sources consulted in Paris, the researcher is forced to trust to the accuracy of typewritten copies.

The records of the two French canal companies that had been amassed in Panama were surrendered to the Americans at the same time. Not all of these have survived, either. When the Canal Zone administration first took possession of the New Company's office building at Galboa, almost half of the inventory was destroyed to gain working space. Further amputations were carried out, for the same reason, at various times between 1905 and 1914. In 1914, the Record Bureau of the Panama Canal, successor to the Isthmian Canal Commission, classified and consolidated the remainder under the heading Record Group 185. This amounts to 208 feet of shelf space. It is further subdivided into sixty-three categories of which the most important are: 1. 'General Matters affecting correspondence with the Paris office' (the American committee first established by the Compagnie Universelle mainly for publicity purposes, and dealing with Nelson and Cromwell and the Colombian government). 2. 'Administrative matters regarding personnel and recruitment of labor'. 18. 'Land matters' of which law suits brought against squatters on company property and counter-suits form the bulk. 37. Panama Railroad Company papers from incorporation in 1849. Since 1967, this consolidated mass of archival material has been located at the Federal Records Center, No. 1, in Suitland, Maryland. The cartographical records, many of which are in a sad state of repair, continue to be in the main building of the National Archives in Washington, D.C.... [12]

The third major location is the Canal Zone, at Balboa Heights which retains a few fiscal and personnel records covering both the French and American periods of construction. As well, there are approximately fifteen hundred glass plate negatives of machinery and excavation sites for the period 1895-1908.

As far as additional manuscript material goes, the researcher finds a disappointing quantity at hand in the nature of private papers. Neither the liquidators nor Lemarquis appear to have left any reminiscences, while the executors of Cromwell's estate have so far refused to allow access to his writings. One collection is available and valuable – that of Philippe Bunau-Varilla. This was presented to the Library of Congress by his son, Etienne, in 1947, and originally comprised about ten thousand items in forty-seven boxes. Smaller additions have been made since, mostly of articles and press clippings by Commander Miles P. Du Val, Jr., Dr. Charles Moore and Mr. R. W. Hebard. Other useful manuscript material in the Library of Congress includes U.S. Department of State Dispatches from Colombia, Vols. 58-60 and Instructions to Colombia, Vol. 10.

The single most important printed source was found to be *U.S. House of Representatives Committee on Foreign Affairs: Hearings of the Rainey Resolution* (Washington, 1913), hereafter referred to by its less cumbersome title, *The Story of Panama*. It is bulky report running to well over 700 pages, and had its origins in a speech delivered by the then ex-president Roosevelt on the Berkeley campus of the University of California on March 23, 1911. There, his boast that he "took the Isthmus, started the canal and then left Congress not to debate the canal but to debate me," gave rise to a storm of partisan protest in Congress and in the press. It was regarded by some as a blatant admission of American complicity in the Panamanian revolution, and it spurred the House Representative from Illinois, Henry T. Rainey, to demand an investigation. The committee heard testimony from a number of witnesses of whom the most important was Cromwell. Though he refused to be drawn on most leading questions, he presented a brief giving a detailed account of his services to the Compagnie Nouvelle, since 1896, and, in particular, his part in the defeat of the rival, Nicaraguan concept.

The technical achievements and plans of the New Panama Canal Company were subjected to exhaustive scrutiny by the Isthmian Canal (or Walker) Commission. The commission's findings, published in 1901, also included correspondence between Maurice Hutin, the Company's first Director-General, and Admiral Walker. The report was first printed as Senate Document No. 54, 57th. Congress, 1st. session, and later, with the addition of maps and diagrams, as Senate Document No. 222, 58th. Congress, 2nd. Session. Unless otherwise stated, the latter is the one quoted throughout. However, it covers only half the period of this study. Estimates of progress on the canal thereafter were given by Walker and consultant engineers, including John Wallace and John Stevens before another U.S. Senate Committee on Interoceanic Canals whose findings are in three volumes, published in 1907, as Senate Document No. 141, 60th. Congress, 2nd. session. Although it must be regarded as a piece of special pleading, the handsomely bound *New Panama Canal Company: Opinions of General Counsel and Documents Showing Title* gives a lucid account of the difficulties involved in framing the New Company's statutes.

It was specially prepared by Cromwell's law firm to impress Congress at a time when the fate of Panama hung in the balance, i.e. 1900-01.

Among printed French sources, the *Rapport fait au nom de la commission d'inquête chargée de faire la lumière sur les allegations portées à la tribune à l'occasion des affaires de Panama* is, as its name suggests, a depository of statements relating to financial irregularities and managerial incompetence which characterized the eight years of the Compagnie Universelle's existence. Its three volumes provided much of the evidence on which the liquidator and *mandataire* made their cases against the *pénalitaires*. A second parliamentary report, in the name of the deputy Valle appeared five years later, in 1898, and was the outcome of a commission's investigation following upon charges made by Arton, one of the most notorious *Panamistes*, in the pay of the original company. Its usefulness in the present context lies in the summary it gives of the liquidation's attempts to force contributions from the guilty parties.

Once the scandals surrounding the Compagnie Universelle had faded from public view, the French press tended to lose interest in the more mundane business of construction by its colourless successor. The affairs of Panama reverted to the business section where they properly belonged. More general interest did revive when the New Company began negotiations with the American government. The fiscal demands of the treasury, to which allusion has already been made, again attracted the attention of financial commentators. *Le Comptant, L'Information and La Vie Financière* devoted considerable space to analyses of the claims of *l'Administration de l'Enregistrement (le fisc)*; and they were unanimous in their expressions of sympathy for the creditors who were directly affected by this unexpected impost. The Colombian press, and in particular

the ultra-nationalist *El Correo Nacional* provide a forceful
if far from neutral expression of popular opinion. In some
ways the Panama *Star and Herald* is the most fascinating.
Not only was the paper the most widely read of all on the
Isthmus by all nationalities because it published in three
languages, Spanish, French and English, but its editor, J.
Gabriel Dubuque, was to play a major part in the events
leading up to the 1903 revolution. It was a spirited, though
not uncritical, adherent to the French cause.

Probably no one wrote more voluminously on the Panama
Canal than Philippe Bunau-Varilla. He had worked for
the de Lesseps company and his autobiographical piece, *De
Panama a Verdun* (subtitled with characteristic lack of modesty "Mes Combats pour la France") and *Panama: la création, la déstruction, la resurrection*, as well as his more
technical works, *Panama, le trafic* and *Comparative Characteristics of Panama* are indispensable for gaining an appre-
ciation of his role in events. Nevertheless, even a superficial
glance at their contents is enough to convince that Bunau-
Varilla was never one to underrate his contribution to a cause
for which, admittedly, he fought longer than anyone. His as-
sertions and theories have to be measured against those of
his contemporaries with which they are often in sharp disagreement.

A chronological method of presentation of this story has
been followed as far as possible. Occasionally, however, because important events occur simultaneously in several locations, the development and outcome of one of them is followed for the sake of clarity. This strictly chronological approach is abandoned in Chapter Four because it was thought
useful to chart the more technical aspects of New Company
history on the Isthmus from beginning to conclusion.

Notes

1. *Les Deux Scandales de Panama* (Paris, 1964), p. 9.

2. The most recent, substantial contribution to Panama Canal historiography is David McCullough, *The Path Between the Seas* (New York, 1979). For an account of de Lesseps's career as canal-builder, see Andre Siegfried, *Suez, Panama et les routes maritimes mondiales* (Paris, 1940 – English edition: Suez and Panama, translated by H. & D. Hemming (London, 1940)), though the author devotes a scant six pages to the New Company. The standard work in French is Andre Dansette, *Les Affaires de Panama* (Paris, 1934) dealing largely with the political scandal. Similarly, Guy de la Batut, *Panama* (Paris, 1931) and Louis Marlio, *La Véritable Histoire de Panama* (Paris, 1932) are concerned exclusively with the Compagnie Universelle. By far the best, single-volume account of Isthmian history from the sixteenth century to the outbreak of World War Two is Gerstle Mack's *The Land Divided* (New York, 1944). Two fairly recent books, Donald Barr Chidsey, *The Panama Canal* (New York, 1970) and Maron J. Simon, *The Panama Affair* (New York, 1971) are readable but make little pretence to deep scholarship.

3. In his foreword to Dwight C. Miner, *The Fight for the Panama Route* (New York, 1940).

4. William J. Jorden, September 29, 1977 quoted in *Panama Canal Treaties: Report of the Committee of Foreign Relations, United States Senate, 95th. Cong., 1st. session* (Washington, 1978).

5. *Op. cit.*

6. Access to Bogota during the entire period under review was by mule train or riverboat. No paved road connected it with other major cities in the country, and the railway from the Pacific coast city of Buenaventura extended only seven miles inland.

7. Quoted in William R. Thayer, *Life and Letters of John Hay* (New York, 1916), Vol. 2, pp. 327-28.

8. D. W. Brogan, *The Development of Modern France* (London, 1940), p. 274.

9. This search is examined in more detail in Appendix C. Quoted in *Story of Panama*, pp. 302-03.

10. *A*(rchives) *N*(ationales) 7 AQ 22, March 1984.

11. *Ibid.*, June 11, 1906.

12. These are included with the American surveys of the site. They comprise 9240 items and are described as *Preliminary Inventory No. 91: Cartographic Records of the Panama Canal* (Washington, 1956).

Chapter 1

The Legacy of the Old Company[1]

The third week of December 1888 witnessed scenes of great confusion along the fifty mile stretch of land on the Isthmus of Panama between Colon on the Atlantic and Panama City on the Pacific side of the coast. There, on the site of a French canal, only partially dug, laborers laid down their tools and ignored the hesitant orders of foremen to return to work. In a few isolated cases violence broke out. In adjacent towns and hamlets banks refused to honour cheques bearing the name Compagnie Universelle du Canal Interocéanique. Contractors made preparations to halt excavation and dismantle machinery. Locomotives and dump trucks were shunted into sidings. Dredges ceased their noisy operations allowing the sounds of the jungle to be heard, undisturbed, for the first time in more than seven years. It was the end of a vision that had been born in Paris, amid scenes of great enthusiasm less than a decade before.

*   *   *

It was not unnatural that the eyes of France should have

turned to Panama in the early years of the Third Republic. The rapid growth of the United States' economy, especially on the west coast, after the gold rush of '49 together with increasing commercial activity between Europe and the Far East had created a demand for a sea route between Atlantic and Pacific that was quicker and less stormy than the Cape Horn passage. Republican Frenchmen reminded themselves that the dead and discredited Second Empire had built the Suez Canal. The new régime, an infinitely finer creation in the eyes of its protagonists, would surpass it. By uniting the seas and dividing the land they would realize a dream as old as the Spanish conquistadors. There were entrepreneurs of other nations who hesitated before the magnitude of the undertaking. Their doubts stemmed from a number of considerations, among them the awful reputation of Central America for disease, and the chronic political instability of the various republics which made investment a risky undertaking.[2] Though it was an exaggeration, it was widely believed that every sleeper on the track of the Panama Railroad, built by the Americans in the 1850's represented a dead laborer. Yet there were those who dismissed all of that as baseless fear, for Frenchmen who still held dear the doctrines of Saint-Simon, social regeneration and universal peace through some great public undertaking could be achieved by France, and it would serve to expiate the shame of Metz, Sedan and Frankfurt in the recently-concluded Franco-Prussian War. If, as Gambetta had declared after the *crise* of May Sixteenth, 1877, the heroic age was over, perhaps the time was opportune for the infant Republic to supplement its moral justification with some material accomplishments.

These somewhat grandiose sentiments obscured very real, practical difficulties in the way of achieving a passage through the Panamanian Isthmus. True, the canal would be only half the length of its Suez counterpart; but whereas the latter traversed flat, semi-desert, a Panama waterway would have to be cut through the Continental Divide in one of the wettest, most swamp-ridden and least healthy parts of the American continent. There was the Chagres River, meandering its way across the narrow neck of land for more than a hundred miles. It could be transformed from a tranquil stream, a few inches in depth, to a raging torrent in a matter of hours. There were malaria-bearing mosquitoes, yellow fever and typhus. What was lacking was a plentiful supply of cheap, docile laborers and a benign ruler close at hand – which had certainly been the case at Suez in Egypt.

None of these arguments could deter Ferdinand de Lesseps, the aging victor of Suez, from attempting to fulfill an ambition. He was, perhaps more than Georges Boulanger, the nearest thing to a popular hero that the early Republic had thrown up. Unlike the general, he was admired by the intelligensia as much as by the populace. Renan had expressed it on his induction into the Academy:

> After Lamartine you have become the most beloved
> man of this century around whom dreams and leg-
> ends have formed.

An equally heartfelt tribute had come from Victor Hugo hearing the news that de Lesseps was considering acceptance of leading a Panama canal company:

> Astound the world with great things that are not
> wars! Does this world have to be conquered? No!
> It is yours, it belongs to civilization. It awaits you.
> Prepare, act, proceed!

For aesthetic reasons, more than anything else, the seventy-five year old victor of Suez was determined to carve another sea-level canal, a second Bosphorus through the

jungle-clad hills of Culebra. This was an error, probably
the most serious of all, but it was not the first. The seeds of
catastrophe had been sown fully two years before when his
name had first been linked with the undertaking. In 1876
the Société Civile Internationale du Canal Interocéanique
du Darien had been formed to explore the region on behalf of the Geographical Society of Paris. Extensive, but,
as it proved, superficial surveying was carried out by one of
its members, Lucien Napoleon-Bonaparte Wyse, an illegit-
imate son of Princess Laetitia Bonaparte. He was assisted
by Lieutenant Armand Reclus of the French navy and Pedro Sosa, an appointee of the Colombian government which
had sovereignty over the region. By February 1878 they had
examined all possible routes save that between Colon and
Panama City. Wyse left his two associates to survey it while
he journeyed to the Colombian capital, Bogota, to secure a
charter sufficiently comprehensive to enable a company to
commence work on this route if it proved feasible.[3] Meanwhile, illness had delayed Reclus's departure for the interior
and it was not until April 2, 1878 that he was fit enough to
leave Panama City. Then, on April 10, Sosa was laid low by
dysentery and was forced to return to the capital. Reclus
continued working on his own until illness again struck, this
time in the form of an ear infection, on April 16. Therefore only two weeks were spent on inspection of the site of
all future French activity. Now, while it is true that earlier
surveys had been made by the Panama Railroad Company,
the requirements for laying a track were obviously different
from those of building a canal. Yet, it was upon this brief
and perfunctory appraisal that the first canal company was
to base its huge enterprise.[4]

The next major error was made at the Congrés Internationale d'études du Canal Interocéanique whose first session
was convened in Paris on 15 May 1879. De Lesseps assumed

the principal role at the outset and found himself supported by the enthusiastic French delegates. He brushed aside the opinions of Godin de Lépinay and Jules Flachat, the only French engineers present who had worked extensively in the Central American tropics. They favored a lock canal to reduce the column of excavation and minimize the risks of subsidence at higher levels. They also recommended the creation of an artificial lake by the damming of the unruly and unpredictable Chagres; but their arguments were dismissed without serious discussion. The atmosphere was one of euphoria as the decision for a sea-level canal was carried by seventy-four votes to eight. All the same, it did not escape the notice of some observers that there were sixteen abstentions and that thirty-eight delegates had departed the conference hall before the final session convened. Of those who voted in the affirmative, only nineteen were engineers and eight of those were involved, in some way, with the Suez company.[5] On July 5, de Lesseps signed an order for the provisional transfer of the concession which Wyse had negotiated with the Colombian government – the so-called Salgar-Wyse concession – to the newly created Compagnie Universelle du Canal Interocéanique, for ten million francs.

Later that same month the first public appeal for capital was made. It was proposed to raise four hundred million francs by offering eighty thousand shares of five hundred francs each. The subscription was not a success with only 60,000 being taken up. The board of directors of the new concern might try to explain this ominous beginning in terms of insufficient press publicity and hard economic times, but the reason lay deeper. Some financiers of repute were convinced that the technical difficulties had been grossly underestimated. Another factor had been ignored: the barely concealed hostility of the United States government. One lesson was learnt for the future: the banks and the press

would have to be courted more assiduously if the tradition-
ally cautious French investor was to be attracted.[6]

Before the next share issue was announced, de Lesseps
visited the United States and Panama. His reception at
the hands of the American press and politicians was polite
and respectful, but their coolness towards his project had
in no way diminished. It was during this journey that de
Lesseps declared excessive the financial estimate given by
the technical committee of the Paris congress. It had put
the cost of the plan at 843,000,000 francs. This he reduced
to 658,000,000, a diminution that was as unwarranted as it
was optimistic. The second appeal for capital was made in
December 1880, but for only half the total requirement of
this revised estimate – 300,000,000 francs – with the remainder to be raised later through bonds. This grave error was
never rectified. Had the full amount been found at this early
date (and there is good reason for supposing that the character of de Lesseps would have been argument enough for
small investors), it would still have been insufficient. As it
happened, repeated appeals had to be made as the decade
progressed. The original investors were dismayed to see their
theoretical share of the profits diminish since they had been
offered much less attractive terms than later subscribers. An
additional, unexpected expense was incurred at the outset
through the need to purchase control of the Panama Railroad Company which, American owned and built, was the
only satisfactory mode of transportation across the Isthmus.
In what has aptly been described as "a real stock exchange
holdup,"[7] ownership changed hands for $25,000,000. In this
way one third of the capital was consumed before a square
metre of earth had been dug.[8]

From this time until the final collapse in December 1888,
the tragedy of Panama was played out on two levels and
in two locales – financial in Paris and constructional on the

Isthmus. The initial contract for complete excavation had been awarded to the Franco-Belgian firm of Couvreux et Hersent which had done sterling work at Suez. As the job was to be executed on a cost-plus basis, no fixed price was publicly stated. However, the press seized on the figure of 512,000,000 that had been casually mentioned by a member of the Couvreux family in an after-dinner speech in Brussels, and no attempt was made to deny it. But within two years Couvreux et Hersent had dissociated themselves from the enterprise on the pretext that a system of employing specialist sub-contractors would be more efficient. In reality, their preliminary surveys had convinced them that the task of excavating to sea level, as the old man wanted, would be a Herculean labor. The company therefore transferred the various tasks to dozens of small firms, few of which had the necessary capital, equipment or expertise. The ensuing difficulties led the directors of the Compagnie Universelle to consider a second change in contracting procedure, late in 1886. This involved hiring six large concerns, *viz.* the American Contracting and Dredging Company (also known as Huerne, Slaven & Co.); Jacob; Artigue Sonderegger et Cie.; Vignaud, Barbaud, Blanleuil et Cie.; the Société des Travaux Publics et Constructions; and Baratoux, Leteiller et Cie.

With the exception of the American concern, the results were disappointing, although it must be admitted, in defence of all six, the natural forces conspired against them. Panama was a real hellhole. Rainfall was heavy at all times on the Atlantic side but it was excessively so in the mid-1880's and caused massive landslides. The proximity of two types of soft soil without any retaining material in between, allowed moisture to seep through and dislodge great masses of earth. At Paraiso, for example, an entire hillside moved into the cut leaving the surface vegetation on it untouched.

Disease was rampant and the origins of malaria were incorrectly diagnosed. For example, to prevent termites eating the legs of wooden beds in the hospitals, these were placed in basins of water which became breeding grounds for the disease-bearing mosquito. One of the chief engineers, Dingler, boasted that Panama was as healthy as France until his entire family was cut down. The three major industries became gambling, prostitution and funeral undertaking. Journalists who visited the scene were bribed to write positive articles on their return.

All but the most sanguine came to realize that a sea-level canal was impossible. Yet, it was not until well into 1887 that de Lesseps gave reluctant approval to the lock idea – and then only as a temporary expedient. To bolster the prestige of the sagging project, France's best known engineer, Alexandre Gustav Eiffel, was brought into the group of contractors. Thereafter, progress was made but slowly and at enormous cost in both money and lives. The original opening date, 1891, had to be abandoned although there was still hope that a partially completed waterway might be open by then for ships of small tonnage engaged in local, coastal trade (as had been the case at Suez). But the world of finance had had enough of M. de Lesseps and his canal. The era of scandal was about to commence.

In financing the venture, the original capital had been raised through two share issues: the remainder was to be obtained by bond issues.[9] Reluctance to invest increased with each flotation. The deeper the Compagnie Universelle sank into trouble, the more lavish were the terms it had to offer – and the heavier the bribes to the press to obtain favorable publicity. Appeals to the French public also fell at a particularly inopportune time. The crash of the Union Générale in 1882 (a Catholic bank created in opposition to the Hugenot-dominated ones), had been followed by a gen-

eral crisis in confidence during which some five billion francs
had been wiped off the value of securities on the Bourse.
Small investors whom de Lesseps had particularly wanted to
court were inevitably the most wary. In fact, the first three
bond issues, dating from 1882, were organized by a financier,
Levy-Cremieux, in concert with syndicates of bankers that
undertook to buy specific numbers of bonds should the general public fail to respond. They were granted options on the
remainder, at discounts ranging from three to fifteen francs
per bond – but with no obligation to buy. In either case,
they lost nothing. The number of those they guaranteed
to purchase was small and, if the demand was slight, the
syndicates merely relinquished their options. A successful
issue, on the other hand, meant that the company had to
pay the agreed discount instead of being able to dispose of all
of them at the nominal rate.[10] The canal company realized
that it had been over-generous and, in an attempt to obtain
a better return in future, its finance committee decided on
independent action for the fourth issue on the Bourse. Unfortunately, speculation and growing unease about the state
of affairs on the Isthmus were enough to guarantee failure.
Only 141,517 of the 362,613 bonds were disposed of. It was
another warning of impending disaster.

The year 1886 also saw the death of Levy-Cremieux and
his replacement by Baron Jacques de Reinach. This flam-
boyant man-about-town was entrusted with several func-
tions: to 'manage' influential senators and deputies in parliament in order to secure their adhesion to future schemes
and to grease the collective palm of the press.[11] Reinach was
soon involved in an operation that was to prove absolutely
ruinous for the company. This concerned the so-called 'syndicats à 2 frs. 50' which guaranteed no purchase of bonds
whatsoever. In exchange for an advance of two francs and
fifty centimes, these syndicates were granted commissions

on the number of bonds they placed. Payment was on a sliding scale of indemnification, and the profits made were huge. On the first of the new series of bonds, dated August 1886, it was 400%; for the second, that of July 1887, it was 300%.

Despite these expedients, financing was always insufficient. Panama continued to swallow money as relentlessly as her jungle devoured sunlight. A desperate expedient was a lottery loan, an idea first mooted in 1885. Although this device had aided the Suez project in its final stages when financing had been difficult, the response of the government to the new initiative had been negative. But 1888 was a year of great crisis for the Third Republic. The spectre of Boulangism was already disconcerting and it would surely grow if the Panamanian enterprise were to flounder through parliament's indifference. Daniel Wilson, the president's son-in-law had been found guilty of trading in state honors, thereby shaking the faith of those who equated the republic with a degree of virtue lacking in a monarchical system. Consequently, a government committee was established to discuss the feasibility of a lottery scheme. It was evenly divided on the merits of the case until one of the deputies, Charles Sans-Leroy, decided in favor. A positive vote in both chambers of the Assembly gave the hard-pressed company what it sought but, *ipso facto*, the methods which had been used to endure success made it inevitable that, if the truth became known, a scandal would ensue. The lottery loan was floated in June for the purpose of raising another 720,000,000 francs of which 120,000,000 would be invested in guaranteed government stocks for amortization and payment of prizes. The fund was to be administered by an independent *Societe Civile pour l'amortissement des obligations à lots.*[12]

Four days before the offer was due to close, false stories were circulated of de Lesseps's death. These certainly damaged its chance of success but they were by no means the only or even the chief reason for failure. The plight of the Compagnie Universelle was gradually becoming common knowledge despite the biased stories in the press and the continuing optimism of the company's own newspaper, the *Bulletin du Canal Interocéanique*, a *moniteur des chimères* as it was dubbed by cynics. And so, of the two million bonds put on sale, less than 850,000 were taken up before the issue closed. On November 29, 1888 a determined effort, an émission d'agonie was made to try and dispose of the remainder, with the proviso that, if less than one third were subscribed, they would all be withdrawn. By the closing date, December 12, fewer than 200,000 had been disposed of. The end of the canal company could not be much longer delayed.

As a result of this unhappy situation, the Minister of Finance, Paul-Louis Peytral, introduced a measure in the Chamber of Deputies two days later requesting a three month moratorium on all company debts and interest payments. Exception was made of the bond issues of March and June of that year for which independent funding had been provided. After heated debate in which the Boulangists, in particular, sought to embarrass the government, it was decided to form a committee of twenty-two deputies to investigate the situation. In its report, Jumel, the chairman, gave three reasons why the moratorium should not be allowed. There were, in the first place, no grounds for supposing that a delay would see any amelioration of the company's perilous fiscal state; secondly, a cessation of payments would discriminate against contractors, entrepreneurs and employees; and thirdly, the government ought not to embroil itself in the fate of a private corporation operating in a foreign country over which France had no jurisdiction. The outcome was that the Chamber voted by 262 to 188 to reject

the request, despite Peytral's protest.[13] This was the proverbial last straw. That same afternoon the Tribunal Civil of
the Seine declared the official bankruptcy of the Compagnie
Universelle and three receivers were immediately appointed
– Denormandie, Baudelot and Hué.

Ironically, they were immediately forced to take the very
steps the Chamber had refused the company. An instant
and indefinite suspension of payment of interest on securities was ordered while authorities in Panama were assured
that cheques in the company's name and other items charged
to current account would be honoured by Paris.[14] To present
a complete stoppage of work on the site, a series of hastily
made arrangements were concluded with five of the seven
contractors whereby each undertook to continue working until February 15, 1889, at the earliest.[15] Some 33,500 shares of
the Panama Railroad Company stood as collateral, and payment was made in ninety day notes. Then, in order to obtain
new financial backing, the three receivers met with Albert
Christophle, governor of the Crédit Foncier, of whom the
Parisian correspondent of the *New York Tribune* had once
written:

> ...although numerous banks here, allured by the
> prospect of gain, have lent themselves to the scheme
> (of the canal company), some men of high stand-
> ing, like M. Christophle, and the Rothschilds re-
> fused to allow their counters to be used for such a
> flytrap.[16]

For all his sympathy for de Lesseps and his failed scheme,
Christophle refused to commit his bank. The best he could
suggest was that he might underwrite in whole or in part
the costs of forming a Société d'études pour l'achèvement
du canal, to a maximum of two million francs. This suggestion the receivers dismissed out of hand as totally unrealistic

observing that, in its heyday, the company was disbursing twenty-five million a month, and that the paltry sum he was suggesting would not even cover the wage bill of the twelve thousand workers on the Isthmus anxiously awaiting developments. What was required was a pledge of such magnitude as to enable digging to continue at a maximum rate while an appraisal of the situation was made. This offer was consequently rejected.[17]

This left the way open for one last, desperate gambit by de Lesseps himself. With the assent of the receivers he tried to launch a new company – la Compagnie Universelle pour l'Achèvement du Canal Interocéanique. Six hundred thousand 500 franc shares would provide its initial capital, bearing an initial yield of five per cent which was to rise to sixteen when the canal was finally open to sea-going traffic.[18] As Mack has observed, since eighty per cent of those purely hypothetical profits were already allocated to existing stockholders of the original company, all dividends owing to the new investors would have to come from the remaining twenty per cent which had been earmarked for founders and directors in the original statutes of incorporation.[19] In the event, the problem was merely academic. When the offer closed on February 2, 1889, slightly less than one and a half per cent of the securities had been subscribed. Two days later, the Tribunal Civil declared the dissolution of the Compagnie Universelle and appointed as permanent liquidator Joseph Brunet, a former minister of public works in Broglie's cabinet. Brunet's unenviable task of attempting to bring order out of the chaos of the previous eight years was to consume his energy and ruin his health. Within a year he was dead. His successor, Achille Monchicourt, was also to find it beyond his capacity, and death claimed him three years later, in 1892.

By the same court decree, Brunet was given broad pow-

ers to transfer or contribute the remaining assets to any
new concern which he might succeed in establishing. Besides the unmortgaged P.R.C. shares there were the unsold
bonds from the June issue of the previous year numbering
some 1,150,751, with a face value of over 400,000,000 francs.
Not even the most partisan of Panamists could bring themselves to believe that an offer to the French public would
now realize anything approaching this figure, but working
capital had to be found somehow, and quickly if the concession were not to revert to the Colombian government. A
law was hastily rushed through the Assembly in July 1889
enabling Brunet to negotiate the totality of these lottery
bonds without restriction as to price, and without payment
of interest. Sums accruing from their sale were to be non-
distrainable to a maximum of 34,000,000 francs. This was
doubly necessary since the courts had confirmed the civil
character of the Compagnie Universelle earlier in the year
and declared that holders of unencumbered bonds had the
right to cease payment on any uncollected sums. Indeed, the
degree of confidence in Panama had evaporated to a point
where Brunet's endeavors were to be completely in vain. He
was able to obtain only ninety-five francs per bond and disposed of only 357,699 of them. With sixty francs of each
going to the Société Civile for prize money and administrative fees, the liquidator was left with a mere 12,543,184
francs.

As was to be expected, the creation of a new canal company necessitated a study of the situation on the Isthmus
from the viewpoint of work completed, relations with the
Colombian government and future plans. The task of making such a report was entrusted to a commission of eleven
prominent engineers under the chairmanship of Henri Guillemain, director of the prestigious Ecole Nationale des Ponts
et Chaussées. Its report was duly presented to the liquida-

tor's office in May, 1890 just two months after Brunet's resignation for health reasons.[20] It dealt a death blow to de Lesseps's original idea of a sea level canal which was deemed too costly. The Commission argued that this concept would not attract extra traffic while construction costs would be more than three times as great as for a lock equivalent. It would also be beyond the ability of any private concern to pay interest on the capital. To raise the necessary capital, a new company was facing a figure in excess of three billion francs. By contrast, the price of a lock substitute was put at nine hundred million. With the revised plan realized, completion should take no more than eight or nine years, provided that wars or revolutions (always a strong possibility in that part of the globe) did not occur and provided that the labor force which had rapidly disintegrated since 1888 could be reassembled and maintained at its original strength. France could have its canal open for business before the twentieth century dawned.

The calamity that had befallen the de Lesseps company raised another, unexpected problem – that of the fate of the 1878 concession. By its terms, a canal had to be open and operating within twelve years of the company's incorporation – which put the expiry date at March 3, 1893. Under the existing circumstances, even the extra year's extension (which the agreement permitted) would be of little value. It was clear that a new understanding would have to be arrived at when and if work was resumed. Therefore, Monchicourt, the new liquidator, asked Wyse to return to Bogota to negotiate a ten year prolongation. The approach soothed Wyse who had been smarting under a grievance for some considerable time. He had confidently expected to play a major role in the affairs of the Compagnie Universelle, but had been ignored since he performed his major service, in 1879. He responded most readily to the letter of reappointment and was on the Isthmus within a month of receiving it.[21]

His first call was on the ailing but influential ex-President Rafael Nunez in Cartagena to enlist his moral support in the forthcoming discussions. Nunez complied only too readily by writing a number of articles in his own newspaper, *El Porvenir* in which he lavished extravagant praise on the renewed French endeavor. Unfortunately, this somewhat heavy-handed manoeuvre encouraged the Colombian government to conclude that Wyse was an agent of the French state, with unlimited money at his disposal. From there, it concluded that, with a bottomless purse, the Republic's government would offer it a lucrative settlement. The acting president, Carlos Holguin, and his foreign minister, Antonio Roldan, were eager to conclude a deal, even after Wyse made the truth known; but the Bogota press and the Colombian congress were more exacting in their demands. A provisional understanding which Holguin and Wyse had reached on August 11, 1890 had to be shelved when the attitude of the assembly became known. After four fruitless months of discussion between the two sides, Congress produced a list of eighteen demands on November 15. Wyse rejected fourteen of them out of hand, and submitted counter-claims on behalf of the defunct company, totalling twenty-five million francs, some of which, as he later admitted, were rather dubious.[22]

Deadlock was broken only by the initiative of a group of Panamanian citizens – including Amador, Peralta and Arango, all of whom were destined to play leading roles in the future independence struggle. Their anxiety was well-founded. Because of her avaricious attitude, Colombia might obtain nothing, and the canal might be built elsewhere, perhaps in Nicaragua where serious surveys were already being undertaken by American interests. The intervention of these men brought matters to a head. Wyse might well have held out for more advantageous terms had not Holguin threatened to prorogue the Congress until the following spring. At the same time, Roldan pressured the legislators to lower their demands. Finally, a draft treaty was framed, passed both houses in the third week of December and received presidential approval on December 26.

From the French viewpoint, the Roldan-Wyse agreement was not an ungenerous one. A ten year extension was granted, commencing on March 3, 1893 with the rider that a new canal company would commence excavations no later than February 23 of the following year. In return, the liquidation undertook to pay the Colombian government ten million francs in gold, and a further five million in the stock of the new company. This involved the Colombians far more intimately in the affairs of canal policy than had been the case in the days of de Lesseps. If it proved impossible to revive the enterprise within the time specified, the canal concession and all fixed and moveable property was to revert to the Bogota government, without compensation. In all other respects, the 1878 entente would remain in force.[23]

The way now appeared open for the establishment of a successor to the Compagnie Universelle that would restore the prestige France had lost. It was a task that was to occupy the energies of a number of able and determined individuals for the next three and a half years, without respite. Against a background of continuing scandal and recrimination, the fate of France's future on the Isthmus of Panama would hang in the balance.

Notes

1. Accounts of the de Lesseps period are numerous. Dansette's work is a most readable account of the political corruption that dogged it. Bouvier's *Les Deux Scandales de Panama* demonstrates, convincingly, that the rapacity of the financial institutions was as great as that of the press or the politicians. American hostility to the French enterprise is the subject of G.

Edgar-Bonnet's "Ferdinand de Lesseps et les Etats-Unis" in the *Revue d'Histoire Diplomatique*, Vol. IV (1956), pp. 289-322.

2. In the late 1870's a severe economic depression coupled with drought in the mid-West had forced the U.S. government to make a number of economies, including the closure of a number of legations in Latin America. This reflected a general lack of political interest in that part of the continent.

3. *Canal Interocéanique: Rapport sur les études de la Commission Internationale d'Exploration* (Paris, 1879), p. 266. This very important contract was signed by Salgar, the Colombian foreign minister on March 20, 1878, and ratified by the Colombian senate on May 17. It is referred to throughout as the 'Salgar-Wyse concession'.

4. Jose Carlos Rodrugues of the New York *World* commented scath- ingly: "It was necessary to play the comedy of science and M. Wyse plated it...in a most grotesque manner. Eighteen days in Panama were enough for such wonderful geniuses as Commander Reclus and a fifth rate Colombian engineer to clear up the scientific mysteries of the Isthmus...." Quoted in Mack, *op. cit.*, p. 284.

5. *U.S. State Department: Interoceanic Canal Congress held at Paris, May 1879*. Testimony of Menocal, p. 20. Menocal was an official government delegate.

6. Bouvier, *op. cit.*, p. 41 *et seq.*

7. Siegfried, *op. cit.*, (Eng. version), p. 250.

8. 68,534 of the 70,000 shares were bought for $17,133,500. The Company therefore paid $250 per share for a security of $100 par value. A further $7,000,000 had to be spent on its bonds, while its directors received a collective 'bonus' of $1,102,000. Even then, operating control remained firmly in the hands of the board in New York.

9. The December 1880 issue which was oversubscribed by 204.5% was supposed to yield 5% on fully paid up installments during construction. After opening, the canal company would distribute 80% of net profit, divided pro rata. For a complete summary of bond issues, see Appendix B (2).

10. Bouvier, *op. cit.*, p. 107 *et seq.* provides some revealing statistics. On the issues made between 1882 and 1888, the

Crédit Industriel et Commercial made a profit of 1,924,719 francs on options which had cost it only 2,244,919. For the Société Générale, the corresponding figures were 3,407,284 on 4,424,534; and for the Crédit Lyonnais.

11. Flory, an examining magistrate during the 1893 inquiry listed payments of 22,000,000 francs made with Reinach's authorization. These went to individuals, and to journals and newspapers large and small.

12. Credit for the establishment of this separate fund was claimed by Hugo Oberndoerffer who had participated in earlier syndicates. A similar Société Civile was set up for the March 1888 issue, with 70 francs 28 of the 460 issue price set aside for investment in 3% rentes to guarantee amortization. There were no prizes in this instance, of course.

13. *Journal Officiel*, Débats parliamentaires. Chambre des Députés, December 14 and 15, 1888.

14. A.N. 7 AQ 12, 'Procès verbaux des négociations 'suivis par les administrateurs provisoires', December 1888 - January 1889.

15. *Ibid.*, pp. 41-43. Vignaud, Barbaud, Blanleuil et Cie. were excluded because it, too, was bankrupt. The seventh, the Société des Travaux Publics et Constructions had filed six suits against the Compagnie Universelle for non-payments and breach of contract.

16. February 2, 1881.

17. A.N. 7 AQ 12, 'Procès verbaux des négociations', p. 5.

18. *Ibid.*, p. 40.

19. *Op. cit.*, pp. 372-73. At a stockholders' meeting on January 26, de Lesseps admitted that a further 450 million would be needed to complete the revised version of the canal. The major banks refused to sell new securities, and they could be bought only at the Company's offices and the Suez Company office in Paris, and the small Banque Parisienne.

20. A.N. 7 AQ 13, *Commission d'études instituée par le liquidateur de la Compagnie Universelle. Rapport Général*, (Paris, 1890). Brunet's resignation was followed by his death the next January.

21. Wyse's account of his commission is in *Canal Interocéanique de Panama. Mission de 1890-91 en Colombie. Rapport général* (Paris, 1891).

22. *Ibid.*, pp. 11-17. These were for loans and other services rendered by the company between 1882 and 1888.

23. The text of the 1890 document is in Appendix D of the *Mission* (supra).

Chapter 2

Abortive Projects – 1890-93[1]

The years from 1890 until 1893 saw the Panama question debated on two levels. While Monchicourt continued to wrestle with the tangled problem of physically reconstituting the enterprise, three deputies, Jules Delahaye, Albert Gauthier and Auguste Le Provost de Launay, all partisans of General Boulanger, and all animated by a hatred of the existing republic, were preparing to fire the opening salvo in the parliamentary scandal surrounding the canal project. They presented sheaves of petitions emanating from thousands of irate creditors who were demanding to know what steps the government intended to take to rescue them from the debacle.

There was, of course, a drastic solution at hand. The Roldan-Wyse concession could be allowed to lapse, the site could be abandoned, and there would follow a distribution of what assets remained. The liquidator certainly had this thought in mind when he prepared to draft his annual report to the Tribunal Civil de la Seine. Yet, this draconian measure had considerable disadvantages. The magnitude of the sums involved, together with the huge number of investors – over two hundred thousand of them whose aggregate claim approached two thousand million francs – would undoubtedly necessitate some form of comprehensive judicial decision to assure fairness. For this reason, Monchicourt recommended the creation of an agency to protect the interests of these unfortunates – and herein lay the genesis of the idea of a *mandataire*, or bondholders' representative. Acknowledging that this was an exceptional procedure for the government to take on behalf of the creditors of a private concern, Monchicourt nevertheless felt that it was the only way to prevent a situation of *sauve qui peut* from which only those with influence and shrewd legal counsel would emerge fortunate. The alternative was to see the gradual but inexorable dissipation of assets in legal wrangles where the only sure outcome would be least for the most deserving at the end of the day.[2]

Monchicourt's pessimism at this time could be attributed, in large part, to the failure of renewed overtures to Christophle. In addition to a reputation for integrity, Albert Christophle had achieved renown for his surgery on the Crédit Foncier when it had been on the brink of collapse in 1877 following irregularities among its executives. His refusal to become involved in de Lesseps's venture during its last, agonizing months of life had, if anything, added to his prestige. He was, in the words of the Paris correspondent of the *New York Times*, "the financier to whom French thriftiness responds with the most eagerness and the greatest confidence."[3] Monchicourt had remained in touch with him since 1890 but he had continued to decline lending his name to any project of reconstitution unless the government approached him directly.[4] No such approach was made for the very good reason that ominous murmurs over the reasons for the collapse of the Compagnie Universelle were growing louder with every week that passed. The premier, Freycinet, was playing politics assiduously, and its conduct, like that of succeeding administrations, was inspired not by a desire to reactivate the canal company but rather by a determination to keep its reputation unsullied.

As a consequence, when the time came for the liquidator to make another appeal to Christophle, and he did so in a letter that was almost embarrassing in its sycophancy, he had to limit his own contribution to a reference to the moral support which the premier had given.[5] Pressure was also being brought to bear on Monchicourt from bondholders of the defunct company.[6] The longer Monchicourt temporized, the greater grew the tumult. The climax came with the revelations of Ferdinand Martin in *Les Dessors de Panama*. A provincial banker, Martin had been charged with organizing a 'spontaneous' petition of stockholders to the government of the day requesting authorization for a lottery bond issue in 1885. He had quarrelled with de Lesseps over the question of remuneration for his part in this. Now, in September 1892, he penned the first of a series of articles under the pseudonym "Micros" in Edouard Drumont's vitriolic, anti-government *La Libre Parole*. By openly accusing a score of deputies and senators of having sold their votes to suit the old company, he effectively destroyed all hopes Monchicourt had of getting Christophle's co-operation.[7]

The liquidator had not staked all on the governor of the Credit Foncier. On 27 July 1892 *Le Jour* was pleased to announce that he was in contact with a M. Charles Leon Hiélard, vice-president of the Paris Chamber of Commerce. Hiélard, who moved in business circles slightly different from but scarcely less eminent than those of Christophle, was to make all haste to establish a new canal company before the year was out, aided by an advance of a million and a quar-

ter francs from the liquidator. The company was to have a
capital of 180 million francs by offering the public shares at
500 francs each. Of these, 50,000 would be registered in the
name of the Colombian government to meet the terms of the
Roldan-Wyse agreement. Investors in the Compagnie Universelle were to be given the first option to subscribe. Any
further contributions from the assets under Monchicourt's
control – including the unissued lottery bonds from 1888 –
were to be made only when the new company had expended
75 million francs of its own capital. Profits from the completed canal would be divided equally between it and the
liquidation.[8]

If Christophle's aid had been solicited under a threatening sky, Hiélard's participation coincided with the breaking
of the storm. Louis Ricard, the Minister of Justice, could
not ignore the uproar that had followed the publication of
Martin's *Dessous* and he ordered an immediate interrogation
of the major personalities named in them. Those who were
summoned to the office of the *juge d'instruction* as witnesses
more often than not emerged as defendants. While this investigation was in progress, Ricard forbade Monchicourt to
alienate any of the one and a quarter million francs which
he had promised Hiélard in a provisional contract. The
death, by apparent suicide, of Baron Jacques de Reinach
on 20 November was the proverbial last straw. A few days
later Hiélard gave up, confessing that he had grossly underestimated the difficulties of trying to raise capital for a
venture whose name had become synonymous with financial
chicanery.[9]

And whilst the failure of the Hiélard *essai* plunged the victims of the scandal into ever deeper despondency, news from
the Isthmus of Panama was no less disquieting. Monchicourt
had already hinted at the gravity of the situation in a letter to Loubet as early as April. He tried to impress on the

then premier the need for immediate action when only ten
months separated the liquidation from the lapse of the concession granted by the Colombian government.[10] Assistance
could take the form of diplomatic support for his agent in
Panama, Francois Mange, who was about to set out for Bogota to obtain an extension of the 1890 concession. Unques-
tionably, there was an earnest desire on Colombia's part to
accede to Mange's request and so avoid losing the economic
benefits a canal would bring, and this despite the sensational
revelations of fraud, mismanagement and corruption which
were almost daily coming to light in the French capital. Yet,
the possibility that the French might not only fail to reactivate the project but try to reach an understanding with
another foreign interest made Bogota suspicious.

Such thoughts were in the minds of Belisario Porras and
a group of Panamanian businessmen when they circulated
a letter urging that an extension be refused except under
certain guarantees. To critics, including the editor of the
Panama Star and Herald who described their anxiety as, "totally or partially insane",[11] they replied by singling out three
ominous developments which they had observed on the abandoned site – the deterioration of wharves and dredges, the
sale of rolling stock to the Panama Railroad Company, and
the faltering efforts of all concerned to make any progress. If
a syndicate was to be formed, it ought to be in a position to
resume excavation in a serious and permanent manner before the expiry of the Roldan-Wyse agreement and so render
its extension unnecessary. In conclusion, wrote Porras:

We love France as a student can love a school where
he his intellectual training; we love her as the second of our minds. We only detest the forces that,
in great and small, some times find room on our
beloved Thus, we must and do, shout, as the Ro-

mans did: 'caveant consules!'[12]

As a terse expression of their apprehensions, this was admirable: but working against the French presence there was
a baser motive. As soon as the Compagnie Universelle had
ceased operations on the Isthmus, there had been a rush of
squatters to occupy the deserted sites. For them, resusci-
tation would mean certain eviction. If, on the other hand,
activity could not be resumed, the land and everything on it
would provide them with a windfall. Considerable quantities
of equipment lay along the length and breadth of the fifty six
miles between the oceans. These suspicions were reinforced
by the sinister appearance of Carlos Roman in Panama City.
A brother-in-law of the Colombian president, Nunez, he had
his own material ends to seek, and he was to be a thorn in
the flesh of the French for the next five years. He began, in
alarming fashion, by threatening to declare the concession
void because the liquidator had, in his opinion, agreed to
the transfer of a few locomotives to the Panama Railroad
Company. He interpreted this as a contravention of Article
VI of the Roldan-Wyse agreement prohibiting alienation of
assets. Two separate protests, by the French ambassador in
Bogota and Monchicourt's agent in Panama proved effective,
for the moment.[13] However, less than two weeks after this
incident had been settled, a letter in the ultranationalist *El
Porvenir* of Bogota repeated the allegation that the foreigners were selling out to the Yanqui-owned railway under the
noses of the unsuspecting Colombian people.[14] In forwarding
a copy of the article to Monchicourt, Mange pleaded for an
exposure of Roman who, he alleged,

> organizes and leads the campaign against exten-
> sion of the concession despite the cordial assur-
> ances which he never stops giving us every time
> we have an occasion to encounter him.[15]

The independent course of action pursued by the New York-based Panama Railroad Company was an additional headache for the harassed Monchicourt. His efforts to bring this delinquent under stricter control were thwarted by American law. Because the railway company had been chartered in New York City, the board "could have no legal existence beyond the boundaries of the sovereignty in which it was created, must dwell in the place of creation and cannot migrate to another sovereignty."[16] In addition, a majority on its board had to be American citizens. William Nelson Cromwell, a powerful Wall Street lawyer who was to have incalculable influence in the Compagnie Nouvelle, was its principal legal adviser as well as one of its major stockholders. He later alleged that enemies of the P.R.C. carried the battle to Bogota where they urged the president not to grant a new concession.[17]

As if this were not enough to dismay the liquidator, the U.S. Department of State posed another threat to the future of a French presence in Panama. It might be difficult to whip up indignation among the American public when the vast majority considered Panama, if at all, as the graveyard of de Lesseps's hopes. But news that Mange was about to set off for the Colombian capital produced a flurry of diplomatic activity in Washington. John Foster, the Secretary of State instructed Jeremiah Coughlan, his agent in the Colombian capital, to lobby against any renewal of the concession in what was, for the U.S.A., "one of the most important and valuable stretches of territory there is in the world."[18] Mancini commented anxiously on the consequences of successful intervention of this sort. Supporters of the rival route through Nicaragua would be immensely heartened and an Isthmian route there would become a real possibility.[19] Unfortunately, Ribot, the premier to whom this note was addressed, was in no position to take the offensive. His finance minister, Maurice Bouvier, the biggest fish the scandalmongers had hooked to date, was implicating himself in the imbroglio with the indiscreet remark that, in accepting money from the Compagnie Universelle for electoral purposes, he had not seen his personal fortune "grow abnormally".[20] The ministry did not survive that shock, and fell on 10 January 1893. Mange and Mancini realized that they would have to fight for the concession unaided in the Colombian capital.[21]

They had only one ace to play – the promise of hard cash – and they played it in what had become a familiar game for canal negotiators. Nunez had achieved victory in the 1892 presidential election by a use of bribery which was startling even by Colombia's generous standards. His support evaporated rapidly as ministers resigned in protest over the repressive measures he sanctioned to muffle the opposition. With his term in office less than a year old, he could repulse further attacks only by buying off trouble.[22] Menage exploited this weakness. Brushing aside a suggestion from Marco Suarez, the Minister of Foreign Affairs, that an inventory of all company holdings should precede the signing of any new agreement, he countered by inscribing a clause in the draft to the effect that neither property nor moveable assets would be alienated even though a new company had not yet been formed. This sufficed to allay Colombian fears that the liquidation might quietly dispose of the assets and then, having obtained the concession, sell it in turn to a private concern.[23] Two weeks of talks followed, culminating in the signing of the second agreement in three years. Nunez appended his signature to it on 4 April 1893, five weeks to the day after the previous one had expired.

Article I granted the liquidator a ten year period for the completion of a canal, to date from 31 October 1894. The concessionary was given until that date to establish a new company. By the terms of Articles III and IV, Colombia was to receive 12 million francs and an additional 5 million in stock in the new concern. In the event that a resumption of work was not possible by this deadline, everything on the Isthmus would revert to the government. In all other matters, the provisions of the 1878 and 1890 charters were to remain in force.[24]

With the signing of the so-called Suarez-Mancini agreement, the liquidator had committed himself to a deadline for the renewal of construction in Panama. More, he had mortgaged the future of the French endeavor to some combination that did not yet exist. Nothing could have been more calamitous for the future than a Paris court decision on 26 January where twenty-five petitioners were given the right to take action against Monchicourt to recover sums invested in bonds in the Compagnie Universelle. Monchicourt naturally appealled this decision but he did more. He addressed himself to Ribot in a long letter which evidenced both anguish and irritation. His previous warnings had gone unheeded. It was inevitable that a government which was intent on defending its reputation to the exclusion of all else would allow such a situation to develop.[25] This time the *cri d'angoisse* was heeded. Ribot introduced a bill in the Chamber on 20 February and it passed both houses in June.

The 'Law of 1 July 1893' as it is commonly referred to, went far to allay the fears expressed above, but it did far more. It suspended all past and present suits and judgments by creditors of the de Lesseps company, and it appointed a *mandataire* or bondholders' representative who would act on behalf of all the investors.[26] The key to the solution of reactivating the canal company lay in the fourth article of this piece of legislation for it allowed the *mandataire* to act in concert with the liquidator to enforce claims based on the personal liability of the founders and directors of the Compagnie Universelle and others for the restitution of monies "unduly obtained".[27] The clause outlining the powers of the liquidator was also pregnant for the future. He was granted the right to transfer or cede assets to a new venture without fear of civil action.[28] Yet, if this law was welcomed for having plugged a hole in the dyke through which the remaining monies of the liquidator might have been allowed to trickle, it did nothing to advance the creation of a new company. Ever since the failure of his talks with Hiélard and Christophle, Monchicourt had been the target of personal abuse.[29] In failing health, burdened by work and frustrated by the complexities of a situation which had driven his predecessor to a premature grave, he requested an assistant. The court complied by appointing an accountant, Jean-Pierre Gautron who was to shoulder an ever increasing burden until his chief's death in March 1894.

*   *   *

So far had the affairs of Panama progressed, or failed to progress when Edmund Bartissol burst upon the scene. Bartissol's credentials were impressive. He had been an engineer with de Lesseps at Suez and had since supervised the construction of railways in Spain and Portugal. He was now a deputy in the Chamber and his professional expertise had given him a seat on several government commissions concerned with problems of transportation. Bartissol's original concept was to forget the canal altogether and concentrate on the Panama Railroad Company. By expanding its termini, he argued, a larger share of interoceanic and transcontinental traffic would be secured for France in Latin America. Only sixty million francs of capital would be required, and it could be raised by public subscription for which he and his colleagues would assume personal responsibility.

Monchicourt would have none of it. The mandate he held from the court and the Suarez-Mancini accord obliged him to act "solely from the standpoint of creating a company for the completion of a canal." The reaction of the Colombian government to such a proposition would almost certainly be one of outright hostility. However, he did not close the door. Presumably M. Bartissol had substantial financial backing when he mooted the idea. Let him submit a canal proposal and he would not find the liquidation unsympathetic.[30] The alacrity with which Bartissol complied ought to have served as a warning; but, with time running out – it was now October – there was an understandable element of clutching at straws. Furthermore, the new scheme, when revealed, was most encouraging to laymen's eyes.

It was a compromise between the sea level canal, an idea to which Lesseps had stubbornly clung until it was too late, and a canal with a summit only thirty-four meters above sea level which the Guillemin Commission had considered feasible. The major problems of cost and time were to be solved by taming the Chagres river, making part of it into an underground channel and dumping forty thousand cubic meters of fill into it each day. The mass of rock and earth would be carried by the river's flow into an open bay. The level would be gradually lowered until the waterway was eventually at sea level. With an estimated cost of 560 million francs, it was only half as expensive as the project considered by the Guillemin Commission.[31]

Monchicourt and the young Gautron remained non- commital until the same technical body had had time to study the plan. In the interim, the anxious Monchicourt commended Bartissol's zeal and even indicated his willingness to sign a contract committing the reserves of the liquidation if the outcome were favorable.[32]

It was not. The commissioners took less than three weeks to reach a decision. They poured some very cold water indeed on the idea. Bartissol's great stroke of attempting to conquer the Chagres was highly impracticable, and rock, which would comprise the bulk of the sub-surface excavation could not be made to flow down the channel he proposed.[33] The short-lived relationship ended amid mutual recrimination. Bartissol charged that the commission was packed with Brunet's old guard, and so they could hardly be expected to approve an idea so superior in conception to their own, without losing professional face.[34] Gautron's relations with Bartissol had never been cordial, and when Monchicourt died on 14 March, the new liquidator threw discretion to the winds. He disavowed any intention of signing a contract and remarked on the apparent lack of faith of the original backers – whoever they were – in their spokesman since they had not come forward to plead his case before the commission. They had been summoned to one on 16 February to hear objections from experts.[35] Bartissol ignored this snub and carried his fight to the bondholders by urging them to demand that a contract be signed.[36] This prompted Lemarquis to issue a circular explaining his support of Gautron and their joint refusal to endorse M. Bartissol's ideas. Nothing was to be gained by prolonging the correspondence. He, the *mandataire*, could only express regret that so much time and effort had been wasted in yet another "Panamanian affair which has already led to far too much deception of the public."[37]

*   *   *

In this catalogue of abortive projects which dogged the efforts of those trying to reactivate the project, that by Philippe Bunau-Varilla deserves attention as much for its conjectural possibilities as for the personality behind it. Bunau-Varilla, the father of Panamanian independence, had been associated with the canal since 1884 when he went out to the Isthmus as chief engineer of the Third Pacific Division at the age of twenty-six. For a brief time, in 1885, he had

been in command of the entire excavations when Dingler
died of fever. When the collapse came in 1888, he immediately launched a campaign to save the nation's honour,
as he put it.[38] He spent three years working on plans for a
canal with locks which, he claimed, could be built for 600
million francs.[39] He was, at this date, implacably opposed
to the idea of American participation, being convinced that
the U.S. government had done everything it could to prevent ratification of the 1878 and 1890 concessions wrung
from Columbia. On the other hand, the current mood in
France made it seem unlikely that "the brilliant influence of
a superior mind" would appear to provide new leadership.[40]

A chance encounter between Bunau-Varilla and a Russian, Prince Tatischeff, in a railway carriage between Dus-
seldorf and Paris sometime in February 1894 promised a
new development.[41] The narrative that follows must be approached with caution. Bunau-Varilla had a fertile imagination and was never hesitant in assigning himself a major role
in the history of the Panama Canal. He had a resolute in-
capacity for admitting the validity of contrary opinion, and
generally remained contemptuous of his rivals. The evidence
at hand to explain this strange interlude is almost entirely
from his own pen.

Talk of canals and tunnels such as the St. Gotthard which
had been built by international cooperation prompted Tatischeff to suggest that his nation might be willing to assist
France in completing Panama as a kind of economic sequel
to the recently-signed Dual Entente.[42] Bunau-Varilla was so
excited by the prospect that he sought and obtained an interview with Serge Witte, Tsar Alexander III's finance minister. The plan he unfolded to the Russian was that on which
he had expended three years of study. For Russia it would
be:

the complement to its great work which has scarcely started, the Trans-Siberian railroad .... By the
same token, the Panama canal, joining the waters
of the Pacific and the Atlantic is the complement to
the Russian transcontinental railroad which unites
the banks of two oceans on the Asiatic continent.
To the venture in the Anglo-Saxon world will be
added the Franco-Russian venture in the northern
hemisphere.[43]

According to Bunau-Varilla, Witte was deeply interested
but added that he would have to leave the initiative to the
French government. Conversations are notoriously difficult
to reproduce accurately, especially long after the event, and
there is nothing in Witte's memoirs referring to any such
event. Russia of the 1890s was far from underwriting foreign venture. She was, on the contrary, desperate for capital
to support her internal financial needs. This thirst had been
one of the overriding reasons for her signing the entente with
France. However, Bunau-Varilla returned to France where
he requested an audience with the premier, Casimir-Perier.
The latter was overjoyed at the news and promised to discuss
the matter with Auguste Burdeau, the minister of finance
who had described Bunau-Varilla as "a Napoleon among engineers." The three met in Burdeau's office on 20 April.

The sole documentation for what subsequently transpired
there is a one page memorandum, "Conference rapide avec
M. Burdeau" in which Bunau-Varilla was apparently advised
that the government was determined to avoid "an industrial Sedan that would be more devastating than a military
Sedan." The premier still found it hard to imagine that Russia was interested, but if that were so, she could be assured
of a cordial reception from the French government.[44]

Bunau-Varilla made the next move by suggesting to Bur-

deau that the Russian offer of help might be linked somehow
to the efforts of the liquidation and the *mandataire* to revive
the enterprise. The presence of the Imperial Government of
the Tsar would give incalculable prestige to any new *essai*.
The engineer pleaded for only fifteen minutes of Burdeau's
time – even a telephone call would suffice. It was all in vain.

There remains one curious facet of this affair. Given these
facts: that the United States would have viewed Russian involvement on the Isthmus with grave suspicion, that Russia
was in no position to render assistance to such a controversial undertaking, and that Bunau-Varilla had been an
employee of Artigue, Sonderegger et Cie, one of the scorned
Panamiste concerns, might he not have sought to use this
visionary notion to draw attention to his engineering talents
in order to head any new company?[45] Evidence, admittedly
thin, is furnished by a letter which he wrote to Gustav Eiffel on 10 March 1894. Eiffel had replied to it by remarking
that, as a forced contributor to the Compagnie Nouvelle, he
had promised the liquidator not to interfere in the choice of
executive officers for the undertaking. The letter concluded:

> You will appreciate, as I do myself, that in the situ-
> ation which I presently find myself, it is impossible
> for me to make the kind of precise and formal dec-
> laration *that you are asking me to make* [author's
> italics] whatever the case may be. And you well
> know what I have always said about your abilities
> as an engineer and about your work experience on
> the Isthmus.[46]

Three days after receiving this, Bunau-Varilla was off to
St. Petersburg with what could well have been his real motive. He may have realised full well that the Tsar could
not involve his nation in the affairs of Panama. But the
publicity resulting from the visit would possibly advance his

candidacy for the leadership of the new venture. By bringing himself to the attention of Witte and Alexander III, he would commend himself to those nearer home who had the power to make appointments to the New Company.

*   *   *

If the years 1890-93 had provided a lesson, it was the negative one that neither a private combination nor an appeal to the French public would succeed. A pragmatic solution lay in an attack on those who had been responsible for or profited from the debacle of the Compagnie Universelle. In appointing a *mandataire* on 4 July 1893, the court had chosen an obscure thirty-two year old lawyer, Georges Emile Lemarquis and elevated him to a position of intimidating power over a large and powerful segment of the business community. No more indefatigable defender of bondholders' rights could have been found. In Gautron he had the perfect foil. Throughout the first eight months of 1894 these two were to labor mightily to bring about the birth of the Compagnie Nouvelle du Canal de Panama.

Notes

1. The technical problems posed in attempting to revitalize the canal project are dealt with in Philippe Bunau-Varilla's *Panama, le trafic* (Paris, 1892), and from a more technical viewpoint in Felix Papinot's *Le canal de Panama: étude retrospective* (Paris, 1890). Bunau-Varilla's unofficial connection with the two canal companies is given in his *Panama: la création, la déstruction, la ressurection* (Paris, 1913). His Russian venture is the subject of Charles D. Ameringer's "Bunau-Varilla, Russia and the Panama Canal" in the *Journal of Inter-American Studies and World Affairs*, Vol. XII, No. 3, July 1970, pp. 328-338.

2. A.N. 7 AQ 42, *Rapport (présenté au Tribunal Civil de la Seine par M. Achille Monchicourt*, 12 November 1891).

3. Issue of 11 September 1891.

4. A.N. 7AQ 42, *Rapport.*

5. *Ibid.*, The text of the letter is in Appendix B.

6. A.N. F30 395. The number of petitions to the Assembly in 1891 alone amounted to 114. Several were addressed to President Carnot. The largest of these bore 100,000 signatures.

7. A.N. F30 396, Cotard to Ribot, 20 December 1892.

8. The complete text is in A.N. 7 AQ 30, "Project Hiélard."

9. Quoted in *Le Jour*, 13 November 1892.

10. A.N. 7 AQ 30, Hiélard to Monchicourt, 30 November 1892. A post mortem was carried out on Reinach but it was done too late to determine whether he had been poisoned, as some alleged.

11. A.N. F30 396, "Deuxième rapport présenté au tribunal par le liquidateur: annexe XIX, (handwritten), Monchicourt to Loubet, 29 April 1892.

12. *Star and Herald,* 12 November 1892.

13. *Ibid.*, 15 November 1892. The letter was headed, "Words, Not Deeds!" but the original was printed in Spanish. The translation is the author's.

14. A.N. F30 396, Coutouly to Ribot, 1 November 1892.

15. An undated press cutting was sent to Monchicourt by Mange.

16. N.A. RG 185/1/1, Mange to Monchicourt, 22 November 1892.

17. *The Story of Panama*, p. 536. Even the company's voting power was limited to the ratio of 1:5 of its stock.

18. In what follows I have relied considerably on Julius Grodinsky, *Transcontinental Railroad Strategy*, 1869-1893 (Philadelphia, 1962).

19. A.N. F30 396, Mancini to Ribot. 27 December 1982.

20. Dansette, *op. cit.*, p. 150. The italics are his. Bouvier resigned on December 13.

21. Mancini was French consul in Bogota at this point. He joined the liquidator's staff in July 1893.

22. For a full discussion of Colombia's internal crisis, see Eusabio A. Morales. "The Political and Economic Situation of Colombia" in *North American Review*, Vol. CLXXV, (1902), pp. 347-60.

23. N.A. RG 185/1/1, Mange to Suarez, 17 March 1893.

24. The full text is in *Sen. Docs.* No. 114, 57 Cong., 2 Sess.

25. N.A. RG 185/1/1, *Rapport présenté au Tribunal Civil de la Seine par M. J.-P. Gautron,* 1894.

26. *Ibid.,* annexe XXIII: *Note publiée par M. Monchicourt à la suite du jugement du 26 janvier* (undated).

27. During debate on this measure, several deputies expressed disquiet that there were no safeguards for *shareholders* rights. Leon Bourgeois, the Minister of Justice offered two reasons for this exclusion: first, the monetary claim by bondholders took precedence by law; and it was unlikely that they would ever be paid in full; secondly, shareholders and bondholders, by their different modes of contribution, might be legally opposed to each other. Shareholders had to bear the risks before bondholders. If the *mandataire* represented the former, he would find himself in conflict with the liquidation who was bound to protect the latter, since they were more in the nature of creditors. *Journal Officiel,* Chambre des Députés (1893), 5è législature, 2 March.

28. A.N. 7 AQ 14, *Loi relative à la liquidation de la Compagnie Universelle du canal interocéanique.* During this same debate in the Chamber, Ernest Vallé, the rapporteur warned that little enough might be recovered from the directors of the defunct enterprise. "On a dit que les administrateurs étaient sans fortune avant de commencer l'entreprise, qu'ils ne sont pas enrichis; ils doivent être aujourd'hui, par conséquent, dans une situation assez modeste."

29. A.N. F30 395. Motions deploring the lack of progress were passed by such self-appointed groups as the 'Union Speciale des obligataires de Lille et Roubaix' and the 'Union Speciale des obligataires de la région du Nord.' See, also, A.N. F30 396, "Rapport du comité des porteurs des titres de Panama" 24 March 1893. Perhaps noisiest of all was Felix Papinot who bombarded the liquidator with vague plans and brought his campaign to a climax with the pamphlet, *Pourquoi la Compagnie a echouée et pour quel motif la liquidation est restée et reste encore dans le 'status quo'* (Paris, 1893).

30. Correspondence between Bartissol and the liquidation is contained in A.N. 7 AQ 42. Several letters are missing.

31. 31 A.N. 7 AQ 30, "Projet d'achever le canal de Panama de Colon à Panama," 20 December 1893.

32. A.N. 7 AQ 33, "Projet de M. Edmond Bartissol. Convention avec MM. A. Monchicourt et J.-P. Gautron" 31 January 1894. Upon a favorable decision by the commission, the liquidation would advance 915,000 francs on a bond issue of 7% on P.R.C. stock, plus the unissued lottery bonds. Profits would be divided evenly.

33. A.N. 7 AQ 42, "Canal interocéanique de Panama: Commission d'études. Rapport," p. 4 *et seq.*, 22 February 1894.

34. *Ibid.*, Bartissol to Gautron, 27 March 1894.

35. *Ibid.*, Gautron to Bartissol, 30 March 1894.

36. This appeal appeared in *Le Messager de Paris* on 1 April 1894.

37. A.N. 7 AQ 42, 4 April 1894. This circular reproduced Gautron's reply to Bartissol in detail.

38. *Panama, la création.* Introduction.

39. *Panama, le passé.*

40. *B*(unau)-*V*(arilla) *Papers*, Box 1. "Note sur le canal de Panama" (undated).

41. *Panama, la création*, p. 180.

42. *Ibid.* pp. 180-181.

43. *B-V Papers*, Box 1.

44. *Panama, la création*, p. 189.

45. *Ibid.*, p. 192.

46. *B-V Papers*, Box 1. Note dated 12 March 1894. I find myself in disagreement with Dr. Ameringer, *op. cit.*, who attributes the government's silence to internal dissension, as well as to the liquidator's personal efforts to form a company at this date. It may be questioned whether Casimir-Perier would have given a guarantee when his ministry was on the verge of falling (it fell on 22 May). Also, the activities of the liquidator and the mandataire had begun to bear fruit as of January of that year, i.e. before Bunau-Varilla set off on his Russian journey. (See Chapter IV *in extenso*), also A.N. 7 AQ 24, "Transaction Eiffel", 26 January 1894.

Chapter 3

The Formation of the New Company[1]

November 1892 saw the scandal of Panama reach its climax in the French capital. At the end of one of the stormiest sessions which the Chamber of Deputies had witnessed since the founding of the Third Republic some twenty-two years previously, a majority of members voted that a commission of inquiry be appointed at once to get to the bottom of the mess. Its terms of reference were to be as broad as the deputies saw fit, and it would certainly encompass the old company's relationship with successive governments, under which it had functioned, its contracts with sub-contractors, its publicity campaigns and the remuneration of its personnel from the directors downwards. The commission was duly established though fears that some sort of witchhunt might result prevented it from having quite as broad terms of reference as might have been wished; nor did it obtain the authority or imprimature of a *bona fide* tribunal from the cabinet of the day for much the same reason. Nevertheless, it was to produce an enormous quantity of material from its sixty-three sessions. A minority of deputies might complain, with justification, that much of the truth was never brought to light because of anxiety among commissioners not to embarrass colleagues and friends.[2] On the other hand, the final three-volume report was a bulky document which Lemarquis was to employ with devastating effect.[3]

Further ammunition was soon at hand with the commencement of the trial (and subsequent conviction) of Charles and Ferdinand de Lesseps, Marius Fontaine and Gustav Eiffel on charges of fraud and maladministration. The verdict, rendered in February 1894, was followed by a second – and far more sensational trial of Charles de Lesseps, Fontaine and the deputies Sans Leroy, Dugue de la Fauconnerie, Gobron, Proust and Baihaut. The last mentioned had been Minister of Public Works and had placed the bill before the Chamber authorizing flotation of the lottery bond issue. In all cases, the charge against the accused was one of accepting bribes. For Gautron and Lemarquis, the verdicts served both to promote and to impede their efforts to form a new company before the fateful date of October 31, 1894. On the one hand, they rendered it inevitable that any further solicitation of the public for funds would be an essay in futility. On the positive side, the charges, as well as the revelations contained in the commission of inquiry's report, were to provide the basis for a series of legal manoeuvres launched by the *mandataire* with the collusion of the liquidator's office in August, 1893.

In his very first month in office, Lemarquis displayed an energy and firmness of purpose which was to distinguish the entire length of his tenure as bondholders' representative. He began by attempting to make contact with as many of his clients as possible, although acknowledging that this was not specifically required by the terms of his appointment. A notice requesting stockholders of the Compagnie

Universelle to identify themselves brought over forty-three thousand replies; but Lemarquis' reaction was one of regret that so few had troubled to make themselves known.[4] Simultaneously, he brought a technical suit against the liquidator demanding payment in full of all sums owing to the bondholders. There was a double purpose behind this: first, he would obtain first title to all the assets as precaution in the event that no combination could be found to resume work before the expiry date of the concession occurred: second, it determined the exact figure of debt and the sums at Gautron's disposal to pay it.[5]

Meanwhile, summonses were being prepared against five distinct categories of delinquent. There were (a) the original promoters of the Compagnie Universelle, (b) its board of directors, (c) the contractors, (d) the financial institutions involved in handling the various share and bond issues, (e) the syndicates. Whatever allegations had been made against the parliamentary commission – of striving to exculpate suspected culprits – had no substance in this new instance. Lemarquis' allegations were blunt to the point of being downright libellous, revealing the personality of the man, absolutely sure of his ground.[6] Very soon the net was to be cast wider to snare those with only a peripheral connection with the ill-fated venture.

When these actions were launched, the intention was to obtain capital for some company to be formed by an independent group of business men and, at that point, the choice appeared to lie with Bartissol. However, when it became clear to Gautron and Lemarquis, following publication of the Commission's report in February 1894, that this plan was impractical, an ingenious proposal was suggested by the *mandataire*. Most of the accused had chosen to deny categorically the charges contained in the summonses. If they were to win their cases, the outlook for future financing of a canal company from that quarter would be bleak. Even their defeat in one court followed by an appeal in a higher court might have no better result than to delay the inevitable or, at best, grant the liquidation some meagre financial recompense after it had ceased to matter. Assuming, however, that the accused lost in a lower court, might this not be taken as proof of guilt, a proof which the government's commission had failed to establish? That, in turn, might lead to a retrial the outcome of which no one could divine. In every one of these contingencies, valuable time would be lost.

The compromise, suggested by Lemarquis, was to take the form of repayment of unjustifiable and/or unearned profits or gifts by making the accused make voluntary contributions to the capital requirements of the new company. The donation would be prefaced by a face-saving declaration of innocence of wrongdoing. For the *mandataire*, it was to render any need of appeal to a higher court superfluous: for the *pénalitaire*, it was an investment which allowed honour to be maintained – and it also held out a chance, however slim, of future profit.[7]

Lemarquis chose a formidable opponent when he decided that Gustav Eiffel would be his first target. He was France's best known, if not most distinguished, engineer with a monument to his talent that had survived initial opprobrium and was fast becoming one of Paris's leading tourist attractions. He had, in fact, been sentenced to two years imprisonment and a fine of twenty thousand francs on February 9, 1894 for dissipating funds entrusted to him for a specific purpose; but the sentence had been quashed four months later on the grounds that the public prosecutor had delayed issuing the summons until November 21, 1892, more than three years after the alleged offence had been committed and therefore *hors de justice* by the terms of the Statute of Limitations. Yet, the mud that had been thrown at Eiffel by the press and the commission of inquiry still clung. There was also another chink in his armour.[8]

In December 1888, he had been one of several contractors paid in 90-day notes secured by the deposit of a quantity of Panama Railroad Company shares enable maintenance to continue on the site.[9] Brunet had afterwards renegotiated with him to retain his services until May 1890, and paid him for the task in lottery bonds. This contract had been homolgated by the court without question. It was while he was sifting through Brunet's correspondence with Eiffel that Lemarquis discovered an item from the former liquidator warning him that

> . . . if I should ascertain that the excessive advantages which were accorded you by the terms of your contract were obtained as a result of compromises made by employees of the (old) company through allocations of funds and promises, let it be understood if I find proof of that, your business transaction will not protect you against this eventuality . . . .[10]

Lemarquis contended that Brunet had been unaware of Eiffel's original sin and that if the court had known of this letter, it would have refused to ratify the subsequent agreement, or demanded further elucidation at the very least. His case was far from watertight, but when Eiffel asserted that he had been acquitted by the Supreme Court, he must have known that what had happened was hardly complete exoneration. Conscious of his weakness, Eiffel made provision to have his accounts moved to various banks in Belgium just as the *mandataire* was preparing to institute proceedings to exercise distraint on them.[11] When efforts were made to institute proceedings to obtain authorization from the government in Brussels to seize them, Lemarquis learnt from his staff that they had been moved to a third, unknown location.[12] Nothing daunted, he sequestered a quantity of iron belonging to Eiffel and valued at 400,000 francs. This cat-and-mouse game was brought to an end on February 13, 1894. Eiffel continued to proclaim his innocence and to regard his dealings with Brunet as "beyond reproach in the eyes of the law"; but, "desirous of coming to the aid of the liquidation, and of the old company, he would put a sum of ten million francs at the disposal of the aforementioned party."[13]

It was a turning point in the fortunes of the liquidator, marking the first real success in raising capital for a new venture. Thus heartened, Lemarquis next turned his attention to the contractors and, specifically, Couvreux et Hersent. This firm's association with the Compagnie Universelle had been of less than two year's duration and had been terminated amicably, in 1882, long before the collapse. The basis of the charge brought related to the estimate of 512,000,000 francs for a completed canal which young Abel Hersent had casually mentioned.[14]

> These statements were doubly inaccurate: at that point no firm contract had yet been made ... and, at the same time, the contract that was finally concluded clearly revealed that MM. Couvreux et Hersent had no intention either of undertaking the enterprise or even of actually completing the work for the sum of 512 millions.[15]

If they were guilty, it was of a sin of omission, a doubtful basis for prosecution. Nevertheless, it was with the contention that they ought to have corrected this misleading impression before it was given official status in the *Bulletin du Canal Interocéanique* that Lemarquis based his case. As he saw it, their failure to deny the statement implied acceptance of a contract on this basis. Couvreux et Hersent decided not to fight – perhaps out of a slight feeling of guilt – and settled for a contribution of half a million francs, all the while disclaiming their responsibility for the ultimate disaster and announcing that their donation was a voluntary one to a project they had always held dear to their hearts.[16]

Excess profits were the grounds for accusations against the other contractors, too. The case against Baratoux, Leteiller and Company was quite straightforward. They had farmed out about one fifth of the ten million cubic meters their contract had called them to excavate, to Artique, Sonderegger and Company. Of the remaining eight million meters, they had managed to remove six and a half million for which they had been paid 37,627,656 francs. The parliamentary commission had calculated their profit on this to be 12,513,382 francs[17] while the company itself had set it lower, at eight million. In this instance, the suit actually reached court[18] and, when they lost, they were ordered to repay 2,270,000 francs to the liquidation. Lemarquis offered them the alternative solution and, on August 8, 1894, they undertook to purchase 22,000 shares in a second canal company for 2,200,000 francs.[19]

With Artigue, Sonderegger there were at once complications and extenuating circumstances. The commission had judged their profits to be the most excessive of all the contractors in terms of amount dug to sums received. However, it was acknowledged that the bulk of their excavations had been on the steep Culebra Cut, the highest and most notorious part of the Isthmus which had broken the back of the Compagnie Universelle. Furthermore, in 1886, they had inherited the contract for this particular stretch from the ailing Anglo-Dutch combine, Cutbill, de Longo, Watson and van Hattum. Again, on what was slippery ground, legally speaking, a compromise was arrived at. Lemarquis, in recognizing "the incontestable technical capacity of the management, appealed to the devotion which they have always manifested for that undertaking, and has asked them to lend their financial aid to succour that great undertaking."[20]

The Jacob company had emerged from the close scrutiny of the parliamentary investigation as the least culpable of all having made no threats or demands for extra payments in the last, desperate months of 1888. Its profit of seven and a half million francs on a payment of 16,540,684 was excessive, nonetheless, and Lemarquis was able to extract a contribution of three quarters of a million from the estate of the late M. Jacob.[21] Of the remaining concerns in this category, only one was to subscribe, and that in an indirect manner. The Société des Travaux Publics led an existence of some complexity. It was controlled by, shared the same quarters as and was partly administered by the Société des Depôts et Comptes Courants, a financial establishment that had implicated itself by dabbling in the syndicates and which counted Charles de Lesseps among its major stockholders. Though it had been established that the Société des Travaux Publics had been paid the exorbitant sum of 76,215,022 francs for excavating just under three and a half million cubic meters of soil, this had not deterred it from getting its parent company to launch suits against the Compagnie Universelle for additional payments. These had not been settled when the debacle occurred and it was not until July 24, 1895, with the Société des Depôts et Comptes Courants tottering on the verge of bankruptcy that Lemarquis was able to secure payment of 1,159,608 francs from it.[22]

Two corporations contributed nothing towards the new venture. The first, Vignaud, Barbaud, Blanleuil was itself one of the first victims of the Panama crash, and the suit against it, for restitution of 8,658,705 francs was a formality.[23] The mandataire was no more successful with the

American Contracting and Dredging Company which the deputies' report had castigated as "one of the enterprises which made some of the most scandalously excessive profits out of Panama."[24] Litigation between its owner H.B. Slaven, and the old company had been pending when disaster struck. Brunet had been able to obtain a partial settlement, but, on December 15, 1890 Slaven had threatened to cash his P.R.C. shares unless a complete payment of his unsettled claims was made. To prevent this disposal of canal company assets which the Colombian government might have construed as a violation of the Salgar-Wyse concession, Monchicourt, Brunet's successor, hastily complied. Slaven returned the railroad stock certificates to the liquidation and received in return one and a half million francs and 7,500 lottery bonds whose prize money was still guaranteed and intact. Both sides thereupon held themselves reciprocally free of further action by the other party.[25] Legality was clearly on Slaven's side and there was no point in Lemarquis pursuing this avenue especially since the American contractor had consistently refused to submit his accounts (all of which were in the United States) to the scrutiny of the commission of inquiry.[26]

To Hugo Oberndoerffer went the dubious honour of being the first of the *syndicataires* to be brought to book in a test case. His guilt had been firmly proclaimed by the public prosecutor who described him as "the individual who had made most out of the affair after Baron de Reinach."[27] If he fell, Lemarquis was hopeful that others in the same category would follow. Oberndoerffer had also participated in the organization of the lottery bond issue both on his own account and in the name of fifty-five foreign banks and trusts. Lemarquis seized on another of his past sins. This was a request to be compensated for suggesting the idea of separate funds for the prize money and the amortization of the lottery scheme, a claim which, when met, brought his total remuneration to 3,931,354 francs. "These allocations of money," read the summons, "constitute liberalities without legitimate cause and the accused is requested to make recompense .... It was in vain that an attempt was made to give these amounts the guise of publicity expenses ...."[28]

The mandataire was sure enough of his ground to approach Oberndoerffer privately, in January 1894, and ask him to subscribe to the Bartissol project, rather than having to go through the tedious and time-consuming business of a lawsuit. Oberndoerffer, with false confidence, had decided to fight, claiming that what he had received up until 1888 was simply extra commission on each bond granted without qualms by the company. This defence failed and on May 10 he had been ordered to make restitution of 3,653,201 francs to the liquidation. A formal agreement now followed on June 26 by which he undertook to purchase 38,000 shares in the New Company.[29] Oberndoerffer's fate was a clear warning to others in the same predicament that recourse to the courts would probably do no more than delay the inevitable now that M. Lemarquis had the bit between his teeth. Within three months of that settlement, sixty-three *syndicataires* had agreed to purchase, on aggregate, 3,285,000 francs worth of stock. Each signed a contract with the liquidator where honour, if little else, was saved.[30]

Gautron and Lemarquis were on even firmer terrain when they turned their guns on the founders and directors of the Compagnie Universelle. The charges had been aired at their trials and were well-known even to the most disinterested of newspaper readers – the excessive price paid for the Panama Railroad Company; the costs of publicity that had turned out to be both misleading and dishonest; the feeble resistance they had offered to the exigencies of the banks and syndicates; and the equally deceptive decision to quote low estimates of the cost of completing the canal. The rebuttals had been uninspired. The railway had been indispensable as the only reliable means of transport across the Isthmus; expenses for launching the company and subsequently keeping it afloat had been proportionately no greater than for some enterprises they could name; the estimates had been based on figures supplied by competent, qualified engineers; newspaper publicity never came cheaply except when a company fell on hard times. But these arguments had not saved the accused in 1893, and they failed to save them now. A scale of contributions was drawn up, based on the length of time each of them had been associated with the de Lesseps enterprise. The founder, or director, in question was then advised that "a transaction by which one would voluntarily bring immediate resources for the new company in course of formation would be preferable to the eventualities of a trial whose outcome could be a long time in appearing."[31]

On June 26 Lemarquis formally concluded a settlement with the final group of penalty stockholders (as they were to become known), the banking establishment comprising the Société Générale, the Crédit Lyonnais and the Credit Industriel et Commercial. Both at the time and in retrospect it appeared as one of his most controversial transactions. Criticism was levelled at him first, for the equanimity with which he was prepared to allow representatives from all three to participate in the administration of the new company by their presence in the boardroom. To some it seemed to run contrary to the intent of the liquidator that none of those who had been responsible, either directly or indirectly for the sins of the past should be allowed to dictate the course of any future canal concern. Georges Thiebaud, an ex-Boulangist, was a particularly vociferous critic. He was especially critical of Lemarquis:

... instead of remaining the aloof, inaccessible jurist for the bondholders, he became the disciple and agent of the Dalai Lama of the Crédit Lyonnais, to wit, Henri Germain. Thus was committed the monstrous piece of immorality which would go far to create the definitive disaster of Panama. It was to be in a position to know that the more one had despoiled the old company, the more one would have of influence in the new, since the number of shares obtained by way of this transaction was directly linked to responsibilities incurred and sums for restitution.[32]

Both Lemarquis and Gautron had anticipated this line of criticism, and they were ready to provide a counter-argument in public.[33] By June 1894, they explained, the expiry date of the Suarez-Mange concession was four months distant. Public interest in subscribing could hardly have been at a lower ebb. At the same time, it was essential to gain the confidence of the business world the better to raise capital at a later date. Neither of them was prepared to be an instrument of the banking fraternity nor were they prepared to "pass under the Caudine Forks where M. de Lesseps had had to tread." But the New Company could not exist in a financial vacuum and it was "wisdom to link the interests of credit institutions with the definitive success of a Panama canal." Even if the public had been willing to contribute on a sufficient scale, it would have been the height of imprudence to have risked their money alone on a venture whose fate was likely to hang in the balance for some time to come. By the same token, the parties which had been forced to contribute would sustain most of the loss were the Compagnie Nouvelle to fail, while its triumph would benefit, in terms of return for past investment, those who had been investors in the original company.[34]

There is no denying the cogency of this argument. All the same, Lemarquis is not above criticism. In framing his charges against the banks, he had mentioned only the profits that they had made from the options on shares and bond issues and from their participation in the syndicates organized for the offers to the public in 1886, 1887 and 1888.[35] Yet, as Bouvier has pointed out, the aggregate of what the Société Générale, the Crédit Industriel and the Crédit Lyonnais had to disgorge in terms of contributions to the New Company just equalled, in round figures, what had been extracted from Eiffel who had made considerably less out of his involvement in Panama.[36] The modesty of their indemnity becomes even more remarkable when it is considered that, in terms of net gain, they made seventy-five million francs profit on capital of 1,335,000,000 and that the latter sum was advanced exclusively by the investing public with the banks acting as mere intermediaries. At 5.6% for this service their profit was, to quote Professor Bouvier, "positively exorbitant" and far in excess of the ratio obtained from any comparable operation in France during the nineteenth century. If the gross profit of these financial institutions is the second scandal of Panama, there may be a case for considering the meagre investment demanded of them for the new company as the third; and Lemarquis's apparent leniency towards them can only help-lend substance to Thiebaud's indecorous allegation.[37]

The mandataire had to admit defeat in the two remaining categories of wrongdoers, the *chequards* and the press. The former comprised those twenty or so deputies and senators who may or may not have been bribed by Baron de Reinach to vote in favor of the lottery loan. The authenticity of the list containing their names was never established. As Lemarquis insisted, it was the baron himself who had committed the original sin, and it was he, or rather, his estate which had been forced to yield up 2,526,754 francs to the liquidator.[38] In the second instance, it proved impossible to devise a formula by which the multitude of newspaper proprietors, journalists and magazine owners could be forced to regurgitate a portion of their alleged expenses for publicity. A test case brought against the *Telegraphe* is indicative of the insuperable obstacles. A member of the mandataire's staff spent weeks poring over each issue of the paper in which mention of the Compagnie Universelle had been made, counting the lineage and advertizing space in an attempt to calculate how much had been paid in bribes in excess of legitimate advertizing. From this it was hoped to gauge the gross paid to the owner and so calculate his liability to the New Company. After all this tedious and time-consuming work, the real owner was found to be not Chaul but Marius Fontaine who had already been caught in Lemarquis's net as a director of the Compagnie Universelle. The expense of setting up a special bureau to investigate journals, some of which had been paid a pittance, others of which were no longer in existence, did not warrant the expense.[39]

The Commission d'Etudes which had been set up to report on the feasibility of a new endeavor and which had reported unfavorably on Bartissol's idea, had also suggested that if ever a canal company came to be formed, its capital ought not to exceed sixty million francs, excluding the sum set aside for compensation to the Colombian government.[40] This limitation on issued capital was proposed in order to avoid undue expenditure on a scheme that might yet prove impracticable from an engineering aspect. Although Gautron and Lemarquis were guaranteed this much in enforced contributions by the end of September 1894, they were prepared to allow the French public an opportunity to reaffirm its faith in Panama by providing the entire capital requirements of the New Company. Those whose loyalty had been put to the severest test – the investors in the original – were given first choice to contribute up to thirty million originally.[41]

Any hopes that the forced contributors might have entertained that their own obligation would be proportionally reduced, or even eliminated, by a resurgence of confidence were dashed when the offer's expiry date arrived. In the three weeks from September 22 when it first opened, only 34,843 of the 600,000 shares offered were taken up, and these by fewer than seven thousand individuals.[42] The blame could not be laid at the liquidator's door. Although Gautron and Lemarquis were rebuffed when they asked for complimentary publicity from those very segments of the press which had been so handsomely rewarded in the time of de Lesseps, they managed to issue seven hundred thousand prospectuses. They also visited more than a score of France's major cities to talk about their hopes.[43] Quite simply, the collective memory of the public was every bit as long and jaundiced as had been feared. Therefore, it was necessary to call in all the enforced pledges and these, added to public contributions, came to 43,484,000 francs. The deficit was made up by Gautron who found himself the largest holder of stock in the Compagnie Nouvelle. A breakdown of stock ownership shows the following:

Public subscription	3,484,000
Eiffel	10,000,000
Societe Generale	4,000,000
Credit Industriel et Commercial	4,000,000
Founders & administrators of the Cie. Universelle	7,885,000
Artigue Sonderegger	2,200,000
Jacob estate	750,000
Baratoux Letellier	2,200,000
Oberndoerffer	3,800,000
Syndicates	3,285,700

Liquidator's contribution   15,895,000
Allotment of 50,000 shares to the Colombian gov't   5,000,000

(Gautron received 158,950 shares and they were purchased in four instalments. A first payment of 3,973,750 francs was made out of cash in hand; the second payment was obtained as a result of suits settled with the Reinach estate, Baihaut, Herz, Barbe and some lesser Panamistes. The third payment was made between 1895 and 1900 from further proceeds from court actions and from the sale of some lottery bonds. Fourth, and final payment was made between 1901 and 1904 from the same source, and it totalled 3,929,478 francs.)

Obtaining sufficient capital proved to be only one hurdle in launching the Company. The constitution of a board of directors was not be achieved until the eleventh hour. Until March 1894 hopes had naturally been placed on Bartissol to whom would have fallen the duty of finding his own administrators. The failure of his plan to materialize left Gautron and Lemarquis with barely six months to come up with alternatives. Nor was this just an internal problem. In a dispatch from Bogota, Bougarel, the resident French minister,[44] left the government in Paris in no doubt as to the negative interpretation the press there was placing on developments – or rather the lack of them – in the French capital. There were leading articles in the Bogota press which insinuated that the Colombian congress would be asked to approve of a third concession when it reconvened on July 30. If that were true, warned Bougarel, it would create insurmountable difficulties. No one who had followed the fortunes of the affair since the days of the first liquidator, Brunet, could forget the odds against which MM. Wyse and Mange had had to struggle. Again the evil disposition of some cabinet ministers supported at one and the same time by biassed and treacherous advice of the United States which has lost no opportunity this year, was in the past, to demonstrate its hostility towards us, and by the confession of powerlessness which will be implied from the liquidation's side by a new demand that, in itself, will set back the accomplishments made thus far; but this time it will not be possible to win out over this opposition.

Let none labor under the illusion that matters can be settled leisurely, warned Bougarel. The canal, as a French interest, had five months of life remaining. Another extension might be obtained, but only on terms so crushing that they would surely bankrupt the fledgling company at birth.[45]

This communique was forwarded to Poincaré at the Finance Ministry, and it was given added urgency by a request for ministerial intervention from the indefatigable Lemarquis.[46] The antecedents to this move can only be sketched in outline owing to the paucity of primary evidence. It would appear, however, that either he or Gautron took the first step in trying to constitute a board of directors by making approaches to prominent financiers, among them Guillotin and Dulau, respectively past and acting presidents of the Chambre Syndicale des Entrepreneurs des Travaux Publics. This occurred soon after publication of the pessimistic findings of the commission on the Bartissol project. They expressed a willingness to assist by putting pressure on certain of their acquaintances. Among them was Jean Bonnardel, destined to become the first president of the Compagnie Nouvelle.[47]

Johnson's epitaph on Goldsmith, *nullum quod testigit non ornavit*, might well be applied to Jean Bonnardel, at least in the financial sense. This Lyons-born entrepreneur had

risen from obscurity in his own city in the dying days of the
Second Empire to become a considerable figure in domestic
and international commerce by the mid-1880's.[48] His biog-
rapher, Jean Beyssac, maintains that the government had
made tentative approaches to him in the winter of 1891-92
in the hope that he might head a second canal company.[49]
The tenor of the correspondence among those trying to enlist
his aid in the summer of 1894 inclines one to the belief that
neither Guillotin, Dulau nor Lemarquis knew of it. Instead,
Guillotin found that he was willing to lend his assistance for
patriotic reasons both in drawing up the statutes of the proposed company and in helping with the negotiations with
the delinquent credit institutions which were still unwilling
to contribute to the new enterprise; but he attached the
rider that he would not be called upon to advance any capital of his own.[50] In common with other potential candidates
who had been canvassed, he said he would prefer a more formal invitation before he, Bonnardel, would commit himself.
Guillotin then suggested that it was incumbent upon the
new government to expedite matters and so rid parliament
of a millstone which had hung round its neck for too long:

> It is a certainty that official encouragement by
> those in public office would suffice to remove the
> last hesitation of this gentleman and would achieve
> the desired result.[51]

One can only surmise that Poincaré or Dupuy, the premier, heeded this appeal, and that Bonnardel's official connection with the new concern began in mid-June, 1894.
He brought two colleagues with him from the boardroom,
Chanove, managing director of the Société des Forges et
Acieries de Hanka-Bankowa (one of four companies Bonnardel had established in Russia in the 1870's) and Souchon,
a director of the Société des Houilleres de Saint-Etienne. In

accordance with the terms struck between Lemarquis and the banks, Brolemann of the Crédit Lyonnais, Saint-Quentin of the Crédit Industriel et Commercial and Le Begue of the Société Générale also joined the board. A fourth bank delegated Melodion as its representative: this was the Comptoir National de'Escompte whose suit with the liquidation was to be settled in monetary terms but without a purchase of stock in the Compagnie Nouvelle. The remainder were recruited by Guillotin and Dulau as a counterbalance to the business interest. These were Jonquier, a public works inspector, Ramet, a former president of the Tribunal de Commerce of Rennes and Baillet, a judge of the Tribunal de Commerce from Orleans.

The bondholders were given an opportunity to object to the format of the New Company by an invitation to reply to a circular issued by Lemarquis and Gautron on June 30.[52] The response was an overwhelming vote of confidence for what the two men had achieved. Of 16,800 letters received, only 118 were hostile and, although many had obviously not bothered to reply, it is highly unlikely that the ratio would have been different if all the creditors had taken the trouble to express an opinion. In all, four injunctions were obtained from the court by objectors. Lemarquis was responsible for the first. His was pure formality, the intention being to allow any bondholder to register his opposition through the mandataire's office and so avoid legal costs to himself. The offer was declined by two creditors, Couailler and Muraccioli who decided to plead their own cases suspecting that Lemarquis's opposition to something that was almost exclusively his own creation would be less than enthusiastic, to say the least.[53] The fourth, brought by Duhamel, and endorsed by several fellow bondholders, begged the court to reject any intervention which had the deferment of the Company's incorporation as its object.[54]

Couailler, the holder of three bonds and one share in the old company, declared at the outset that he was not opposed, in principle, to the idea of a successor. But he maintained that the resources at the disposal of the liquidation, namely the unissued lottery bonds and the P.R.C. shares were sufficient collateral for the purpose of initial financing. He deplored the low valuation that had been placed on these bonds by various liquidators, and he particularly objected to the provisions which had been made for disposal of the railroad shares in the New Company's statutes. They were to be put in trust by Gautron and title was not to pass to the New Company until after a special stockholders' meeting as provided for in article 75. If a decision not to continue with the building of a canal were taken or if it proved to be impossible to complete it before the expiry date of the Suarez-Mange concession, legal title to these securities would then be vested in the New Company but it would pay the liquidation twenty million francs compensation. This figure, contended Couailler, was a far cry from the ninety-three million that had been paid for control of the railroad in 1881. Eiffel and his confreres could justifiably been forced to put up additional capital, rather than hazard the pitifully weak resources of the liquidator at all. As matters now stood, those who had been driven to contribute would sooner or later become the masters of the company since their investment comprised the bulk of the paid-up capital of the concern; and policy would surely be in their hands.[55]

The other contender was Muraccioli, a Colombian contractor who had won a court decision in 1893 to be reimbursed for a small debt of less than thirty-five hundred dollars incurred for services to the de Lesseps company five years previously. The judgment had, however, not been executed by July 1 of that year, the date when the law halting all actions against the Compagnie niverselle had been promulgated. Murracioli held that this law not only contravened the court finding, but it also discriminated against those creditors who did not have the good fortune to be bondholders as well. He therefore asked the court to disallow all contracts entered into by Lemarquis and to redefine the assets at the disposal of the liquidator as belonging to all creditors, without distinction.[56]

These objections, Lemarquis pointed out with not a little asperity, were either frivolous or betrayed a lack of understanding of the function of the liquidator and the mandataire. It could not be said too often that unilateral action was not within their powers and that, in any case, the poisonous reputation that Panama unfortunately enjoyed doomed such action to instant failure. The lottery bonds, for instance, had been negotiated at what was their current market value. If they were to flood the market again, as M. Couailler seemed to be suggesting, they would be subject to the kind of speculation and manipulation so distressingly familiar to the hapless investors of the original company. As for the railroad shares, the most recent financial balance sheet (for 1893) had revealed that assets stood at only $1,800,000 (nine million francs). In that circumstance, the estimate for this particular property was not unrealistic. Anyway, the necessity of having to reimburse the liquidation was purely hypothetical. As for Muraccioli, his claim was as much contrary to the spirit as to the letter of the law which he had condemned. It had been passed by parliament specifically to prevent seizure of funds by sundry creditors, and to discourage suits of this very nature.[57]

In his summation, the procureur, Cabat, agreed that there were safeguards in the statutes to insure against a misapplication of resources. While the Compagnie Nouvelle had been formed in great haste, he did not believe it was "in the interests of justice to paralyze an effort after which there would

be nothing left to attempt."[58] Both plaintiffs were required
to pay token costs of fifty francs each. With this last barrier removed, the way was clear for the formal incorporation
of the New Panama Canal Company with temporary headquarters at 65 rue de la Victoire. This duly took place on
October 20, 1894.[59]

In framing the statutes, pains had been taken to ensure
that the Company would be divorced, as far as possible,
from the old concern. The prospectus had intimated that
its board and executive officers would not include any officials who had been associated in any official capacity with
the Compagnie Universelle. Strictly speaking, this was not
adhered to since Maurice Hutin, the Director-General, had
seen service under Charles de Lesseps in 1885 and had actually replaced Dingler as head of works in September of that
year just prior to the arrival of Bunau-Varilla.[60] On the other
hand, the participation of Paul Leroy-Beaulieu had been actively canvassed. This eminent businessman and economist
had been a persistent critic in the past, and he was invited
to head the sub-committee charged with supervising expenditure. The duties of the directors were strictly defined,
and Article 21 made it clear that, unlike de Lesseps and his
friends, they would receive no financial or personal benefits
by reason of their status.[61] The same studious care had been
taken in matters of financing to avoid past errors. To prevent speculation in stock, for example, Article 13 declared
that the original shares had to remain nominative until the
canal was completed or until an alternative procedure had
been settled by legal deed. They were not quoted on the
Bourse, bore no guaranteed dividend and, in the fourteen
years of their existence, no dividend was declared.[62]

As previously stated, the shares of the P.R.C. in Gautron's
hands were to remain in trust pending a decision taken by
the shareholders of the New Company under the terms of

Article 75. This stated that once thirty million francs of capital had been expended, they would be in a better position to decide the future of that enterprise. In the election of directors to the railway company's board, the Compagnie Nouvelle was to continue to exercise its will through its proxy in New York. The decision on whether to wind up the concern would be reached at a special stockholders' meeting and would be based on the report of a technical commission of five experts. Otherwise, the entire holdings of the liquidation were transferred. Article 6 fixed the registered capital at sixty-five million francs of which five million, representing fifty thousand unencumbered shares were assigned to the Colombian government in conformity with the prolongation legislation of December 1890. It is to be noted that, although the liquidation had contributed slightly under one quarter of the registered capital, it was to receive sixty per cent of the net profit, rather than the fifty which had been stipulated in the abortive contract with Bartissol.[63] With assets amounting to a ridiculously low 7% of the figure that the Guillemain Commission had reckoned would be necessary to complete the canal, a prime necessity was to establish the New Company's credibility as a working concern. By Article 31 of the statutes, the board was compelled to appoint a technical commission of its own at the outset to decide upon a new plan for completion of the waterway. Again there is a striking contrast between the old ways and the new. The criterion for membership in what came to be known as the International Technical Commission (I.T.C.) was not, as in the past, a readiness to acquiesce in the opinions and aesthetic concepts of superiors, but rather competency and experience in the field of public works.[64]

The first shareholders' meeting was a boisterous affair although entirely concerned with the mundane matter of verifying the declaration of subscriptions to the Company and evaluating the exact contribution to the liquidator. A vote condemning the banks for past behaviour was passed, and the two representatives from the Crédit Lyonnais and the Comptoir d'Escompte were forced to withdraw from the verification committee.[65] This – coupled with the agenda for the next stockholders' meeting that included acceptance of the slate of candidates for the board – almost guaranteed that it would be equally tempestuous. Sure enough, ill-feeling was displayed from the start. By what right, asked Thiebaud, did Lemarquis occupy the chairman's seat which ought to have been reserved for a major contributor to the New Company? This quibble was followed by a more serious objection to the method whereby the board had been chosen and was now to be presented and elected. The ten directors were presented en bloc to the sixteen hundred or so present who were instructed to raise their hands only if they disapproved of the choice. There were cheers mixed with groans as the ever voluble Thiebaud rose again to comment on the incompatibility that could exist between their duties as directors and their commitments in their own respective spheres of business. He quoted from letters he had received from concerned parties demanding to know why the public appeal for funds had been terminated after only three weeks. There were many who might have contributed, including some living abroad, if only more time had been made available to allow them to convert from other stocks or find capital by some other method. Was this indicative of collusion between the financiers and the mandataire to shut out "les petits porteurs de Panama"?

Lemarquis kept his composure, knowing that he held the whip hand. He coolly observed that M. Thiebaud and his friends, assuming they were in the majority, could vote the New Company out of existence by refusing to accept the board as constituted. The concession would then become invalid in a matter of eleven days and all would be over. If, on the other hand, they hoped to save something of their investment – and of tens of thousands who were not present – they had better realize that unanimity and homogeneity were vital among the board members and that

> if the persons who appear on the list before you know each other and know that they are of one mind, they will accept their roles as part of the administration, something which will not happen if there are developments to the contrary.[66]

This blunt ultimatum carried the day. When the vote was taken adopting the motion of the chair, there were fewer than a hundred contrary voices. As *La Patrie* wryly commented, only a handful of the people who had gathered in the Horticultural Society auditorium that afternoon could have known anything about the men into whose hands the destiny of a French presence in Panama was being placed.[67] *Le Soir* concurred, adding that if they and the stockholders of the old company were of a mind in thinking that it was all a case of plus ça change, they were right, but it was difficult to see how the outcome could have been different.[68] These sentiments were to be repeated in six years' time when an unexpected chain of events would lead to a boardroom revolution.

*   *   *

News of this eleventh hour reprieve was warmly received in Bogota and on the Isthmus although for reasons which were hardly altruistic. For the Colombian government, in particular, the prospect of more cash could not have arrived at a more opportune moment. Mancini had earlier reported that the treasury was "bone dry". Only troops and police had been paid regularly for the past six months and that to maintain their shaky loyalty to the Nunez regime. On a prophetic note he speculated that Panama's dissatisfaction with the central government might one day lead her to seek complete autonomy. Until that happened, he advised that any request on the part of Colombia for a loan or subsidy as an expression of French goodwill be resisted to the hilt because it would be dissipated in futile military ventures. He also doubted whether the regime's unpopularity would permit it to complete its term in office, especially if President Nunez were to die suddenly.[69]

Three days after the stormy meeting that had seen the Compagnie Nouvelle launched, Gautron received the text of a letter which Mange had sent from Panama City. It read simply: "Work actively resumed since October 1 by 1,300 workers of whom 800 at Culebra."[70] After almost five years of adversity it was no small triumph that a canal across Panama was again being dug.

Notes

1. The so-called 'first Vallé report' provided the bulk of evidence against those guilty of misdemeanors against the Compagnie Universelle. Its official title is: *Chambre des Députés: 5é législature, session de 1893, No. 2921. Rapport fait au nom de la commission d'enquête chargée de faire la lumière sur les allégations portées à la Tribune à l'occasion des affaires de Panama. Rapport général par M. Ernest Vallé, député* (Paris, 1893), 3 vols. Further evidence came to light as a result of the interrogation of Arton in 1897, and was published as: *Chambre des Députés: 6è législature, session de 1898, No. 2992.* In La véritable histoire de Panama (Paris, 1932), Louis Marlio concludes that Eiffel's reputation sank lower than Ferdinand de Lesseps's when the public learnt that he had sold the prestige of his name at an exorbitant price in the knowledge that the company was desperate. Jean Bonnardel's career is summarized in Jean Bouvier, "Une dynastie d'affaires Lyonnaise aux XIXe siècle" in the *Revue d'histoire moderne et contemporaine*, Vol. 2, 1955, pp. 185-96.

2. Vallé report, Vol. 1, pp. 242-44. A group of nine dissentient deputies made thus charge of 'whitewashing'.

3. His own, heavily annotated copy is in A.N. 7 AQ 15.

4. A.N. 7 AQ 42, "Premier rapport trimestriel adressé par M. Lemarquis à M. le Procureur de la République", October 30, 1893.

5. *Ibid.* This revealed 228,000 bondholders possessing 2,937,000 bonds with a face value of 1,780,000,000 francs.

6. *Journal des Débats*, August 9, 1893. Of the original founders, for example, it was said: "...que la tactique de ces promoteurs a, du premier jour, jusqu'au dernier, consiste tantôt à taire completement, tantôt a dissumuler sous d'habiles reticences les charges de l'entreprise, et a vanter pompeusement, sans cesse, sans relâche ...."

7. Just when the idea was exactly mooted must remain conjectural. A suggestion that Lemarquis was considering Oberndoerffer as a test case appears in A.N. 7 AQ 42, "Deuxième rapport trimestriel", January 8, 1894.

8. Marlio, *op. cit.*, pp. 48-49.

9. *Chambre des Députeś: 6è législature, session de 1898.* No. 2992, Vol. 3, "Déposition – Lemarquis", pp. 56-57.

10. *Ibid.* The contract referred to in this extract was the one he had signed with de Lesseps in 1887.

11. A.N. 7 AQ 42, "Troisième Rapport Trimestriel", April 8, 1894.

12. *Gazette de France*, August 13, 1893. A.N. 7 AQ 24, "Transaction Eiffel." Two hypotheses were foreseen. If a new company was formed, Eiffel was to contribute ten million in capital and return the P.R.C. shares, then valued at seven million francs. The liquidator would then pay him for work done under Brunet with 56,000 lottery bonds whose current market value was 95 francs each. If a company could not be formed, he was to pay the liquidator 5 million francs, abandon claim to the P.R.C. shares, receive no bonds, but have his iron returned. In either case, his contribution was to be 11,680,000 *in toto*. This exchange of bonds for railroad shares was also to be made in settlements with other contractors: Baratoux – 18,270 bonds for securities valued at 2,269,009 frs.; Artigue – 15,657 for bonds

at 1,921,004, and Jacob – 17,122 for bonds at 2,126,366. See
A.N. 7 AQ 22, "Quittance des entrepreneurs pour solde de leurs
comptes", November 29, 1894.

13. See Chapter 1.

14. A.N. 7 AQ 22, "Demande en responsabilite à raison des assig-
nations que ont accompagné le placement des obligations", July
1894.

15. A.N. 7 AQ 42, "Transaction Couvreux et Hersent" (undated).

16. *Chambre des Deputes, 5è législature, session de 1893.* No.
2921, Vol. l, pp. 75-81.

17. A.N. 7 AQ 23, "Poursuites contre Baratoux, Letellier et Cie,"
(undated).

18. *Ibid.*, "Nouveau contrat avec Baratoux, Letellier et Cie," (undated).

19. B-V Papers, Box 18 contains an English version of the contract
dated September 30, 1894.

20. A.N. 7 AQ 23, "Transaction – heritiers Jacob". Jacob died in
July, 1893.

21. *Chambre des Députés: 6è législature, session de 1898.* No.
2992, Vol. 1, annexe 2, pp. 144-45. Since the New Company
was flourishing by this time, the award went into the liquidation's cash reserves.

22. A.N. 7 AQ 23, "Faillité Vignaud, Barbaud, Blanleuil et Cie"
(undated).

23. *Chambre des Députés: 5è législature, session de 1893.* No.
2921, Vol. 1, pp. 467-68.

24. A.N. 7 AQ 12, "Transaction entre M. Achille Monchicourt et-
break[3]M.H.B. Slaven," January 10, 1891.

25. *Chambre des Deputes: 5e Legislature, session de 1893.* No.
2921, Vol. l, pp. 467-68.

26. Quoted in Bouvier, *Les Deux Scandales*, p. 196.

27. A.N. 7 AQ 42, "Poursuites contre les syndicataires," (undated).

28. *Ibid.*, "Contrat Oberndoerffer." At his second trial, Charles de
Lesseps testified that Oberndoerffer was a figure of note on
the Bourse and that his hostility would have been a serious
obstacle.

29. A.N. 7 AQ 29. Altogether, 120 *syndicataires* were charged of whom 93 had settled by 1897 ("Note remise à M. Albert Martin, February 28, 1898). The standardized form, of which dozens were printed, reads: "M. Lemarquis, prétendant que ce benefice n'était pas juridiquement acquis, a, suivant exploit de 'X', huissier, assigné le – a l'effet d'en obtenir la restitution." M. – a protesté, et renouvelle ici ses protestations contre la prétention de M. Lemarquis. Il considere que sa participation aux Syndicats de Panama est à l'abri de toute discussion et ne saurait donner overture contre lui à aucune restitution des sommes qu'il a legitement encaissés. Mais, se plaçant à un tout autre point de vue, M. – reconnait qu'apres les efforts déja tentés, l'abandon definitif de l'oeuvre du Canal de Panama constituerait pour les interêts nationaux à l'etranger un echec moral qu'il importe d'éviter. Que ce devoir moral s'imposait selon lui plus directement à ceux qui avait receuillé des bénéfices dans la première entreprise et que, pour sa parte, il est prêt, pour faciliter la constitution d'une Société d'achevement, à exposer une somme égale au profit légitime qu'il avait retiré de sa participation dans les syndicats de l'ancienne Société."

30. A.N. 7 AQ 42, "Négoçiations avec les administrateurs de la Compagnie Universelle" (undated). Lemarquis spared no effort in pursuit of the accused, seizing property in Greece belonging to General Turr who was then involved in the construction of the Corinth Canal. He even went as far as opposing payment of honoraria to Ferdinand, Charles and Victor de Lesseps by the Suez Company, maintaining that it ought to go to the liquidator's funds. See A.N. 7 AQ 19, "Comité de Defense du Canal de Suez." Avis aux actionnaires, February 20, 1894. A means had to be devised to pay them so that the mandataire would not garnish the amounts. Even so, Ferdinand's stock in Suez was sold in order to make payment to the New Company.

31. A.N. 7 AQ 35. *La perte de Panama* was published as a six page supplement to *La Vie Financière* on January 19, 1904.

32. These were made by Loustenau and Martin, the liquidator's agents, in an interview in *Le Droit* on August 12, 1894.

33. *Ibid.*

34. A.N. 7 AQ 30, "Conventions avec les établissements de crédit" (undated).

35. *Les Deux Scandales.*

36. *Ibid.*, pp. 116-17.

37. *Chambre des Députés: 6è législature, session de 1898.* No. 2992, Vol. 3, "Déposition – Lemarquis," p. 58. Cash payments to the liquidation were made by those who (a) did not want New Company shares; (b) administered the estates of deceased *pénalitaires*; and (c) had settled after the Compagnie Nouvelle was in full operation.

38. *Ibid.*, p. 65.

39. A.N. 7 AQ 42, *Canal Interocéanique de Panama. Commission d'Etudes. Rapport,* February 22, 1894.

40. The prospectus is in A.N. 7 AQ 31.

41. A.N. 7 AQ 42, "Sixième rapport trimestriel", January 5, 1895.

42. A *pro forma* letter was sent to all bondholders on September 12.

43. Bougarel had succeeded Mancini when the latter replaced the elderly Felipe Paul as Gautron's agent in Bogota. Mancini then became officially associated with the Compagnie Nouvelle from October, 1894. See N.A. RG 185/1/1, Gautron to Paul, July 8, 1893.

44. A.N. F30 395, Bougarel to Hanotaux, June 4, 1894.

45. A.N. 7 AQ 30, Lemarquis to Burdeau, June 11, 1894. The letter was received after Casimir-Perier's ministry had fallen.

46. *Ibid.*, and a copy of the original, dated March 15, 1894, is alone in a file marked "Negoçiations Guillotin-Bonnardel."

47. Bouvier, *Une dynastie d'affaires lyonnaise*, pp. 185-86.

48. *Ibid.*, p. 197, footnote 5.

49. A.N. 7 AQ 30, Guillotin to Lemarquis, April 27 and May 8, 1894.

50. *Ibid.* Unsigned 'Note confidentielle' dated April 12, 1894.

51. A.N. 7 AQ 42, *Communication a MM. les obligataires de la Compagnie Universelle en liquidation.*

52. A.N. 7 AQ 36, "Affaires contentieuses – Couailler, Muraccioli" (unsigned and undated).

53. *New Panama Canal Company. Opinions of General Counsel and Documents showing Title Deed, compiled by Nelson and Cromwell* (privately printed, New York, N.Y., 1902).

54. N.A. RG 185/1/1, *Rapport présenté au Tribunal Civil de la Seine par M. J-P Gautron* (misprinted as P.A. Gautron), 1894.

55. A.N. 7 AQ 36, "Jugement sur les tierces oppositions au jugement d'homolgation des statuts", August 8, 1894.

56. *Ibid.*, "Plaidoiries de la liquidation."

57. *Le Droit*, August 12, 1894.

58. Permanent offices were secured at 7 rue Louis-le-Grand in December 1894, adjacent to Lemarquis's residence.

59. Hutin was to succeed de la Tournerie in 1896. See Mack, op. cit., pp. 325 and 409.

60. A.N. 7 AQ 37, *Statuts de la Compagnie Nouvelle du Canal de Panama*.

61. Article 14 referred solely to "une parte proportionelle dans le propriété de l'actif social, dans les bénéfices à distribuer comme interets ou dividends ...."

62. Article 52.

63. This commission was entirely divorced from that provided for in Article 75.

64. *Revue Economique et Financière*, October 6, 1894.

65. A.N. 7 AQ 31, "Compagnie Nouvelle du Canal de Panama: Deuxième Assemblée Générale Constitutive" (undated).

66. Its account began: "La Nouvelle Société a debuté sous de facheux auspices." (issue of October 23). The police were called to restrain one or two speakers.

67. Issue of October 21, 1894.

68. A.N. 7 AQ 33, Mancini to Gautron, August 23, 1894.

69. N.A. RG 185/1/1, Mancini to Gautron, October 23, 1894.

Chapter 4

The New Company on the Isthmus[1]

The record of the Compagnie Nouvelle during its ten year presence in Panama may be divided into three periods. The first, from October 1, 1894 to the winter of 1898-99 was devoted to renovations on site and to the continuation of the most essential excavation begun by the original workforce. The second period dates from the publication of the International Technical Commission's report, which resulted in the company working to a modified plan, until the summer of 1902, by which time the United States government had virtually committed itself to the Panamanian route. The final period, terminating in May 1904 with the transfer of the property, was one of gradually diminishing activity by a severely reduced labor force whose duties were confined, especially in the last twelve months, to routine maintenance of excavations.

Caution was the hallmark of the New Company throughout its entire existence. It was an attitude that was to exasperate bolder spirits, such as Bunau-Varilla who persisted

in his vision of a French canal to the end of the century
and perhaps beyond. It also displeased those directors of
the Panama Railroad Company who visited Paris looking
for assistance less than a month after activity had recommenced on the Isthmus. Their feud with Pacific Mail was
still raging,[2] and the Americans were anxious to obtain monetary support for the building of a wharf at La Boca as an
additional weapon in the fight. When constructed, it would
enable ocean- going vessels to discharge and load cargoes directly alongside the railway track. Oppenheim, who led the
delegation, reported on what he found in Paris:

> Bonnardel and the members of the Board ... very
> attentive and courteous listeners. We also found
> them absolutely ignorant either of the present sit-
> uation of the Road or of its past history. We ex-
> plained everything and urged on them the need to
> come to a swift decision, but they needed more
> time, so novel and absolutely contradictory were
> the ideas presented. I told them the commodity
> 'time' was costing them $33,000 a month. They
> admitted this but said that, being new to the busi-
> ness, they would rather face a loss than come to a
> hasty decision.[3]

Further entreaties were met by Bonnardel's polite observation that there was "such a thing as a mental process
of ripening a conviction, and we have not yet had time to
ripen ours." A full year was to elapse before a decision was
made to advance five million francs for quayside facilities,
the largest single expenditure the New Company was to
make outside its commitment to the canal itself.[4] 1895 did
witness a gratifying reconciliation between the P.R.C. and
Pacific Mail with the former abandoning its steamship service between Panama City and San Francisco. By then its

profits had plunged from \$266,248 in the previous financial
year to \$62,944, and the track had been neglected.[5] Echoing
the sentiments of the late Monchicourt, Bonnardel deplored
the serious inconveniences being caused by this subsidiary
enterprise that was allowed to operate under independent
control. He blamed it for its willful pursuit of selfish policies
while the parent company remained impotent.[6]

General conditions along the length of the canal were less
depressing than had been feared.[7] From its projected point
of entry, at Colon, on the Atlantic side, to km. 21.7 near
Bohio Soldado, the waterway was actually open, although
depths varied, an important factor being incursions of the
Chagres River.[8] It had left its original bed and now flowed
down a man-made route that offered it a more direct route
to the Caribbean. Vegetation had completely covered much
of the excavation; but this proved to be less disastrous than
might have been expected in that it cemented the earth on
all but the steepest slopes and so prevented major landslides.
The state of moveable equipment depended very largely on
its location and composition. Termites had consumed everything non-metallic that had been left in the open from
wooden dump trucks to pick handles. Dredgers, locomotives, wagons and other items of iron and steel manufacture
had stood up well, especially where precautions had been
taken to protect them from the tropical rains. The greatest loss in this category was a quantity of metal intended
for lock gates in the revised 1886 plan for a sea-level operation. This had been dumped on the beach near Colon
and had consequently suffered severe corrosion. In the same
way, temporary accommodations made of wood or grasses
had deteriorated badly; but permanent structures were quite
habitable, notably the two hospitals, at Ancon and Colon.
On the whole, the skeleton maintenance staff had done re-
markably well in preventing loss despite the fact that even

it had been progressively reduced until it numbered only a few score by the time operations resumed.[9]

One of the most serious and persistent problems to plague the Compagnie Nouvelle was a shortage of labor. This was not immediately apparent since work remained at a modest level until the end of the rainy season in 1895. Indeed, at the outset, there was an excess of workers, mostly West Indians who, for various reasons had not returned home after activity had ceased in 1888. Those who had chosen to remain were given priority when recruiting began again. The initial labor surplus created a feeling of false optimism among the section chiefs; and when Mange rashly asserted that the wages currently being paid by the Company were sufficient, he was immediately forced to eat his words.[10] November 1894 saw the first of a series of stoppages to protest the high cost of living and against the differential in wage rates between those paid by the Company and the P.R.C. – amounting to almost fifty per cent in the case of unskilled laborers.[11] These strikes became more frequent and culminated in a general shut-down on March 25, 1895 which lasted for three weeks.[12]

The parsimony of the second company was a studied reaction to previous practice. However, it undoubtedly served to dissipate initial enthusiasm that had been generated throughout the Isthmus when a resumption of activity was first announced, and it contributed to the general air of disillusionment which soon pervaded labor and citizenry alike.[13] Mange spoke bitterly of certain journals and newspapers that were fostering the rumour that nothing was happening, and he emphasized the need for an energetic denial of such allegations.[14] In part, theirs was a natural response to the modest manner in which the work had been restarted, without the fanfares, banquets and general hoopla which had heralded the advent of de Lesseps. Yet, for Mange, this false impression had to be dispelled. Profiteering was rampant. Landlords and hoteliers were raising their rates to the extortionate levels prevailing in the 1880's; and the entire population appeared to be animated by a desire to have the Company "spend its money without counting the cost, as in the past so as to enrich itself with the same facility."[15]

There was a serious aspect to this unrest beyond the obvious disruptions it was causing on site. On February 9, 1895, Suarez summoned Mancini to the Ministry in Bogota to acquaint him with a disquieting report that he had received from the Isthmus that work was progressing "only in a half hearted and lethargic manner". Mancini emphatically refuted the charge explaining that it was not his employer's intention to throw its money out of the window as in past times. But he wondered, afterwards, whether it would not be politic to issue some sort of newsletter publicising the more positive attributes of the enterprise without necessarily indulging in the spurious optimism of the *Bulletin du Canal Interocéanique*.[16] However, this suggestion was not taken up for what one assumes was reason of economy.

The wage settlement eventually arrived at in April 1895 was not a generous one. Laborers' pay was increased to 96 centavos, with the semi- skilled receiving between 1.35 and 1.80 – rates that were still below comparable ones being paid by the railroad. These meagre concessions by the management was answered by yet another outbreak of industrial unrest in August.[17] By then the workers were in a much better bargaining position. The original pool of labor had been exhausted by resignations and desertions and Paris was anxious to increase the scale and intensity of operations once the dry season began, usually around the end of December.[18] The workforce at this juncture numbered around two thousand while Vautard, one of the section chiefs, saw the need for an additional two thousand if targets were to be met. His experience with the old company led him to believe that the best solution lay in utilizing the services of labor agents abroad. He regarded the local population as lazy or indifferent to the opportunities for employment offered; and while a few of them might be taken on, there was no guarantee that they would not disappear when they felt so inclined.[19] Accordingly, arrangements were made with labor agents in Cuba, the British West Indies and West Africa. The Panama *Star and Herald*, always an enthusiastic ally, offered to alert its correspondents and agents throughout Central America as to the opportunities available, and at no charge.[20]

Nevertheless, these efforts were to prove inadequate for a number of reasons. For one, the 1890s were a decade of unparalleled activity in the field of mineral prospecting and discovery. There was less likelihood that the type of penniless itinerant who had gravitated towards Panama in the days of de Lesseps (of whom Paul Gaugin was the most celebrated) would return when more lucrative rewards seemed to beckon in Australia, South Africa, Alaska and the Yukon. For another, there still hung a pall of gloom cast by the lurid and exaggerated accounts of death and disease as retailed by Drumont, Dr. Wolfred Nelson and others with scores real or imaginary to settle with the old company.[21] Yet, in terms of health, the record of the Compagnie Nouvelle was to prove vastly superior to its predecessor's, and not even inferior to that of the United States during its first three years of tenure. Taking the period 1895-1903, the mortality rate per thousand employees averaged 25.5 annually, reaching a high of 34.5 in 1900 and a low of 18 in 1901.[22] Not a single white employee died of yellow fever in the first five years of the New Company's occupation.[23] A third reason for workers' disinclination to go to Panama lay in the fate of the fourteen thousand who had been marooned there when the Compagnie Universelle had failed. The destitute had been forced to look to their own governments for assistance;[24] and as early as 1892 the *Official Gazette* of Barbados had carried the following stern warning:

> As it is possible that work on the canal will resume shortly, warning is hereby given that the Government of Barbados will not assume any responsibility for those who have contracted to work on the canal, and those who go to the Isthmus of Panama do so at their own risk, and they will neither be repatriated nor supported by the Government if they become financially indigent.

A company complaint had been sent to the British consul, Arnold Mallet, in Panama city that notices of this nature would be most detrimental to recruitment. Mallet countered that his consulate, in common with others, had been gravely inconvenienced by the events of 1888-89, and that Her Majesty's Government was determined to avoid their repetition by attempting to dissuade family men, at least, throughout the British West Indies from signing contracts. For the rest, he suggested that repatriation certificates, entitling the holder to free passage home, might be given to all foreign workers on arrival.[25]

Three years later found the British colonial authorities still manifestly hostile. It was charged that the governor of Jamaica had dashed hopes of obtaining a thousand men for work at Culebra, the principal location of New Company activity, with an edict specifically prohibiting emigration to the Isthmus.[26] In January 1896, however, Mallet's idea of a repatriation certificate was put into practice as the result of a formula reached between the Jamaican government and one of the Company's recruiting officers. This pledged the Company to deposit twenty-five shillings per man with the Jamaican treasury to be used for his return voyage in the event of a termination in operations before his contract had expired. For victims of injury or disease, a scale of compensation was to be fixed after consultation between British and French consuls in Panama City, and the cost of their repatriation was likewise to be borne by the Company.[27] Despite these elaborate precautions, the Jamaican presence was not to be a happy one.

Within weeks of the arrival of the first shipload, there were complaints from the section chiefs about local police having entered the encampment at Las Cascadas to demand payment of municipal taxes. Those who had refused to contribute had been jailed on the spot and, upon release, they had deserted, thereby violating the contract.[28] Matters came to a head in March 1898 when racial tension between coloured and white workers – coupled with dissatisfaction over pay and working conditions – resulted in a riot in which three were killed and several dozen injured.[29] Thereafter, the number of Jamaicans declined as demands for repatriation were met; but problems with them were still causing Mallet headaches as late as 1901.[30]

The Company mounted its greatest effort to recruit personnel in 1896 by securing the services of a seasoned labor agent, Etienne Famin. Unfortunately his grand tour of Central America and the Caribbean islands was to prove less fruitful than had been hoped. He found no surplus in Mexico, the most populous of the republics, and he dismissed the natives of the French West Indies (who would at least have a language in common with their employer) as

> unquestionably the laziest and least disciplined of all those in the Antilles, constantly disposed to regard themselves as the equals of their superiors, insolent and even violent when they think they can behave in this way with impunity.[31]

In Barbados he found the authorities adamant on the strict observation of an 1893 law which prohibited migration of laborers even for the purpose of temporary employment. A fellow agent in Trinidad, Nurse, was able to offer four or five hundred plantation workers but here again the crown agent made it clear through press notices that these prospective migrants could expect no assistance in the event of sickness, injury or redundancy.[32] One of the Company's few successes, the hiring of a hundred Cubans, had the unforeseen and disagreeable consequence of incurring the displeasure of Sanclemente, Colombia's president. It was claimed that these men were revolutionaries, fresh from prisoner-of-war camps or else guerilla fighters lately in action against their Spanish masters. It was further asserted that they would join rebel bands in the Colombian countryside.[33] Though there was no substance to these allegations, a government order swiftly followed from Bogota forbidding the importation of any others from that island.

The shipment of five hundred and seventy Africans from Sierra Leone and Liberia was to have an even more disastrous outcome. In the first consignment of eighty-three, thirty-six were found to be suffering from beri-beri and a further forty had symptoms of cardiac trouble. Dr. Lacroisade, the Company's director of medical services who prided himself on maintaining a good health record, advised that the entire complement be returned to their place of origin.[34] This suggestion was not acted on, however, until the authorities made the alarming discovery that several discharged patients (who had been treated at Company expense) were trying to find employment in cafes and hotels in various towns and cities along the canal route. They were immediately thereafter deported *en masse*.[35]

The instability of the labor force, small though it was by previous (or future American) standards, can be ascribed in large part to the absence of family life. Experience had taught railroad and canal builders in North America that married men were more likely to be sober and industrious and to remain on the land as settlers once the original job had been completed than footloose bachelors. The nature of the country precluded this in Panama, and circumstances were to force the Compagnie Nouvelle in to offering more attractive wages, although they were grudgingly given. It was characteristic, for example, that in authorizing an increase in the basic rate from 96 centavos to 1 piastre 20, the section foremen were advised to tell their workers that the newly found munificence of the Company necessitated an increase in productivity on the part of all concerned.[36]

Ironically, at the same time as the French were searching for workers, they were engaged in a wearisome effort to rid their property of others. As mentioned earlier, hundreds of families had taken up residence along the deserted canal site after 1888 where they engaged mostly in subsistence farming. Wyse had foreseen the problem that these squatters might pose, and he had insisted that a special article be included in the 1890 concession agreement by which the onus for their eviction would be Colombia's responsibility when the time came.[37] The process ought to have been put into motion in the summer of 1894 when it was clear that excavation would recommence, but frequent appeals to the governor of Panama, Casabianca, went unheeded, and it was not until November of the following year that Mancini formally requested intervention.[38] As in so many cases of dispute, where recourse to local powers became necessary, a pattern was set. Events were to move with painful slowness.

Had the squatters been limited to poor farmers living at bare subsistence level, a solution would probably have been achieved with more ease. But it was the Company's misfortune to have to deal with local politicians and civic dignitaries, as well. Santiago Samudio, the city treasurer of Emperador, was a not untypical example. According to Le Cornec, the section chief there, he, together with the more affluent of these illegal and unwelcome tenants had had recourse to bribery and threats in their determination to stave off eviction, a practice which had apparently worked smoothly in the days of de Lesseps. Wrote Le Cornec:

> Besides, I ought to warn you, in the event of a campaign of slander against the Company that blackmail attempts were made aimed at me, and after these failed, their authors promised that the press would threaten me with a series of articles that would be hostile to the whole enterprise we are undertaking here.[39]

While such tactics failed to shake the resolution of Company officials, they were employed to better advantage with the local judiciary. According to Mange's ample evidence, an Emperador magistrate had granted Samudio a stay of execution of eviction proceedings. In the same letter he supplied Mancini with confirmatory evidence of Cornec's charges of press interference by including a collection of xenophobic articles from November issues of *El Mercutio* of Panama City.[40]

There was no improvement in 1896. Although Bogota had promised to appoint an investigator with legal powers, he, too, seemed to have succumbed to the blandishments of the local establishment. How else could one explain the extraordinary behaviour of judge and prosecutor in the case of a landowner named Huertas? In this particular case, both men had vied with each other in their concern that the accused should receive every consideration. Although two full years had elapsed since the resumption of digging in his section, Bélin concluded despairingly that not a single squatter had been moved – or gone of his own account.[41]

The answer lay in a compromise. It was clear that it would be a long time before the New Company required all of the disputed land, given the modest scale of its operations. Furthermore, it had already been demonstrated that when tenants were forced off one portion of land, they frequently settled in another nearby. It was therefore agreed to let them remain provided that they agreed to pay rent and arrears of rent dating back to October 1, 1894.[42] Even so, this procedure involved more than twelve hundred separate contracts and a mass of paperwork. Throughout the remainder of 1896 and well into the following year there was a constant stream of complaints from section chiefs: some leaseholders were refusing to acknowledge liability for retroactive debts claiming that they had not been there since official day named; some had vanished at the mention of payment but had since returned; some were so poor that legal action against them would be an exercise in futility while still others were boldly initiating countersuits against the New Company for trespass! Bélin was particularly incensed by the impertinence of one Martha Brown, whose property was adjacent to his own. He was certain that her establishment had ministered most adequately to the grosser physical needs of his employees, but she had adamantly refused to pay a single piastre in rent. He angrily concluded that

> to put an end to the nasty example furnished by this resistance on the other inhabitants of Bohio who have come to the conclusion that our long-standing condescension of Madame Brown is a confession of impotence, I feel that it is urgent that we take strong measures against her.[43]

This same lack of harmony between the Compagnie Nouvelle and the local authorities was evident, too, in the question of security and crime prevention. The depredation of

thieves were by no means an uncommon occurrence during the de Lesseps era, and a provision had been written
into the Roldan-Wyse contract by which Colombia was to
furnish two hundred and fifty troops for policing duties on
payment of ten thousand piastres a month.[44] It was perhaps inevitable, with the federal government fighting for its
very survival at that time, that the soldiers sent were not
always the most professional. Drunkenness, desertion and
open pilfering of stores resulted in yet another protest to
the Panamanian governor; and when no satisfaction could
be obtained from that quarter, the dreary pattern of appeal
to Bogota had to be repeated.[45] The gradual expansion of
operations planned for the winter of 1895-96 made the issue
a pressing one; but, by November the situation had deteriorated even further. Le Cornec gave the startling news
that the law was no longer being enforced along his section,
troops having been withdrawn on the pretext of widespread
disease. However, their commandant had had the effron-
tery to request that the monthly payroll be sent as usual
"appealing to our humanitarian sentiments." Le Cornec was
convinced that this was nothing more or less than a clumsy
ruse to obtain money for no services rendered since all the
soldiers had disappeared at the same time and none of his
own workers had been afflicted by this mysterious ailment.
As far as he could see, the best answer lay in a police force
of the Company's own which would have the merit, among
others, of saving thousands of francs.[46]

The Company was inclined to agree although it foresaw
fresh difficulties in defining the limits of their jurisdiction.
It was willing to settle for a local constabulary with strictly
limited areas of operation.[47] Frustrated by the procrasti-
nations of Bogota, Mancini decided to raise this suggestion with the Panamanian governor personally. Casabianca,
as anticipated, immediately vetoed the idea of a French

canal company police force, but he promised to refer the proposal to his advisory council.[48] Nothing had been decided by December at which time Casabianca had been replaced. His successor, Jose Arango, agreed that government soldiers should be replaced by seventy-five constables for whose services the Company undertook to pay 4,000 piastres monthly. The regular troops were to return in the event of major civil disturbance or war. Even so, this substitution was only a partial success: the problem of law enforcement was to plague the administration for the remainder of the Company's tenure. The files contain many thick dossiers of agents' letters to the director of administrative services complaining of laxity and unpopularity of these so-called guardians of the law.[49] It became somewhat less of a problem after 1902 when the workforce was gradually reduced. However, the whole, sad experience was not lost on the Americans. In abrogating its first treaty with Colombia relating to occupation of the canal zone, the United States insisted on obtaining complete autonomy within the Canal Zone as properly constituted.[50]

An equally thorny problem, that of liability for payment of taxes, served to alienate the Compagnie Nouvelle still further from its host. The history of this particular issue goes back to 1886 when tentative and sporadic demands had been made for municipal taxes. For once, the old company had stood its ground and had justified its refusal on the basis of Article IX of the Salgar-Wyse agreement as well as on previous ordinances granting exemption to foreign corporations.[51] There matters rested until June 1894, when the provincial authorities received the news of the imminent formation of the Companie Nouvelle. It was an opportunity that the isolated, near-bankrupt province was eager to exploit, having had to deal in *vales*, inconvertible paper currency, since 1886.[52] The departmental assembly rushed through legislation to levy a duty on all imported merchandise, intentionally ignoring the exemption granted to the canal company and the P.R.C. in the late 1870's. An appeal was immediately launched against this to the supreme court in Bogota; but, in anticipation of an adverse verdict, the provincial legislators approved another motion on November 20, 1894, which the Company claimed was nothing but a rehash of the original.[53] Emboldened by their own daring, they next demanded payment of municipal taxes and sent collection agents, accompanied by squads of police into the workers' encampments on March 26, 1985. Vautard, the chief supervising engineer, advised they pay up because, as he put it, he did not want "either to expose the workers to violent measures or to give the government the satisfaction of using them."[54] A protest to the governor was duly ignored and, in the face of this *force majeure*, the whole knotty problem became a matter for mediation between the board in Paris and the Colombian government.

In the interim, the local politicians concocted a third scheme worthy of Grenville at his most exigent. This specified that all future correspondence of the New Company's emanating from the department of Panama must be written on stamped paper supplied by the taxation department. As a consequence of this action, Colombian officials found themselves being bombarded by letter from irate officials demanding that a halt be called to these illegal expedients.[55] Partial satisfaction was obtained from one decree exempting all employees from municipal tax levies, except for those who had taken out Colombian citizenship.[56] By 1897, however, both the notorious stamp act and the import duties had been dropped although the Panamanian politicians were bent on returning to the attack by claiming taxes on premises rented by the French to private citizens who had no connection with the Company.[57] In consequence, litigation dragged on until

1904 as both parties wrangled over precedents, valuations, legal definitions and treaties; but, generally speaking, the amounts the Company had to pay were small, rarely exceeding five piastres.[58]

*   *   *

When the time came to resume excavation in 1894, plans for a completed canal were not a prime consideration. Initial efforts were directed towards continuing what had been started in the modified lock scheme, specifically the cutting through the Massif Central from Las Cascades at km. 48 to Paraiso, at km. 57 with particular attention to the summits at Culebra and Emperador. The choice of this location was dictated by two considerations. First, it was the most difficult portion to attempt and one whose conquest was vital for the remainder of the operation. Second, the final depth of the trench here would establish the height above sea level at which the completed waterway could be conceived. The deeper the cut into these hills, the less work there would be to perform elsewhere, on lower segments of the canal. The first year was spent making multiple borings and taking soundings to permit a comparison between the new data and that on which previous calculations had been based.[59]

Although this slow, deliberate mode of approach was to earn the warm commendation of the Isthmian Canal Commission three years later, it disturbed Lemarquis and Gautron. They had heard disquieting reports from the Isthmus of continued American interest in the rival Nicaraguan route, and they feared that unless the Colombian government saw much greater activity along the whole length of the strip, it might use the excuse provided by this unspectacular beginning to revoke the concession.[60] Yet, with the chronic labor shortage there was little the chief engineer, de la Tournerie, could do beyond exhorting his subordinates to utilize the manpower at hand to the best advantage.[61] As a

result, the target of a hundred thousand cubic meters of ex-
cavated material per month was not to be reached until well
into 1897.[62] This disappointing record aggravated an existing state of tension between de la Tournerie and the board
and led to his resignation in February 1896. Needless to say,
this incident dealt the Company's image another blow that
it could ill afford.

The source of this conflict lay in Bonnardel's determination that complete independence of action be granted the
technical committee envisaged by Article 31 of the statutes.
The board refused de la Tournerie's request that he be allowed to preside over it as long as he held his position as
chief engineer. It was argued that this dual control would
render impossible a critical and impartial study of the work
already completed. Overall direction of excavation was then
assumed by his chief assistant, Maurice Hutin whose ambi-
tions were more modest.[63] The International Technical Commission at first belied its name being composed entirely of
Frenchmen under the chairmanship of Robaglia, a retired
inspector of public works. Wisely, the board decided to
widen its ranks with the inclusion of other nationalities, and
eventually engineers from six nations were induced to accept positions.[64] Between February 3, 1896 and September
8, 1898 it held ninety-seven sessions and many more informal
meetings. Its report was presented to the board in November 1898.

In deciding on a canal without locks, de Lesseps had been
faced with two major difficulties. First, there was the problem of cutting through the Cordilleras, the backbone of hills
and mountains stretching down the length of Central America. On the projected canal line they reached a maximum
height of one hundred and ten meters. Secondly, there was
the difficulty of regulating the Chagres which periodically
became torrential. When the idea of a lock canal was re-

luctantly accepted by the 'victor of Suez', a third obstacle
presented itself – a water supply for the lock basins. The
higher the summit was raised, the greater would be the difficulty in supplying these basins with water, and the stronger
the foundations of the locks would have to be. These were
the issues facing the Guillemain Commission when it came
to consider a new plan capable of execution within the ten
year limit allowed by the 1890 concession. The problem reduced itself to the relatively simple question: what depth
could be reached at Culebra, the summit, in the ninth and
final years of operations? The limit had been set at 25.5 meters above sea level by Guillemain. In his proposed scheme,
water would be supplied by the Chagres whose level would
be raised by means of a dam at San Pablo, at km. 38. The
construction of two locks there would create a large lake to
act as a regulating reservoir of which the summit level of
the canal would form an integral part. This summit level
would end at Paraiso, km. 57, followed by a descent to the
Pacific through another pair of locks. Excess water would
be allowed to drain into a second lake, formed by building a
dam of smaller dimensions at Bohio, km. 24 from which it
would escape to the sea through diversionary channels.[65]

The I.T.C. objected to the proposed location of the main
dam on the grounds that it would lack the necessary rock
foundation from Bohio to the point where the Chagres met
the canal line, at km. 45. Even if it were feasible, the Commissioners had grave doubts as to the ability of the channels
to dispose of the river's freshets. A thorough study of flood-
ing statistics based on ten years of observation led them to
conclude that an allowable maximum flow of 1,200 cubic meters could result in an excess of 250,000,000 cubic meters instead of the 60,000,000 that the Guillemain Commission had
calculated. It was also felt that the period of time allowed
for construction on that design was inadequate, considering,

too, the need to divert the railway line.[66]

The revised plan, to which the Compagnie Nouvelle adhered, called for the construction of an artificial lake-cum-reservoir in the upper valley of the Chagres, at Alhajuela, fifteen kilometers below the canal line, to feed another dam at Bohio which would be reached from the Atlantic side by a flight of locks. The lake thus created would extend to Obispo, km. 46, and it would be sufficiently large to take flood water – the excess being carried to the ocean by diversionary channels, as before. The flow of water below Bohio would be kept within the capacity of these channels by the building of sluices above Alhajuela Dam and Lake Bohio. The highest point in the entire waterway, between Paraiso and Obispo, would be reached by another flight of locks. The descent on the Pacific side would be made in a similar manner. The total projected length of the canal, from sea to sea, would be 74 kilometers. Regarding the number of locks, the Commission opted for four on each side of the continental divide, giving a summit level of 20.75 meters above sea level at mean tide.[67] A supplementary project was also suggested, omitting the uppermost level and cutting through the divide until the summit was progressively lowered to 10.00 meters above sea level. This would have the advantage of omitting one pair of locks at either side. The estimated cost of this alternative, five hundred and thirty-one million francs was only nineteen million more than for the initial scheme; and it had the advantage that all work done on the first plan would be equally useful for the second.[68] The Company therefore decided to adopt it, time permitting; and it was on this understanding that Mancini sought a third extension of the concession from Colombia.[69] All locks were to be double, 230 meters in length and 10 meters deep. One basin of each pair would be 25 meters in width, the other 18. The dams were also to furnish electric power.

As events transpired, the plan was to remain a purely theoretical one, to be superseded in 1906 by the American conception. Yet, there is little doubt that, from an engineering
viewpoint, a perfectly adequate waterway could have been
constructed, based on this conception. Its main defect, that
of scale, is attributable to the time and funds available and
not to any lack of skill on the part of the French engineers.[70]
Ever faithful to its frugal principles, the New Company
ordered a severe contraction of activity when the final verdict of the U.S. Isthmian Canal Commission in favor of
Panama became known. In 1902, in a highly confidential
note to Vautard, the board advised that work on every section should be closed gradually with only surveillance being
carried out with a skeleton staff.[71] There was, of necessity, a
large measure of deception implicit in this. It was designed
to maintain a level of industriousness sufficient to appease
the Colombian government while ensuring a radical reduction in expenditure.[72] The statistics speak for themselves.
The total volume of earth and rock removed annually fell
from a high of 1,210,000 cubic meters in 1899 to 430,000 in
1903, the last full year of operations. The labor force declined from 3,100 to 1,300 in the same period.[73] The American administration was to complain about this rundown
when it inherited the property. John Frank Stevens, the
chief engineer in those early days, described the railroad as
two lines "which, by the utmost stretch of the imagination
could not be termed railroad tracks."

These facts do not constitute a condemnation of the Company's policy after January 1902 when the sale was impending. At that date there was every reason for thinking that
a prompt entente would be included between Colombia and
the U.S.A. to allow the transfer to take place. It would have
been financially imprudent to have continued at the same
intensity. Few could then have forecast that more than two

years would elapse before the Americans were in a position to take possession.

This unforeseen extension in the period of French occupation led the Company to ask for further remuneration from the American government, additional to the forty million dollars originally negotiated. It was maintained that the U.S. evaluation had been based only on the quantity of work completed until 1901, at which time the I.C.C. had made its report. Since there was a continuation of activity for a further two years, it was argued that the new owners would find their task proportionately reduced. In March 1903 the attention of President Theodore Roosevelt himself was drawn to this appeal.[74] When Walker, Burr and Waines, all American members of the I.C.C. arrived in Panama a month afterwards, French hopes were high that these veterans of canal affairs would appreciate the justice of the request. Marius Bô who had replaced Bonnardel as Company president advised his staff of the need to create a favorable impression on the guests since all they could count on was the benevolence and sense of fair play of the U.S. government.[75] Past experience ought to have prepared the Company to expect the worst.

Walker had an even greater aversion to spending money than his hosts. According to William Gorgas, the chief medical officer for the Canal Zone during the American construction period, he was to carry his meanness to pathological extremes once established as chairman of canal administration by Washington. He is said to have declined to open letters from subordinates lest they contain some request or other for additional funds to meet an emergency.[76] On this occasion, he refused to commit himself or his fellow commissioners when pressed by the New Company officials, and the French had to await the arrival of the entire complement of the Commission in April of the following year, 1904. Even this brought little solace. Some felt that there was merit in the claim for upward revision; others were opposed, and still others argued that the decision ought to be left to Congress.[77]

A sequel to this trip – and one which was to have negative results for the New Company – was a deterioration between two of its members, Walker and John Findley Wallace whom Roosevelt had appointed as supervising engineer. For a year Wallace fought against the petty economies imposed by Walker from Washington, and he finally resigned on June 25, 1905. When he was asked to testify before a Senate committee on interoceanic canals a year later, he had a perfect forum in which to vent his bitter feelings on the project as he had come to it in 1904. He had also a sympathetic interlocutor in Senator John T. Morgan, chairman of the Committee whose unswerving opposition to Panama will be discussed at length in subsequent chapters. In answer to Morgan's leading questions about conditions as he found them when he first came to the Isthmus, he replied that the French "were simply spending the least possible in order to retain possession of the franchise" and that what he had witnessed on landing was a scene of "chaos from one end to the other."[78] Whatever credence Roosevelt attached to this testimony, it later provided ammunition for a last ditch appeal by William Nelson Cromwell, the Company's chief lawyer. The President pointed out that any cessation of work would have given the Colombians the right to step in and revoke the concession there and then.[79] For him the matter was settled. Not for the first nor the last time, the United States demonstrated its inflexibility and obduracy in matters of canal diplomacy.

Notes

1. Documentation on the New Company's operations in Panama is sparse. I have summarized the findings of the commission constituted in accordance with Article 31 of the Compagnie Nou-

velle statutes and contained in the *Final and Définitive Report (of the International Technical Commission* (New York, 1898)). This body produced the plan followed by New Company engineers. An interim summary of progress was provided by the Commission Technique set up by the liquidation in 1889. Etienne Famin's *Mission de 1896 aux Antilles* (Paris, 1896) reveals some of the difficulties encountered in recruiting laborers.

2. See Chapter 2, p. *et seq.*

3. N.A. RG 185/37, Oppenheim to Newton, December 4, 1894.

4. A.N. 7 AQ 31, *Compagnie Nouvelle du Canal de Panama: Rapport (du Conseil d'Administration)*, December 15, 1896. The final cost of this facility was 5,599,826.18.

5. N.A. RG 185/37. *Forty Seventh Annual Report of the Board of Directors for the year ending December 31, 1896.* It was an uneasy truce that lasted only until 1900 when the P.R.C. recommenced charter shipping on the same route. This was discontinued in June 1902, following which another accommodation was reached.

6. A.N. 7 AQ 31, Compagnie Nouvelle. Rapport.

7. N.A. RG 185/1/1. *Troisième rapport (de la Cie. Universelle en liquidation, présenté au Tribunal Civil de la Seine par M. J.-P. Gautron)*, October 1894, pp. 2-6.

8. All distances are from Atlantic entry point. Readers may find the plan of the side elevation in Appendix A useful.

9. *Troisième rapport.*

10. N.A. RG 185/1/1, Mange to Mancini, November 12, 1894.

11. *Ibid.* Vautard to Mancini, March 12, 1895. The P.R.C. paid laborers 1 1/2 piastres a day. The New Company paid 80 centavos (100 centavos = 1 piastre = 4 francs). This was deliberate policy. Gautron had asked for a table of P.R.C. rates in July for the purpose of fixing Company rates and he knew they would and should be less. See *Canal Zone Library* 2-1338, Vautard (?) to Gautron, July 2, 1894.

12. N.A. RG 185/1/1, Vautard to Mancini, April 25, 1895.

13. In 1895 alone, there were 71 *notes de service* concerned with possible overpayment of staff: e.g. No. 4 where a M. Donon

had been paid 1,786.70 travel allowance for himself and wife. She had remained in France and so he was ordered to repay 893.95 in monthly instalments. No. 57 comprises 13 closely-typed sheets of overtime claims where totals seem excessive.

14. 14 N.A. RG 185/1/1, Mange to Mancini, October 23, 1894.

15. *Ibid.*, Mange to Mancini, October 26, 1894.

16. *Ibid.*, Mancini to Mange, February 10, 1895.

17. *Ibid.*, Vautard to Bonnardel, August 1, 1895.

18. N.A. RG 185/1/2, Ramet to Vautard. The dry season extended from then until the end of May.

19. *Supra.*

20. N.A. RG 185/1/1, Vautard to Bonnardel, September 30, 1895.

21. Edouard Drumont, *La Dernière Rataille* (Paris, 1890): Wolfred Nelson, *Mes cinq ans a Panama* (Paris, 1890).

22. The U.S. death rate between 1904 and 1906 was 29 per 1,000 though it did drop sharply thereafter. See Mack, *op. cit.*, pp. 528-29.

23. N.A. RG 185/11, *Issuances of the New Panama Canal Company to the Isthmian Canal Commission*, 1899.

24. *Messages and Papers of Presidents* (Washington, 1899), Vol. III, p. 852. The American government had been forced to apportion $250,000 for the repatriation of citizens.

25. N.A. RG 185/1/1, Pourquie to Monchicourt, November 20, 1892.

26. *Ibid.*, Vautard to Bonnardel, September 30, 1895.

27. CZL 2-1244 contains specimens of the detailed, three-page contracts.

28. For administrative purposes, the canal was divided into three parts, each supervised by a *chef de section*. The first extended from the Atlantic to km. 45; the second from km. 45 to 56; the third from km. 56 to the Pacific. See N.A. RG 185/1/2, "Ordre de service – 27", November 29, 1895. Also N.A. RG 185/1/1, Renaudin to Vautard, February 20, 1896. Legal matters, health and local recruitment were also the responsibility of *chef de section* 2.

29. *New York Times*, March 3, 1898.

30. N.A. RG 185/1/1, Mallet to Renaudin, April 11, 1901. He had received complaints of unprovoked attacks by the police on pay days and the refusal of jailers to release "offenders" until they had paid for their "crimes".

31. Famin, *op. cit.*, p. 69.

32. *Ibid.*, p. 73.

33. N.A. RG 185/1/19, Saurine to Vautard, June 12, 1896.

34. 34 N.A. RG 185/1/14, Lacroisade to Royer, June 23, 1897. Thirty-seven of eighty-three died.

35. *Ibid.*, em Avis aux ouvriers africains, September 1, 1897. Though some had technically broken their contracts by acting in this manner, it was decided that all would be allowed free return passage on the S.S. *Holyrood* which left Colon on September 15.

36. N.A. RG 185/1/1, Ramet to Vautard, May 16, 1896.

37. A.N. 7 AQ 31, *Mission de 1890-91 en Colombia*: Appendix D III.

38. N.A. RG 185/1/1, Mancini to Holguin, November 8, 1895.

39. *Ibid.*, Le Cornec to Renaudin, November 8, 1895.

40. *Ibid.*, Mange to Mancini, November 22, 1895.

41. *Ibid.*, Bélin to Mancini, November 25, 1896.

42. N.A. RG 185/1/2. Notices to this effect appeared in local papers in the first week of July 1896.

43. N.A. RG 185/1/8, Bélin to Mancini, November 25, 1896. Vautard forwarded a list of defaulters to Paris on September 24, 1897. Two of these counterclaims were to cost the Company dear. See Chapter 9.

44. *Supra*, Article III, para. 1.

45. N.A. RG 185/1/18, Le Cornec to Casabianca, September 1, 1896.

46. N.A. RG 185/1/2, Le Cornec to Marie, November 11, 1895.

47. *Ibid.*, Vautard to Mancini, January 9, 1896.

48. *Ibid.*, Marie to Vautard, May 6, 1896.

49. See, for example, a letter from Renaudin to the Chef du Corps de Police, dated May 5, 1903, asking that constables return to duty as workers' anger had now abated (N.A. RG 185/1/2).

50. Miles P. Du Val, *Cadiz to Cathay* (London, 1940) compares the Hay-Herran and Hay-Bunau-Varilla treaties in this respect (in Appendix L).

51. N.A. RG 185/1/1, Berges to Brunet, September 18, 1889.

52. The currency crisis is dealt with in Miner, *op. cit.*, pp. 50-51 and 55.

53. N.A. RG 185/1/1, Vautard to Mancini, January 19, 1895.

54. *Ibid.*, Vautard to Bonnardel, March 27, 1895.

55. *Ibid.*, Bonnardel to Uribe, April 20: Mancine to Uribe, May 21: Bonnardel to Mallario, May 27, 1895.

56. N.A. RG 185/1/19, "Avis – Compagnie Nouvelle: Division du Secretariat et du Personnel", April 21, 1895.

57. N.A. RG 185/1/1, Mancini to Vautard. The decree granting tax exemption was issued on April 27; the other, abolishing stamp duty, on May 24.

58. N.A. RG 185/1/18, Belin to Ardilla (New Company lawyer in Bogota), April 25, 1899. The file contains reports on claims at Gatun, Obispo, Bohio and elsewhere.

59. N.A. RG 185/1/30, "Note pour Dr. Roman", May 19, 1897.

60. N.A. RG 185/1/1, Lemarquis to de la Tournerie, June 13, 1895. The letter spoke of the need to retain the workforce, ". . . evidemment, si nous les laissons partir, nous commetrions une lourde faute, car il en coutera moins pour les retenir que pour les rappeler."

61. *Ibid.*

62. Only 797,000 had been removed by November 1896. See A.N. 7 AQ 31, "Rapport du Conseil d'Administration", December 15, 1896.

63. *Ibid.*, also N.A. RG 185/1/2, Chanove to Ramet and Mange, February 8, 1896.

64. These included the following: Skalikowski (Russia), Sosa (the Colombian who had assisted Wyse in 1877-78), Koch and Fulscher (Germany) formerly associated with the Kiel Canal, Hunter (England) of the Manchester Ship Canal, and, on Cromwell's urging, two Americans, Abbott of the U.S. Army Engineering Corps and Fteley.

65. A.N. 7 AQ 13, *Commission d'études institutées par le liqui-dateur de la Compagnie Universelle. Rapport générale* (Paris, 1890), Vol. 1.

66. *Ibid.*, Final and Definitive Report, pp. 2-5.

67. *Ibid.*, p. 20 *et seq.*

68. *Ibid.*, p. 30.

69. See Chapter Five.

70. For opinions on the French plan, see W. Leon Pepperman, *Who Built the Panama Canal?* (New York, 1915). Pepperman was chief officer of the second U.S. Isthmian Canal Commission, and the book is a collection of diverse professional opinions. Width of the French canal (with final U.S. equivalents in parenthesis): 81.25' (110) and length: 731.25' (1,000).

71. N.A. RG 185/1/2, Choron to Vautard, January 22, 1902.

72. A.N. 7 AQ 31, "Rapport général du Conseil d'Administration", June 30, 1903. The phrase used was "diminuant nos dépenses dans toute la mésure de possible."

73. *Isthmian Canal Commission. Official Handbook of the Panama Canal* (4th ed.) (Washington, 1913), p. 43. In terms of total excavation, the New Company was responsible for 11,403,409 cu. yds.; the Compagnie Universelle for 66,743,551.

74. 59 Cong., 2 sess., *Sen. Doc. Vol. 33. Hearings before the Committee on Interoceanic Canals of the U.S. Senate* (Washington, 1906), pp. 3079-83.

75. N.A. RG 185/1/2, Bô to Renaudin, March 13, 1903.

76. Mack, *op. cit.*, p. 488.

77. A.N. 7 AQ 38, Cromwell to Bô, November 15, 1904.

78. *Supra.*, Vol. III, p. 2013.

79. A.N. 7 AQ 38, Roosevelt to Cromwell, April 18, 1906 (French trans. of Eng. original).

Chapter 5

The Challenge of Nicaragua[1]

From 1898 onwards, the history of the Compagnie Nouvelle was inextricably bound up with the strategic and economic requirements of the United States in Central America. On April 28, 1898, the U.S.A. declared war on Spain. Exactly four weeks later, the U.S.S. *Oregon* arrived in Key West, Florida to join Admiral Dewey's fleet for the forthcoming Battle of Santiago. The 14,760 mile voyage from San Francisco, via Cape Horn, which had taken sixty-seven days underlined America's problem of policing both Atlantic and Pacific as a result of recent acquisitions. To voices who had long advocated an isthmian canal under American control for commercial purposes were now added those who saw a military advantage in such a waterway. Shipping companies, chambers of commerce and individual citizens responding to patriotic feelings deluged congressmen with letters and petitions. Even as ostentatious an anti-imperialist as William Jennings Bryan was inclined to rest quiet, sensing in this outburst an expression of the national will.

For most Americans intimately concerned with canal policy, it meant an examination of the Nicaraguan route. The champion of this passageway, and lifelong opponent of Panama was the Democratic senator from Alabama, John T. Morgan. A former Confederate cavalry officer, he was deeply concerned with restoring prosperity to the ravaged South, a task which involved, among other things, the expansion of coal and cotton exports from the Gulf states. Morgan's predilection for Nicaragua was twofold: from the outset it would be under American control since the land would be bought outright and with it full U.S. jurisdiction; and, for another, it would give the ports on the Gulf of Mexico an advantage over their eastern seaboard rivals, in terms of proximity to West Coast and Far Eastern Markets, even more so than in the case of Panama as the following table reveals:

Route	via Panama	via Nicaragua	distance saved
New York-San Francisco	5299	4922	377
New Orleans-San Francisco	4698	4119	579
New York-Shanghai	11007	10752	255
New Orleans-Shanghai	10406	9949	457
New York-Yokahama	10087	9832	255
New Orleans-Yokahama	9486	9029	457

(distances in miles)[2]

Some preliminary survey work had been done there by the American-financed Nicaraguan Canal Construction Company in 1889, immediately following cessation of French activity. It, too, had had to weather financial difficulties as well as hostility from powerful U.S. transcontinental railway interests which insisted that it would never be able to compete. When Congress rejected two requests for aid, it was wound up in 1893. Morgan, undaunted, supported legislation to guarantee financing for a successor when it was introduced in the Senate the following January. But the only positive outcome was the appointment of the Ludlow Commission to investigate anew the pros and cons of the Nicaraguan route. Its report appeared in 1895, and gave qualified approval to the plan of the defunct company. It also estimated the cost at $133,472,893, a significant figure, as events were to prove. Two years later the first Walker Commission attempted to carry out a more extensive survey but was prevented from doing so by border skirmishes between Nicaragua and Costa Rica near the proposed site.[3]

Since the hastily-formed Maritime Canal Company had no hope of completing the project before a concession it had obtained from the Nicaraguan government expired, the latter granted a 'promise of contract' to yet a third contender known as the Eyre-Cragin-Grace syndicate, on October 31, 1898.[4] This called for construction to commence within two years, with completion before April 1912. With the backing of giants of commerce such as John Jacob Astor and Levi P. Morton, its prospects did not look unfavorable; but Morgan and his friends had reckoned without the determination of the Panama lobby and its chief protagonist, William Nelson Cromwell which suddenly appeared in the corridors of power in Washington.

Cromwell could boast a highly successful career before he became associated with the Compagnie Nouvelle. At the age of thirty-six, he had become a partner in one of Wall Street's leading law firms, and in 1891 had brilliantly reorganized the giant Northern Pacific Railroad Company. Since 1893 he had been legal counsel for the Panama Railroad Company in which he held a few shares, and it was in this capacity that he was to be involved with its parent body. In 1895, Whaley, the P.R.C. legal agent in Panama

City, invited him to express his opinions on the future of the
second canal company.[4] Cromwell's analysis was distinctly
pessimistic. Not only had it a past to live down, but it was
virtually unknown in the United States. Most Americans, if
they knew anything at all about transisthmian projects, automatically thought of Nicaragua, and they would continue
to do so unless there was a radical change of attitude among
those who controlled the Compagnie Nouvelle.[5] Impressed
by such frankness, Whaley recommended the Brooklyn-born
lawyer to Bonnardel as legal representative of the Company
in the United States.[6] From the outset, Cromwell's role was
to be far greater than originally mooted in Paris. Within
weeks of his appointment, he was advising the board of the
shortcomings of the Nicaraguan route and the necessity of
publicizing the adverse comments on it which had been made
by Ludlow so that

> ... the opponents in Congress who oppose the (US)
> Government assuming such vast obligations will be
> promptly and quietly roused ... A little attention
> at this time will make a vast saving and difference.[7]

But, as if to typify the inertia of the board in those early
years, there was no response.

Undeterred, Cromwell worked zealously on his own
throughout 1897 both to obstruct all pro-Nicaraguan legislation and in urging the Company to adopt a more aggressive posture. Quite early he seems to have sensed that it
was madness for any private company to contemplate building a canal anywhere in Central America if the American
government should decide to do the same elsewhere in the
area.[8] Bonnardel was eventually made to see the trend in
Washington and, at Cromwell's urging, he wrote President
McKinley on February 18, 1898, giving an outline sketch of
his Company's progress since its inception, its lack of bonded

indebtedness and, most significantly, its independence of the French government.[9] Cromwell was particularly anxious that an energetic demonstration be made before the Walker Commission filed its report on Nicaragua. There was also a need to soothe American public opinion which had been offended by the pro-Spanish tone of certain segments of the French press in reporting the international scene.[10]

The outlook for the New Company did not look good when the Senate adopted a resolution in May inviting the Maritime Canal Company to fix a price for the possible sale of all its assets to the U.S. government. The stockholders responded with alacrity and the board provided a figure of $5,500,000 by June 21 whereupon Morgan introduced a bill for the immediate construction of a canal through Nicaragua.[11] Cromwell was not yet prepared to admit defeat. The International Technical Commission was due to make its report public in November; and he knew from preliminary findings that it would be favorable to the New Company and the choice of Panama as the better route. If the U.S. could somehow be induced to postpone its decision as to the location and then be persuaded of the superiority of Panama, it would solve two pressing problems. Not only would the spectre of a Nicaraguan rival be banished, but the New Company would have a partner, and there would be no need to negotiate a fourth concession treaty with the Colombians. The onus for gaining additional time would fall more heavily on the much broader shoulders of the United States government.

In Paris, the board drafted a letter to Delcassé at the Ministry of Foreign Affairs appraising him of the situation and requesting that the French ambassador in Washington be instructed to lend all assistance to Cromwell. Reference was made to Delcassé's immediate predecessor, Hanotaux, and to the encouragement he had given when the situation

was much less critical.[12] Meanwhile, Cromwell was organizing a publicity campaign of his own, replete with articles
and news items for the daily press, all of them designed to
flatter his client's achievements.[13]

When the I.T.C. report duly appeared, its conclusions
were every bit as favorable to Panama as he had hoped. The
French property was valued at four hundred and fifty million
francs, and the cost of completing the canal at between six
hundred and twelve million and seven hundred and twenty
million depending on height above sea level and dimensions
of the locks.[14] The iron was hot and Cromwell determined
to strike. The director of operations on the Isthmus, Hutin,
was to cross the Atlantic in November after consultations in
Paris. On December 2 he had an interview with McKinley
where he presented him with an English translation of the
I.T.C. findings.[15] The Company's fortunes appeared to have
revived most promisingly, but they received a setback only
two days after Hutin's meeting with the President when the
State Department announced that the Bogota government
had refused to grant the French an extension of their 1893
concession.[16] This was not strictly accurate, but the truth
lay buried in the labyrinth of Colombian politics and would
be hard to unearth.

Frequent reference has already been made to various political figures with whom the French negotiators had had to
deal since the 1870's. Present purposes now require a more
detailed examination of the background to events which were
about to take place in the Republic of Colombia. The original state of Colombia had also comprised the present nations
of Panama, Ecuador and Venezuela. However, separatist
sentiment and resulting civil war had caused Ecuador and
Venezuela to go their separate ways by 1832. The remaining
fragment took the name New Grenada. Though its constitution gave wide powers to the federal government in Bogota,

formidable natural barriers militated against any real sense of national unity, and the Liberal party secured changed whose result was to create semi-autonomous provinces, like Panama. The 1860s saw an almost classical nineteenth century liberal attack on the Catholic Church, with the expulsion of certain religious orders, confiscation of ecclesiastical property and the introduction of a civil marriage ceremony, all of which provoked counter-action. This was led by the Conservatives who espoused limited suffrage, restoration of church property and greater centralization of government.

Initial French activity under de Lesseps had coincided with the rise to power of a Liberal, Dr. Rafael Nunez. Once in office, though, he quickly disavowed his previous political allegiance and began attacking particularism and anticlericalism. The climax to this Becket-like *volte face* was the introduction of a new constitution in 1886 which renamed the country the Republic of Colombia and presaged a return to strong, federal government. A concordat was signed with Rome, and the president was vested with extensive emergency powers. The years 1888 to 1892 were marked by increasing discontent, to which influential Conservatives, no less than disillusioned Liberals were a party. Corruption and inefficiency brought the nation to the verge of bankruptcy, while mishandling of foreign debt obligations had practically ended the flow of capital from abroad. A splinter group, calling itself the Historicals, was formed and drew support from the disgruntled of both old line parties. It advanced the candidacy of General Marcelino Velez against Nunez in the presidential election of 1892. Despite a lot of Liberal support, Velez was beaten in a campaign that was corrupt, even by Colombia's deplorable standards. Nunez remained in office, but only by resorting to police state methods and lavish subsidies to the armed forces.

The death of Nunez in 1894 triggered off a rebellion since

the opposition considered his successor, vice-president Caro, every bit as dishonest. The next presidential contest, in 1897, saw all three parties providing candidates. Caro, convinced that even massive bribery would not overcome his popularity, proposed the aging but respected Dr. Manuel Sanclemente as the Conservative choice. The Historicals nominated General Rafael Reyes, a popular soldier and one-time explorer, while the Liberals, in advancing the candidacy of Manuel Samper, warned that a repetition of the 1892 contest would inevitably lead to revolution. Sanclemente won over a divided opposition but the real power was still Caro. When the former asked to be relieved of his duties, he was moved to the outskirts of Bogota where he could sign decrees but remain isolated from the pressure of cabinet and press.

Meanwhile, the economy went from bad to worse. One third of the budget went to the military and the currency was subject to frequent devaluation. By 1898, the opposition was preparing for war, angered by the repeated use of the Nunez constitution and specifically Article 121 by which the president could ignore Congress and rule by decree. Such was the situation when Mancini requested a third renewal of the New Company's concession.

His request was based on the International Technical Commission's recommendation that it would be preferable to cut deeper than the thirty- five meters above sea level originally planned by de Lesseps, or even the twenty-five meters suggested by the Guillemain Commission. He was at pains to point out the considerable advantages that would accrue to Colombia from the increased traffic which would use the canal if the transit time was less (and it would be if the new plan were adhered to).[17] Molina, the Finance Minister, was not in a position to act independently; he said he had to consult the President which meant, in effect, obtaining Caro's consent. Therefore, it was not until December 21 that Cromwell was able to inform the U.S. government and, specifically John Hay at the State Department, that he had erred: the prolongation *would* be granted, subject to approval by the Colombian Congress.[18] McKinley's annual message to congress on December 5 contained no reference to Panama. It did review the situation in Nicaragua and recommended that steps be taken for the planning of a canal there.[19]

Morgan's elation at this announcement was tempered by the certainty that neither Cromwell nor Hutin would accept it as final; and he publicly denounced the Panama interest for conspiring to deny the American people of a canal of their own so that they might offer one that was under alien ownership.[20] What Morgan had forgotten was that a waterway through Nicaragua built, owned, managed and fortified by the United States would contravene an Anglo-U.S. agreement of long standing, the Clayton-Bulwer Treaty of 1850 which specified that any such project must be a joint venture of the two sig-natories.[21] Cromwell naturally seized on this and, in correspondence with Hay and McKinley, dwelt at length on the illegality of the proposed Nicaraguan legislation. At the same time, he arranged for New Company and Panama Railroad Company staff to testify before a House Committee on Interstate and Foreign Commerce on the absence of such a barrier in the case of Panama. Nevertheless, Morgan's bill was adopted by the Senate on January 21, 1899 on the legislators' assumption that the Clayton-Bulwer Treaty could be abrogated without too much fuss from the British.[22] Everything now rested on the House of Representatives, and it was there that Cromwell concentrated his attention. "If," as he put it, "a vote could not be deferred, the fate of Panama was sealed."[23]

Providential aid came from two sources. First, the House

Committee, chaired by William Hepburn, was tepid as far
as the bill was concerned, having had an opportunity to consider the ramifications arising from any unilateral attempt
to change the 1850 Treaty. It was also perplexed and wor-
ried by the legal confusion surrounding the various commercial interests active in Nicaragua. Not only had the Eyre-
Cragin-Grace syndicate been granted a concession, but the
Maritime Canal Company had lost its rights relating to inland water transportation in 1894. It had ceded these to
the Nicaragua Mail and Steamship Company which had, in
turn, sold them to the Atlas Steamship Company. Thus, the
question of who owned what in the proposed area was far
from clear, as various witnesses before the Committee had
made evident.[24] Secondly, there existed a personal rivalry
between the Democrat, Morgan, and the Republican, Hepburn. It is fair to say that both men assumed that Nicaragua
was bound to triumph; but each wanted the credit for party
and self.

This *furor canaliensis*, as Dwight Miner has described it,
continued unabated though Congress had only three weeks
of the session to run. The solution adopted to break the
deadlock was the establishment of yet another commission to
investigate both routes and define, more precisely,
Nicaragua's legal relationship with her various concession-
aires. Since the long-term consequences of this move were a
triumph for Panama, the identity and motive of the author
of this idea is of much significance in the present context.

Determined not to be outflanked by the Hepburn committee, Morgan attached his legislation to a Rivers and Har-
bors Bill with the House had already sent up to the Senate.
The canal commission idea was seen as an amendment to
Morgan's supplementary legislation. Philippe Bunau-Varilla
claims with characteristic lack of modesty that it was he who
laid the ground work for what followed during the fall of

1898 when he converted his old friend, John Bigelow, a former U.S. ambassador to France and Lieutenant-Commander Asher Baker, to the plot. On their return to the U.S.A. from Paris, as his story goes, Bigelow influenced Hay and Baker talked to his friend, Thomas Reed, Speaker of the House. In this way "light fell on the government itself."[25] To accept this as the genesis of the Isthmian Canal Commission would be to deny the value of Cromwell's work nearer the scene. His knowledge of the workings of the capital and his business connections with prominent members of both parties cannot be ignored. He had reason to believe that the longstanding rivalry between Morgan and Hepburn would continue and was perspicacious enough to see that the New Company could, indeed had to, exploit that rivalry.

Since McKinley had been as consistent as anyone in his attitude to Nicaragua, Hutin's letter to him may not have been without effect, either. Writing on February 28, only a week after testifying before Hepburn's committee, the Director-General of the New Company asserted that it had never sought and did not now seek financial assistance from the American government. But it recognized that national sentiment in the U.S.A. was in favor of acquiring an interest in a transisthmian canal. In that case, the French company would not be averse to reincorporation under the laws of the State of New York (under whose jurisdiction the P.R.C. had functioned for close to half a century), or any other state if the President so desired. In such an eventuality, his board would "... accord to the United States such representation as might be permitted by its charter," and further, "... if the United States should desire to perpetuate or enlarge on existing rights and privileges, acquired under the said Treaty of 1846,[26] the Company (would) conform to such supplemental treaty as may be entered into between the United States and Colombia."[27] This declaration of interest may

have helped allay American fears regarding the 'foreignness'
of the Compagnie Nouvelle. As early as 1880, President
Hayes had voiced such apprehensions, though in a slightly
different context:

> The United States cannot consent to the surrender
> of this control to a European power. The capital
> invested in such an enterprise must, in a great de-
> gree, look for protection to one or other of the great
> powers. No European power can intervene for such
> protection without adopting measures on this con-
> tinent which the United States would deem wholly
> inadmissible.[28]

The House then accepted the brief from the New Company
as sufficient reason to reexamine all possible routes; but the
Senate stood firm by its earlier decision to give preference to
Nicaragua. Republican leaders grew anxious over the date
for adjournment, and with good reason. Their forces were
in control in both houses following the 1896 elections, and
so responsibility for canal legislation lay with them. So it
was that, at the crack of the party whip, the Republican-
dominated Senate Committee abandoned the Democrat
Morgan.[29] In the dying days of the session, a committee
report in favor of setting up an Isthmian Canal Commission
became law. It was instructed by the President to "determine the most feasible and practical route under the control,
management and ownership of the United States."[30] These
terms of reference constituted a victory for a foreign company that had been an unknown quantity to Americans only
two years before.

The next hurdle facing the French – and this, too, was the
responsibility of the men on the spot in Washington – was to
prevent the appointment of ostentatiously pro-Nicaraguan
individuals to the I.C.C. Hutin assured McKinley that his

board welcomed this most recent development but he begged to suggest that it be composed of men with the widest experience, not "embarrassed by public committals or previous records favorable to either one or the other project."[31] Cromwell, for his part, furnished a list of engineers which he had prepared as soon as he knew the idea for a Commission had been approved. He was particularly anxious to see the exclusion of pro-Morganites, such as Professor Haupt. This gambit failed and both he and Walker were among its members. Given this check, Cromwell did what he could to influence subsequent moves. He suggested that, instead of proceeding directly to Central America, the Commissioners might find a visit to Europe enlightening. Consequently, they spent the summer of 1899 inspecting the Kiel and Manchester Ship Canals before arriving in Paris on August 17.[32] This was the first occasion the Company had had to acquaint these technical experts with its achievements and future plans. The hospitality was lavish, and the tireless Cromwell was on hand to guide Admiral Walker and his colleagues as they sampled the attractions of the City of Light.

*   *   *

The cordiality of their reception concealed serious internal dissensions which had arisen within the New Company a few months previously. On March 25, Lemarquis had written Bonnardel to explain his letter of resignation from the board. He regretted having to terminate a collaboration that had lasted since 1894, but he was exasperated by the lethargy of the directors:

> We have already lost, and I am convinced that we are going to lose even more precious time in sterile discussions, time which ought to have been used in taking action. I can no longer share in the respon-

sibilities which have accumulated for this committee whose inertia I have failed to shake.[33]

The irascibility of the mandataire was due, primarily, to the
lack of action on the Company's part following receipt of
its own Technical Commission report on February 28, 1899.
It will be recalled that this body had been constituted, according to the articles of the Company, when one half of its
paid-up capital had been expended[34] – a condition that had
been reached in December, 1898. Though this Commission
reported at some length, it did little beyond confirming the
findings of the I.T.C. including advocacy of a canal design
based on an altitude of 20.75 meters above sea level. Lemarquis felt that its optimistic conclusions as to what had been
achieved since 1894 ought to have been given immediate exposure throughout France in the offchance that additional
funds could yet be raised via public borrowing. Instead, the
board had seemed content to wait upon developments on the
other side of the Atlantic. The full report of the Technical
Commission was not to be made public until November 30,
1899 but even then, Lemarquis and Gautron alleged, it was
"in a manner that can best be described as most discreet."[35]
     The liquidation was soon to discover additional reason for
irritation. The fate of the Panama Railroad Company's own
stock depended on the attitude of shareholders, once they
were appraised of the conclusions of this Technical Commission. If the suggestion was for a continuation of work on
Panama, the share rights, vested in the liquidator's estate
were to become the property of the New Company without any monetary compensation going to the liquidation as
long as the canal was completed. A negative decision, on
the other hand, would leave the railroad in the hands of the
Company, but it would have to pay the liquidation twenty
million francs and half of any surplus on sale of assets.[36] The

prospects for the enterprise were still not all that bright, and they received a double blow. The first came from the publicity given to the death of Cornelius Herz in exile, in July 1898. He had been the blackmailer of Reinach and a typical relic of the bad old days of Panama. Soon afterwards, the second Vallé committee of inquiry, set up by the Chamber of Deputies, published its findings, based on the unsavoury revelations of Emile Arton who had also played a role in the era of the Compagnie Universelle as embezzler and bribery agent.[37] Naturally, these events made the board less inclined than ever to ask shareholders for a decision on what immediate course to take or to appeal to the public for the six or seven hundred million francs still required to complete the canal (if it was to be exclusively a private, French effort). One small expedient was to try to persuade Gautron to exchange his rights to the assets of the P.R.C. for a quantity of shares in the New Company, the number to be decided by mutual agreement. There were also the remainder of the lottery bonds which, it was hoped, he might be persuaded to 'release' at the 'bargain' price of seventy-five francs each.[38]

Gautron showed Lemarquis the letter which he had received from Bonnardel outlining these suggestions. The mandataire's response was distinctly lukewarm and Gautron was inclined to agree with his conclusions. There was no objection, in principle, to the cession of the lottery bonds for additional capital; but the price mentioned was quite unacceptable. Furthermore, the P.R.C. shares constituted one of the most considerable assets belonging to the creditors of the old company.[39] This joint reply caused Bonnardel to comment, with some acerbity, that unanimity was vital "at the very moment when the fate of the enterprise will depend on whatever perception the United States puts upon our behaviour."[40] It would be highly impolitic to attempt to raise capital and risk a rebuff of the kind sustained in 1894, the only occasion on which the Compagnie Nouvelle had made an appeal for public monies. The enemies of Panama would not miss that opportunity to exploit the Frenchman's lack of faith in a venture of his own compatriots.

The American decision to establish the Isthmian Canal Commission and its impending visit to Paris altered matters considerably. Gautron recognized that its report might take as long as two years to prepare and submit to Congress and the President; and, until that time, the Company had had to have sufficient funds to show continued vigour. He therefore informed the board that, in the light of these changed circumstances, he was ready to discuss the cession of the 670,000 unissued bonds with a view not only to determining their market worth but also to discuss the conditions under which they might be offered to the public either now or at a later date. He was still adamant that no transfer of P.R.C. shares would be made.[41]

On this understanding, negotiations continued throughout the summer of 1899 and terminated on August 9 in a tentative understanding among the parties concerned. To preclude any possibility of a negative decision by the shareholders, it was decided to postpone the extraordinary general meeting required by the statutes. The Company would continue to function, using the remainder of its capital. Payment by the Company for the rights to the P.R.C. stock would also be delayed. This agreement was not to become legal until ratified by an ordinary meeting of the shareholders and thereafter confirmed by a court decision.[42] But no such development occurred – for a reason that was to shake the New Panama Canal Company to its very foundations.

For an understanding of what followed, two facts need to be restated: the first is that the Salgar-Wyse concession forbade the sale of the concession to a foreign power, as distinct from a private concern: the second is that Arton's disclosures to the parliamentary commission made the possibility of a return of public confidence in the Panama company a remote possibility. Given this situation, Cromwell, Bonnardel and the directors were of a mind in thinking that the best solution to all their problems lay in the immediate Americanization of the Company. As early as 1896, Bonnardel had talked of "the common interest which exists between the Company and the United States and the legitimate interests which the United States have to safeguard."[43] The plan mooted in 1899 seems to have envisaged an American-based corporation so constituted that its capital would ensure the French half the shares and a majority of members of its board. Cromwell was obviously the one best suited to look after the details, and a decision giving him the requisite authority was taken at a board meeting on October 10 while he was still in the French capital.[44] Gautron and Lemarquis knew nothing of this until the end of the month. The only inkling they had that something radical was afoot was a rather vague letter from Cromwell to Lemarquis written on the eve of his return to New York in which he regretted not having had the opportunity to meet with the mandataire but informing him that Hutin and Edouard Lampré, the New Company's secretary would explain the details. He would only go as far as to say that:

> ... we are working for the interests of the beneficiaries of the Canal, rather than allowing strangers to do so, and, in this important work, I expect you to take an important part – if it develops. This I can only determine upon my return, and I shall report to you.[45]

The scheme, in fact, called for the flotation of a corporation with a common stock of forty-five million dollars and preferred stock to a maximum of sixty million. Three fourths of the directors would be U.S. citizens and the head office would be located in either New York or the state of New Jersey. The Compagnie Nouvelle would transfer all of its assets to it, receiving in exchange, a majority of shares in the new body.[46]

The note to Gautron containing the details of this startling development contained few details, and, in referring it to Lemarquis, he observed that the board seemed to have abandoned all basis for agreement they had made heretofore.[47] A request for additional information was met with the reply that the directors did not consider that their latest move invalidated that understanding at all. They maintained that the new proposal would be submitted for approval when the shareholders gathered on December 30. As to the Americanization, the board was ready to enlighten both men as to its essentials. However, it would be best if they would formulate their objections in advance as time was pressing and action would have to be taken very soon.[48] The degree to which liaison had broken down between the two parties was shown in a subsequent communication to Gautron on December 18. Bonnardel and his colleagues had consulted their legal counsel in New York, i.e. Cromwell, and he had opined that the New Company was acting within its rights in going ahead on its own initiative, without reference to the liquidator or the mandataire.[49]

There was no ignoring this challenge; and the two men who, more than any others, had nursed the fragile Company through birth and infancy did not intend to do so. On December 23, Gautron fired off a reply which left Bonnardel in no doubt that he and Lemarquis were diametrically opposed to all that had been done and also to the claim that the board could act independently. He implied, too, that legal action would be taken if that was the only way of halting the scheme. Since he was not only responsible for the bondholders of the old company but also held a sixty per cent interest in the profit of the New, he had no intention of allowing anyone to be enticed into voting for a measure whose consequences would be fatal to both.[50]

Meanwhile, Cromwell was on the point of registering this mysterious corporation under the laws of the state of New Jersey; but it was one whose base differed significantly from that that had been mooted in October. The object of this revised concern was not to be confined to the achievement of the canal, but might extend into shipbuilding and transportation. Its capital was fixed, at least on paper, at three million dollars represented by three hundred thousand ten dollar shares. Provision was made for creating extra capital to a maximum of fifteen million in preference shares.[51] Whether this peculiar organization was ever intended seriously to finish the Panama Canal is a matter of conjecture. Certainly, its miniscule capital precluded such an idea.

In the event, the intransigence of Gautron and Lemarquis won the day. On December 28 they met Bonnardel before a judge in the chambers of the Tribunal Civil de la Seine. Lemarquis warned that if the American scheme came to be discussed at the shareholders' meeting on the 30th, the resulting outburst (for outburst there would surely be) would damage the New Company's image irreparably. He and M. Gautron were prepared to fight this thing to the very end.[52] The board met on the 29th, and, though there is no detailed account of their deliberations, they issued a communique at the end, announcing that they would not

> continue to fight against the liquidation ... for the interests which we have devotedly served for the past five years will suffer less by our retreat than from discussions whose consequence is difficult to measure.[53]

Bonnardel then went to the office of the Tribunal Civil and tendered the resignation of the entire board. This extraordinary move was announced to the stockholders at the ordinary general meeting the following afternoon. The extraordinary meeting planned for the same day to decide the events on the other side of the Atlantic did not take place, of course, and the August agreement fell into abeyance. Thus, as 1900 dawned, the Compagnie Nouvelle was in a state of disarray.

It may be questioned whether those involved in the scheme to transfer the Company to the U.S.A. were really clear as to what purpose they expected the move to serve; and certainly no two were in full agreement on all the points. But all could find features to justify their conduct or their interpretation of events. Bunau-Varilla, for instance, claims that the American syndicate which Cromwell tried to create with Bonnardel's blessing had but one aim – to sell out to another group, perhaps Morgan's Nicaraguan interest, and retain a major portion of the profit from the enterprise for very little effort.[54] This is refuted by Cromwell's later claim that the abortive company was simply a manoeuvre to remove the stigma of 'foreignness' from the French enterprise, without depriving the original investors of control. Moreover, he maintained, the project "never was consummated, either by subscription or assent .... It had no life force or being ... did not exist and has never existed."[55] When the press contacted the so-called 'founders' of the American concern, the statements they gave were equivocal, to say the least, and they were certainly at odds with the confident expressions Cromwell had made to the New York *Daily Tribune* only a few days previously.[56] It would appear that Cromwell had acted independently, even of the board in Paris. As late as December 28 when Gautron and Lemarquis issued their ultimatum, it was still in the dark as to the structure of the proposed corporation from that agreed to in October. Bonnardel cabled the lawyer's Wall Street offices on the 27th requesting such information for the benefit of the stockholders. The reply given explained the alteration in form in terms of the sudden financial panic on the New York Stock Exchange which had made it impossible to raise money on any firm engaged solely in canal construction. Nowhere in Cromwell's reply is there any mention of the strenuous opposition of Gautron and Lemarquis.[57] It may be that he misjudged the situation while in Paris and felt that he had what amounted to a *carte blanche* from that end. In correspondence with Navarre, the New Company's temporary head, and with Lemarquis, immediately afterwards, he certainly evidenced a remarkable degree of contrition.[58]

A more recent interpretation sees the whole Americanization incident as a subtle and effective plot to remove Bonnardel and his supporters on the board without necessarily opposing the principle of U.S. ownership.[59] It was the Lyonsborn entrepreneur who had conducted negotiations with the three banks, the Crédit Lyonnais, the Société Générale and the Crédit Industriel et Commercial which had culminated in their making unwilling contributions to the New Company's capital. He had had successes in a number of ventures prior to his association with Panama, and these had earned him the enmity or jealousy of certain influential French businessmen. Linked with him in this new undertaking were his close friends, Chanove, Brolemann and Souchon. By 1898, therefore, there were several who would welcome his fall. There exists an undated, unsigned "Note pour répondre aux lettres de Monsieur le Liquidateur et á la communication adressee par MM. Gautron et Lemarquis aux actionnaires" in the Paris archives which Bouvier feels convinced is by Bonnardel. The note claims that Henri Germain, president of the Credit Lyonnais, was in the plot to overthrow him and

that both the liquidator and the mandataire laid great store
by his, Germain's, opinions. Germain himself, it continues,
had shown himself

> absolutely opposed to our conduct. (This was) un-
> usual intervention especially since the representa-
> tives of the Crédit Lyonnais on our board had al-
> ways shown themselves to be very much partisans
> of the Americanization plan.[60]

This line of argument is substantiated by three additional
sources. First, an analysis of the membership of the new
board which took office on February 12, 1900, reveals that
it ws dominated to as great a degree as in the past by representatives from the three banks which had been among
the ranks of the *pénalitaires.* Immediately following its first
meeting, it gave instructions to the Company's agent in New
York to "Reassure Mr. Hay, the Secretary of State that our
previous declarations still stand."[61] Second, among some private papers of Joseph Caillaux, then Minister of Finance in
the Waldeck-Rousseau administration, there appears a brief
note on a conversation between "the Minister"[62] and Maz-
erat, vice-president of the Crédit Lyonnais, on February 16,
1900. In it, the former appears to be speaking from a position of knowledge and authority as he strongly advises sale
of the canal concession, especially in view of Hutin's cautious, possible fatal, attitude.[63] The implication is that the
Crédit Lyonnais was in a position to dictate policy. That
Hutin was to go the way of Bonnardel within two years because of pressure from the new board will not go unnoticed,
either. Third, Lemarquis was to castigate the old group
of directors before the assembled stockholders in February
as "a collection of incompetents, lacking in character, will
and energy ... these were people who would not have shrunk
from any manoeuvre to circumvent you ...."[64] And yet, as

noted already, the composition of the new board did not differ radically from its predecessor.

There is one final consideration. As the nineteenth century drew to its close, French high finance was increasingly concerned by German rivalry in Africa and the Middle and Far East, despite some cooperative efforts in Europe itself. By coming to terms with its American counterpart and abdicating the last of its influence on the continent of the Americas, it might have sought to assure itself of future support in those areas where the Monroe Doctrine did not hold sway but where U.S. influence could nonetheless be useful. In neither country was there a clear division between the worlds of big business and high finance. Men like Cromwell, Casimir-Perrier and Waldeck Rousseau slipped easily from the one to the other.[65] In the sphere of international diplomacy, as well, France could discern the genesis of an anti-German coalition with Russia and England as partners. She had, as a consequence, no desire to antagonize the Americans over a lost cause such as Panama. In this light, the eagerness of Third Republic politicians and financiers to accommodate Washington and Wall Street becomes understandable, as does the increasing cordiality between Delcassé and the Republican administrations of McKinley and Theodore Roosevelt.[66] By 1906 it might have been surmised that American support for the French position at the Algeciras Conference would not be entirely fortuitous. In the meantime, there was a mammoth task in hand to defeat the proponents of Nicaragua once and for all and sell Panama as the only alternative for a Central American canal.

Notes

1. Some account of the agitation for a transisthmian route by U.S. interests is to be found in Julius W. Pratt, "American Business and the Spanish-American War" in *Hispanic American Historical Review*, Vol. XIV (1934), p. 180 *et seq.* The motives of the

Nicaraguan lobby are examined in *The Fight for the Panama Route* by Dwight C. Miner (New York, 1940). The best full-length survey of Colombian history in the nineteenth and early twentieth centuries is by Jesus Maria Henao and Gerardo Arrubia, *The History of Colombia* (trans. J. Fred Rippy) (Chapel Hill, S.C., 1938).

2. Source: I.C.C. *Preliminary Report,* 56 Cong., 2 Sess., *Sen. Doc. No. 5,* November 1900.

3. Mack, *op. cit.,* pp. 221-23.

4. An initial payment was made to the Nicaraguan government of $100,000, but the syndicate defaulted on the second, of $400,000, and the contract lapsed on August 9, 1900.

5. A.N. 7 AQ 37, Whaley to Cromwell, April 4, 1895.

6. *Ibid.,* Cromwell to Whaley, October 11, 1895. He entered New Company service in January 1896.

7. A.N. 7 AQ 37, Cromwell to Chanove (?), February 1, 1896.

8. He expressed these sentiments, at length, in a letter to Whaley on October 11, 1895. See also his testimony before the Rainey Committee on the same theme in *Story of Panama,* p. 206.

9. A.N. 7 AQ 30, Bonnardel to McKinley.

10. *Story of Panama,* p. 219.

11. *Congressional Record,* 55 Cong., 2 Sess., pp. 4923-24.

12. A.N. 7 AQ 31, "Note remise a M. Delcassé", August 17, 1898 (unsigned).

13. A good example is Henry L. Abbot, "The Panama Canal and the Nicaraguan Canal" in *Forum,* Vol. XXVI, No. 23, November 1898. Abbot was a member of the I.T.C.

14. These figures included interest on capital.

15. *Story of Panama,* p. 221.

16. New York *World,* December 5, 1898.

17. A.N. 7 AQ 38, Mancini to Molina, November 1, 1898.

18. 57 Cong., 2 Sess., *Sen. Doc.* No. 34, Cromwell to Hay: also A.N. 7 AQ 38, Mancini to Cromwell, December 20, 1898.

19. James D. Richardson, *Messages and Papers (of the Presidents, 1789- 1908)* (New York, 1909), Vol. X, pp. 101-02.

20. *Congressional Record*, 55 Cong., 3 Sess., p. 107.

21. The full text is given in *Sen. Doc.* No. 367, 61 Cong., 2 Sess. Article I forbade the signatories to "obtain or maintain ... any exclusive control over the said ship canal ... or to occupy or fortify or colonize or excercize any dominion over Nicaragua."

22. Senate attitudes are discussed in A.E. Campbell, *Great Britain and the United States, 1895-1903* (London, 1960), pp. 48-51.

23. *Story of Panama*, pp. 204-05.

24. *House Reports*, 55 Cong., 3 Sess., No. 2104, February 13, 1899.

25. *Panama, la création*, p. 208.

26. This referred to the Mallarino-Bidlack Treaty of December 12, 1846 which defined U.S. – Colombian relations.

27. A.N. 7 AQ 33, Hutin to McKinley.

28. Richardson, *Message and Papers*, VIII, pp. 585-86.

29. Miner, *op. cit.*, p. 90.

30. *United States: Statutes at Large*, Vol. XXX, p. 1150.

31. A.N. 7 AQ 33, Hutin to McKinley, March 11, 1899.

32. *Story of Panama*, p. 228 *et seq.*

33. A.N. 7 AQ 34, Lemarquis to Bonnardel, March 25, 1899.

34. By Article 75 of the statutes.

35. A.N. 7 AQ 34, "Situation financiere de la Compagnie Nouvelle" (unsigned, undated). By this time, the precise expenditure was 29,628,187 francs 89.

36. *Ibid. Communication du liquidateur de la Compagnie Universelle du Canal Interocéanique et du mandataire des obligataires à Messieurs les actionnaires de la Compagnie Nouvelle du Canal de Panama* (Paris, 1900), p. 1. Article 5, paragraph 3 of the statutes applied.

37. *Chambre des Députés: 6è legislature, session de 1898.* No. 2992.

38. A.N. 7 AQ 34, Board to Gautron, March 17, 1899.

39. *Ibid.*, Gautron to Board, April 20, 1899.

40. *Ibid.*, Board to Gautron, April 26, 1899.

41. *Ibid.*, Gautron to Board, June 20, 1899.

42. *Ibid.*, "Accord entre le liquidateur et le Conseil d'Administration de la Compagnie Nouvelle," August 9, 1899.

43. A.N. 7 AQ 31, "Rapport du Conseil d'Administration", June 30, 1896.

44. A.N. 7 AQ 34, "Procès verbaux des deliberations du Conseil d'Administration."

45. *Ibid.*, Cromwell to Lemarquis, October 12, 1899.

46. *Story of Panama*, pp. 229-30. Also, Mack, *op. cit.*, pp. 423-34.

47. A.N. 7 AQ 34, "Note remise a M. Gautron" (undated and unsigned); also Gautron to Lemarquis, November 13, 1899.

48. *Ibid.*, Conseil d'Administration to Gautron, December 1, 1899.

49. *Ibid.*, Conseil d'Administration to Gautron.

50. *Ibid.*

51. *Ibid.*, Canal de Panama. Communication du liquidateur, pp. 7-8.

52. A.N. 7 AQ 34, "Procès verbal de la déliberation du Conseil d'Administration", December 29, 1899.

53. *Ibid.*

54. *Panama, la création*, pp. 219-22.

55. *Sen. Doc.* No. 401, 59 Cong., 2 Sess. (Cromwell's testimony).

56. On December 27 Cromwell had mentioned that "a number of merchants, financiers and capitalists of well-known financial ability, standing and repute" were involved. When contacted, they supplied the following answers: Jacob H. Schiff – "I know nothing about it."; J. Edward Simmonds – "I refuse to answer that question!"; Jefferson Seligmann – "I have always been interested in Panama ....."; Harry Seligmann – "I may become interested in it. I have not decided yet." These statements were quoted in the New York *Daily Tribune* on December 28.

57. A.N. 7 AQ 38, Cromwell to Board, December 28, 1898.

58. A.N. 7 AQ 34, Cromwell to Navarre, January 18, 1900, and to Lemarquis on the same date.

59. Bouvier, *Une dynastie d'affaires lyonnaise*, pp. 201-05.

60. The Crédit Lyonnais representative was Brolemann.

61. A.N. F30 395, Conseil d'Administration to Boyard.

62. Waldeck Rousseau?

63. A.N. F30 394. In a small collection of notes headed "Confidential – Panama, mes notes personnelles." This one is dated February 16.

64. *Ibid.*, undated.

65. Waldeck Rousseau was legal adviser to both French canal companies.

66. This theme is developed in Charles W. Porter, *The Career of Théophile Delcassé* (Philadelphia, 1936), pp. 118-32.

Chapter 6

Preliminaries to the Sale[1]

The disappearance of Bonnardel and his fellow board members occurred at a crucial period in the history of Colombia and the United States. In the former, a particularly vicious civil war was imminent. For the Americans 1900 was an election year, and this carried with it the possibility that a new president – and one holding quite different views of canal projects from McKinley – might be elected. Thus, it was vital that the Compagnie Nouvelle display firmness of purpose and, above all, not remain leaderless at such a time. For this reason, the Tribunal Civil de la Seine made haste to appoint a temporary administrator, Eugene Navarre. He was to act as president of the board until such time as a new group of directors could be found and the selection ratified by the stockholders.[2] Navarre's immediate concern was to reassure the United States government that the organization he headed was still a viable one. Accordingly, Hay and McKinley were informed that there had been no fundamental change of attitude towards possible sale of the property and that all the information given to the Isthmian Canal Commission was still valid.[3]

Navarre then turned to the onerous task of creating a new board. There is, as in the instance of 1894, a serious lack of documentation regarding approaches made to specific individuals. However, it seems evident that when he consulted Gautron and Lemarquis, he found them anxious to secure a combination of financial expertise and technical experience.[4] In the first category, the banking establishment was again well represented with Marius Bô, a director of the Crédit Lyonnais, destined to inherit Bonnardel's presidential mantle. In the second, much reliance seems to have been placed on the advice of Edouard Alexandre Badois, secretary of the Engineering Society of France.[5]

There was much truth in the editorial verdict on the new board, as expressed by the *Revue Economique et Financière* that the efforts of Navarre, Lemarquis and Gautron had resulted in nothing more than a palace revolution of little interest to the public. It would, continued the editorial, be of little interest to the financial community, either, except for its impact in the fate of the enterprise in Panama.[6] It also reprinted one of the several letters it had received from disgruntled shareholders who felt that, in being summoned to a special meeting of the Company on February 12, 1900 to vote the new slate of directors, they were being presented with a *fait accompli*. Yet the same journal felt constrained to point out that, even if hours were to be spent in earnest discussion of their merits, the outcome would be little different. Since the banks were among the largest stockholders they were unlikely to relinquish control.[7]

It was felt necessary to take precautions against a repetition of the impasse which had precipitated the crisis of the previous December when board and liquidation were at loggerheads. Navarre vetoed Lemarquis's suggestion that a specific limitation of powers be imposed on each new board member as a condition of appointment. He felt that such a limitation would be detrimental in the recruitment of the best men; and, in addition, it would probably require the revision of the original statutes.[8] Only two days before this extraordinary general meeting was convened, a compromise was arrived at. In future, no policy decision of major consequence would be taken without consultation with the liquidator and mandataire. In the event of a divergence of opinion, recourse would be had to a consultative committee. Two of its members would be chosen by the Compagnie Nouvelle, two by the liquidator and mandataire acting in concert. There would be a fifth, independent chairman, and his vote would be decisive in the event of a deadlock. It was on this understanding that the individuals contacted were offered directorships.[9]

Among a number of external problems needing attention, none was more pressing than the need to obtain an extension of the 1893 concession, due to expire in less than five years. Negotiations for this purpose had begun as early as November 1898 when Sanclemente had agreed to submit Mancini's request to the subsequent session of the Colombian congress. Before it was due to meet, however, Carlos Calderon, the Minister of Finance had dispatched an envoy, Nicolas Esguerra, to Paris to investigate the New Company's financial health and, by implication, its ability to pay for the privilege. There he was joined by Samper and by the Colombian ambassadors to France and the United States respectively, Rafael Reyes and Dr. Climaco Calderon. The summer in Paris was a frustrating one in that the board refused to be co-operative. In part, its attitude could be attributed to the fact that it was preparing to receive the Isthmian Canal Commission members; but its reluctance to talk to the Colombians about money had another explanation. This lay in information relayed by Mancini from Bogota.

The political crisis which had been caused by the corrupt manner in which the Conservative Sanclemente had been elected president was deepening with every week that passed. In August 1898, the first of many reports of revolt in the remote interior was received in the Colombian capital. Soon, the administration was in desperate need of money just to retain the army's loyalty.[10] The Company was forewarned that the arrival of Esguerra and his two friends should be construed in only one way:

> We ought to conclude, then, that the funds of the Compagnie Nouvelle are going to undergo a formidable assault – that is what was plainly stated in a cable from the Finance Ministry to the governor of Panama.[11]

In these circumstances, Esguerra's suggestion that the French might have to come up with as much as thirty million francs for the right to have the Suarez-Mange agreement extended until 1910 should be regarded as exorbitant.[12] The Company was certainly not prepared to underwrite the costs of a counter-revolutionary offensive. It was held that, if the situation there continued to deteriorate, the Conservatives might be driven to settle for a reasonable amount with Mancini in Bogota. In December 1899 a series of government defeats and desertions from the armed forces put the future of the ramshackle regime of Sanclemente in even greater jeopardy. To pay him, or his administration would be foolish since their fall from power might see the Company's money vanish with them. On the other hand, a victory by the Liberals and their Historical allies – both lukewarm to transisthmian developments – was an equally bleak prospect. Chauvinism had become one of their watchwords. One of their generals had often expressed his hostility towards foreigners of any stamp in Panama maintaining that they were intent on selling out to the Yanqui government at the first opportunity.[13]

It came as no great surprise to Mancini when he was summoned to the Ministry of Finance on December 23. Without ceremony Calderon acknowledged the desperate straits in which the government found itself, and he then asked whether the New Company was willing to make an immediate cash advance of five million francs for what it wanted, with the balance to be decided after Esguerra and Samper had had talks with the Board in Paris. Mancini replied that he was in no position to commit his superiors but he was sure that a transaction as vague as this would take time to execute. He then asked for time to contact Bonnardel.[14] However, guerilla bands had been active in the area between Bogota and the Pacific coast, and they had cut the cable lines by which Mancini's message was to be transmitted to the French capital. As a result, it did not reach its destination until December 30, by which time the board was in the midst of its domestic crisis. So exigent had the government's needs become, however, that Calderon requested a second meeting with Mancini on January 8, 1900 even though Paris had not replied. This time he promised that the prolongation would definitely be granted by using the emergency powers available to the President. There was no mention of Congressional approval or, indeed, of sums additional to the five million that had been suggested in December. Calderon did point out that, for a million less than that, a certain French Match Company had been sold a lucrative trading monopoly, to the satisfaction of both parties.[15]

If communication between Mancini and the Compagnie Nouvelle was erratic, that between Esguerra and his government was infinitely worse. From mid-December the diplomat had heard nothing from Bogota and was forced to act on his own initiative, knowing little or nothing of what Calderon was doing, bewildered by the disappearance of the board and trying desperately to negotiate with its replacement. He was still convinced that he could wring a sizeable amount from it.[16] Meanwhile, the Conservatives were in a predicament. On the one hand, they recognized that it was rash to settle with Mancini for five million as long as Esguerra was in Paris and, as he had boasted, could extract a good deal more. On the other, there was the precarious military-cum-political situation literally at the palace gates to consider. In an unavailing attempt to crush the insurgents, military spending had been increased to the limit with the result that the treasury was completely empty. Thus, obtaining the New Company's gold involved far more than the re-negotiation of a canal treaty: their political future was at stake. Beyond this, again, there was the impression which this civic turmoil was creating on the mind of the American administration and Congress. If the United States was convinced that Colombia was in a semi-permanent state of insurrection, it would have no compunction in pressing ahead with the Nicaraguan alternative. In that event, the French would, in all probability, allow their concession to lapse. No one would have gained.

Faced with these unpalatable alternatives, the Conservatives' strategy was to conceal from its left hand what the right was doing. Esguerra was ordered to cease trying to negotiate and confine himself to the role of observer, for the moment. Simultaneously, a decree containing acceptance of the five million franc offer was being prepared at the Finance Ministry in mid-February.[17]

The matter might have been settled there and then had not the Compagnie Nouvelle decided that six years might be insufficient time for completion of the canal – and an eight year alternative would be more attractive to a prospective buyer. It therefore asked Mancini to sound out the possibilities for this extension by two years. The new submission was conveyed to Sanclemente in person but he replied that he would not budge from his original decision and, anyway, the paperwork on that had been completed. He added that he might well revoke what had been agreed upon unless payment was made within one hundred and twenty days of the signing of the decree.[18] There was still unease in Paris over the six year limit and Marius Bô, the new chairman of the board, issued Mancini with new instructions. He was to make a new offer, sweetening the pot by offering seven million for an eight year extension, retarding the expiry date to October 31, 1912. Five million would be delivered immediately with the balance at the end of six years.[19] French government assistance was promised by Delcassé.[20]

As soon as Esguerra learnt of the machinations of his government, he tendered his resignation. It was refused and he was given thirty days in which to conclude a more lucrative arrangement.[21] Talks between Mancini and Calderon in Bogota were halted in the hope that those in Paris would result in something better. But the Company refused to be drawn. Esguerra was given to understand, in the plainest of terms, that an entente would be concluded only in terms of what Mancini was negotiating in the Colombian capital. An incensed Esguerra insisted that nothing would be signed unless it conformed with his estimate of the situation and this would be "dictated in the interests of (his) political affiliation."[22] The French remained firm, heartened as they were by further communiques from their Colombian representative. By now it was all too obvious that the Conservative administration was playing a double game. On March 15 Calderon told Mancini that Esguerra was no longer empowered to speak on behalf of the government, and that he was prepared to accept the five million already discussed and regard the matter as closed.[23] Thanks to this bungling, Bô was able to confront the hapless Colombian envoy and dub his original claims "exaggerated demands, neither fair nor serious."[24] But the idea of an eight year extension had had to be abandoned. On April 23, Sanclemente put his signature to the last concession treaty the French were to have to negotiate. The time period was extended from 1904 to the last day of October, 1910.[25]

Native reaction to what the president had done was immediate and hostile. Indeed, three days before the signing took place, one of the rebel commanders, Vargas Santos, warned the New Company that the Conservatives no longer had the support of the people and that, whatever the contract, it would surely not be recognized by the "legitimate government of the nation." President Sanclemente was a tool in the hands of the Conservative Clique and had no mandate to enter into such a transaction without a plebiscite.[26] The insurgent Liberals even went as far as sending one of their number, Antonio Jose Restrepo, to Washington to plead their cause for diplomatic recognition. On May 8 Vargas Santos issued a second caveat to the French urging them to reconsider their policy. They would be misguided if they delivered their money into Sanclemente's hands because the revolutionaries would never recognize his "act of criminality."[27] Esguerra, still in Paris, found himself completely outpaced by events; but he also denounced the treaty as prejudicial to his nation and one which he must, for the sake of his honour, assail.[28] The Historicals who had been nursing their wrath since the presidential election of 1898 had found another reason to draw still closer to the Liberals for the purpose of unseating the government and dealing afresh with the foreigners.

By putting his signature to the concession agreement, Sanclemente had, indeed, sealed the fate of his regime. A rumor steadily gained ground that the presidential seal had been counterfeited and was being used by a clique of ministers and civil servants for their own ends.[29] When the Bogota supreme court rejected a plea to declare legislation carrying the deal invalid on the grounds that he had been coerced into affixing it to documents, the two opposition groups began to plan a coup. It was successfully staged on July 31. Marroquin, the Historicals' choice, was proclaimed head of the new administration as a concession to middle-of-the-road opinion which regarded the Liberal program as too extreme. Foolishly, he refused to reform the electoral system, and he conspicuously excluded Liberals from decision-making in his cabinet despite their repeated demands. It was all too much for revolutionary tempers still hot. By the beginning of October hostilities had broken out between the victorious parties, and Colombia was to suffer a more violent upheaval than ever as the three groups vied for power. By a supreme irony, Marroquin now found himself in the same position as the man whom he had replaced in his need for French monies.

*   *   *

Since private enterprise was unlikely to achieve the goal of building a canal across either Panama or Nicaragua, it was clear that the United States government would have to become involved. However, as has been noted, its freedom of action in this regard was circumscribed by the Clayton-Bulwer Treaty of 1850. The need for its abrogation led to the opening of diplomatic talks between Hay and Lord Pauncefote, the British ambassador in Washington in December 1898.[30] Hopes that a new settlement would be ready before Hepburn introduced his bill in Congress were dashed when the British demanded that an agreement on the Alaska Boundary Dispute between Canada and the United States must be a pre-condition of any modification of the 1850

Treaty. Hay refused, and instructed the American ambassador in London, Joseph Chaote, to do what he could to bring about a change in attitude on the part of the British Foreign Office.[31] This was not too difficult. At that moment the Fashoda crisis was erupting while the German Naval Law and the amount of world sympathy generated outside Great Britain for the Boers conspired to make her policy of splendid isolation less grand than it had once been. For these and other reasons which are not relevant to the present study, Lord Salisbury, the British prime minister, seized the chance to improve relations with the United States. Canadian interests were sacrificed and the first Hay-Pauncefote Treaty was drawn up on February 5, 1900.

The Senate was expected to ratify it within six months. As ill luck would have it, a member had leaked a copy to the press and, within a few days, it had become a hot topic of discussion in Washington. Controversy mainly centered on Article II which, in revising Article VIII of the original protocol, stated that any Isthmian canal was to be open to vessels of all nations on equal terms in both peace and war, and that no fortifications would be built for its defence.[32] Opposition to this clause was expressed by the statesman who, more than any other, would guide his nation to the control and eventual ownership of the Panama Canal – Theodore Roosevelt. His objections were based entirely on strategic considerations. Writing to Hay some two weeks after the leak, he maintained that if a canal had been in existence in 1898 and operating under the terms of Article II, the *Oregon* would certainly have reached her destination more speedily; but this would have been far outweighed by the ability of the Spanish fleet to use it as well, and to menace both coasts of the United States.[33] In another letter, he enunciated the principle of canal policy which was to guide him during his presidency:

> If the Monroe Doctrine means anything, it means
> that European powers are not to acquire additional
> territorial interests on this side of the water. I am
> not afraid of England, but I do not want to see
> Germany or France given a joint right with us to
> interfere in Central America.[34]

The Senate found itself in a somewhat embarrassing position by the publicity being given to the Hay-Pauncefote Treaty at a time when it was anxious to avoid controversy in international affairs – namely an election year. Therefore, it decided to postpone debate on ratification until December, by which time McKinley, or his opponent, would have been elected. Meanwhile, Morgan and Hepburn pressed ahead with preparation of their Nicaragua bill, confident that the treaty would be modified to their satisfaction.

Cromwell's penitential pose, following the debacle of his Americanization plan for the New Company did not deter him from returning to the fray. Less than three weeks after the board's resignation, he warned Lemarquis that the future of the French enterprise was in as grave danger as it had ever been. Any further attempts to locate the Company in the U.S.A. would almost certainly fail but there was a new consideration: the necessity of finding a means to delay or destroy the legislation which Hepburn and Morgan were planning so confidently. Seen from his vantage point, something might be made of the pending treaty with England, and the Nicaraguan bill might be delayed until the Isthmian Canal Commission had issued its full report. But these were feeble, negative avenues of approach unlikely to convert the majority who honestly believed that their nation had to have a canal as soon as possible and that Nicaragua offered the better prospect. A positive step might be to publicize the findings of the International Technical Commission and have

two of its members on hand to expatiate on the rosy conclusions of its report. But something would have to be done
quickly.[35] Another warning followed a week later. Politics,
cabled Cromwell, counted for more than the theories of engineers in Washington; and Congress would act with little
regard for the *pourparlers* held between Walker's commissioners and a board of governors that no longer existed.[36]
He pleaded for the presence of a Company representative in
Washington before it was too late. His advice was taken and
Hutin crossed the Atlantic in March. From this point until
the eventual sale of the French interest in 1904, the fate of
Panama was to be decided in Washington, Bogota and the
Isthmus, rather than in Paris. Increasingly, the board would
be presented with a series of *faits accomplis*.

The move soon bore fruit. In April Admiral Walker contacted Hutin requesting specific answers to three points: was
his company disposed to sell its property and its concession
outright rather than invite outside, e.g. American, participation in an essentially French venture? Did it have the
legal right to dispose of its assets? What figure did it have
in mind in the event that the U.S. government might be
prepared to buy? While this was not to be construed as
an indication of an American offer to purchase, it could be
taken as an indication of his government's determination
to have all aspects of construction and operation under its
exclusive jurisdiction.[37] Cromwell grasped this straw in his
effort to impede the rival camp by writing directly to the
President. He observed that the Compagnie Nouvellle had
dealt with the Isthmian Canal Commission on the assumption that it would investigate all possible routes impartially.
It also expected, reasonably enough, that no Congressional
action would be taken inconsistent with the aims expressed
in his own Message to Congress of March 1899 in which he
had said as much. Now, said Cromwell

... on the contrary, however, and presumably without the knowledge of the foregoing facts, measures have been introduced in Congress and are to be acted upon in the House of Representatives on May 1st and 2nd, 1900, having for their purpose the adoption of another Isthmian route, without awaiting the recommendation of the President and the report and conclusions of the Isthmian Canal Commission. We respectfully request that the President advise Congress of the facts of the case.[38]

Although this elicited no response from McKinley, it did drive Morgan to fresh fury and convinced him that it would be politic to sink any differences between himself and Hepburn to ensure rapid passage of the bill. This was achieved in the House on May 2 by a vote of 224 to 36. To enhance its chances in the Senate, Morgan tried to commit individual members of the I.C.C. to advocate the Nicaraguan route. A special Senate committee was hastily convened for the purpose. Its hearings began with a round castigation of the French Company and its evil genius, Cromwell. Morgan described his letter to McKinley as

... an insolent invitation to the President to control the action of Congress .... It is a spectacle that is, happily, without precedent, that this foreign corporation, acting in a foreign country and without recognition, even of the honesty of its dealings while it has all the while been subject to distrust by our government, should ask the President to 'advise' Congress of the facts of the case.[39]

Even so, Walker and his colleagues refused to be drawn pleading lack of evidence for their inability to endorse the Senator's choice of the Nicaraguan route. Pressure of other

business prevented a Senate vote being taken before the summer recess just when it seemed to Morgan that victory was
within his grasp (having heard of the confused situation in
Colombia that was causing his rival even more grief). He
had to be content with a motion to give it top priority when
Congress reconvened in December. Adjournment took place
on June 7 and both parties turned their thoughts to the
forthcoming election.

The next six months were to see a slow but perceptible
change in attitudes towards Panama in the case of several
leading Republican politicians. The most notable example
was that of Senator Marcus Alonzo Hanna who had been on
Morgan's improvised committee. His *volte face*, like that of
others, was attributed at the time to further Machiavellian
maneuvers by Cromwell. The first sign of a change was a
motion carried by the Republicans at their June convention.
In its omission of any mention of the Nicaraguan route as the
more acceptable solution, it differed markedly from a declaration on canal policy made by the Republicans four years
previously.[40] Hanna, who was later to become a staunch advocate of Panama, was chairman of the party's National
Committee. His efforts there, and later in the Senate would
ensure the ultimate approval of the majority for the purchase of the French holding. It was perhaps inevitable that
allegations would be made that New Company money had
accomplished this end. While Cromwell made no secret of
the fact that he actively lobbied at the convention on his
client's behalf, he denied charges of outright bribery, and
the accepted evidence for this allegation has rested on information supplied to Don Seitz, editor of the New York
World.[41]

An analysis of Company payments to Cromwell certainly
reveals that his expenditure was heaviest at this period.[42]
A French court decision of 1907 when the lawyer sued his

former employer for its refusal to pay what he thought was a reasonable commission on the money received from the U.S.A. includes the following judicial comment:

> The itemized list of expenses incurred since 1900 by Mr. Cromwell contains portions insufficiently justified to be conventionally audited, and from this arose difficulties which were finally resolved by the deduction of the above-mentioned expenses from those in the account which were properly audited, and the allocation of an honorarium, supplementary in nature, to indemnify Messrs. Sullivan and Cromwell for this deduction.[43]

Whether the bulk of this ended in the coffers of the Republican party may never be known for certain.[44] But, even if one assumes that there was a donation from the Compagnie Nouvelle, there are other motives to be considered for the party's reluctance to show the same wholehearted support for Nicaragua then as it had done in 1896. Hanna's presence on Morgan's committee did not mean that he endorsed the opinions of the Senator from Alabama.[45] Furthermore, the establishment of the I.C.C. by a Republican administration surely implied a belief in the possibility of an alternative route. To have chosen Nicaragua would have been to make its recommendations, even its spadework, redundant. In brief, through McKinley's action, the party had committed itself to an impartial investigation. Nor, finally, should it be forgotten that Cromwell himself, had been a Republican adherent for many years before he came to be associated with the French company.

The state of confusion in Colombia subsequent to Marroquin's seizure of power prevented the French from answering Walker's pointed questions. By the middle of 1900 the Bogota government had still not taken any steps to satisfy

Mancini's latest request. This was for the repeal of the article in the original concession agreement forbidding transfer
of the property to a foreign power. Consequently, when
Hutin did reply to Walker, he had nothing to add to what
he had told the U.S. President in February 1899. The Company was still of a mind to turn itself into an American
corporation and accord U.S. government representation on
its board. Alternatively, it could offer the government the
opportunity to acquire a controlling interest by increasing
its capital substantially, as its by-laws permitted and allowing the Americans the opportunity to buy stock. But either
of these moves would require Colombian consent. Any unilateral action on the part of the French might lead to the
immediate nullifications of the Calderon-Mancini so recently
concluded and with so much effort. Hutin therefore suggested that the next, logical step was for the United States
to make approaches to the Colombian government with a
view to feeling out what the attitude of the latter might
be.[46]

Walker had been anticipating such a response, and it
only served to confirm the verdict on Panama which had
been contained in his commission's preliminary report which
appeared only four days after he received this letter from
Hutin.[47] It dismissed all routes except the Nicaraguan and
Panamanian. In turning to the Compagnie Nouvelle it issued a caveat. Not only had the Commission discovered
that it was unable to cede or mortgage its property under
pain of forfeiture, but the disturbed condition of the country
had made it impossible to visit Bogota in order to ascertain
the views of the various political factions on any proposed
American purchase. The report concluded that

> ...in view of all the facts, and particularly in view
> of all the difficulties of obtaining the necessary

rights and privileges and franchises on the Panama
route, and assuming that Nicaragua and Costa
Rica recognize the value of the canal to themselves...the Commission is of the opinion that the
most practicable and feasible route for an Isthmian
canal to be under the control, management and
ownership of the United States is that known as the
Nicaraguan
route.[48]

This body blow to Panamanian hopes was greeted with
jubilation by Morgan and his supporters. So confident were
they of success that, when Hepburn's bill was delayed yet
again in the Senate, they were content to leave it on the
table until the following January. Everything seemed lost
as far as the Compagnie Nouvelle was concerned and talk
of a 'worthless ditch' was heard in the capital. Yet, closer
scrutiny of the report would have revealed that it was less
an indictment of Panama than an acknowledgement of the
New Company's inability to offer its concession for outright
purchase by a foreign government. From a technical aspect,
Nicaragua suffered from a number of liabilities. There was
a lack of suitable deep-water termini at either end: neither
Greytown nor Brito possessed facilities for handling large
vessels whereas Colon and Balboa did. In terms of distance
from Caribbean to Pacific, Panama was shorter by over a
hundred miles; and a not inconsiderable amount of excavation had already been executed there.[49]

As soon as the directors obtained a copy of the I.C.C.
report, they called an emergency meeting. There was a
unanimous feeling that all thought of Americanization of
the concern must be abandoned, as must U.S. involvement
in a French one. A telegram was sent to Hutin in New
York on December 12 instructing him to "enter into talks

with the United States for consent in principle to the transfer of all rights, privileges and franchises, and work of any description".[50] Any engagement made was to become definitive as soon as the United States and Colombia had reached an understanding which would allow the sale to take place. The financial papers in Paris were also urging the same course, without delay.[51]

The onus for saving the situation rested once more on the shoulders of Cromwell and Hutin. Cromwell made the next move. Bogota in December 1900 was not a haven of tranquility to be sure, and he recognized the difficulties the Americans, not to mention his employers would face if they tried to negotiate under the threat of rebel attack and inter-party squabbling. But the Colombian legation in Washington had been closed since the coup and official business had to be conducted through a consul-general in New York, de Brigard. Cromwell's plan was to get Marroquin to send an accredited minister to Washington empowered to deal both with the United States government and with the New Company's agents. He asked de Brigard to send an urgent message to this effect on December 23. Four days later, Marroquin replied that no less a person than his Minister of Foreign Affairs, Martinez Silva, would assume those responsibilities, with the title of minister and envoy extraordinary.[52]

It was not until February that this Colombian envoy reached the U.S.. He had talks with Cromwell and Hutin which again caused their hopes to plummet. Silva told them bluntly that his government had never had any faith in the ability of the French to do much on the Isthmus even before the concession expired. Far more alarming was his appraisal of the threat posed by Nicaragua and the recommendation of the I.C.C. to that end. He airily announced that Panama had undeniable advantages, that the Americans were perfectly aware of them and that raising the spectre of a rival

route was nothing more than a Yanqui red herring designed
to wring the most advantageous terms from his government
and Cromwell's employer. His conviction seemed to be reinforced when Lord Lansdowne and the British Foreign Office
chose that very moment to lodge an objection to the preliminary draft of the Hay-Paucefote Treaty. This referred to
matters of jurisdiction in the proposed canal zone located in
an area over which Costa Rica and Nicaragua exercised joint
control. Silva pointed out that the Nicaraguan alternative
had its diplomatic snares no less than the Panamanian. He
ended by asking Hutin what steps the New Company directors intended to take to dispose of their holdings, assuming,
of course, that his government gave permission for a transfer
of the concession to the Americans.[53]

The reply he received was evasive, and for good reason.
Hutin was under pressure to conclude a definite sale, but
he did not have an exact price and, as one who had been
associated with the enterprise since the mid-1880's, he was
unwilling to be panicked into disposing of it for a pittance.
From February onwards he was to encounter increasingly severe criticism from the board. They felt that his talk about
'arbitration' – in the event that buyer and seller could not
agree – a matter of undue importance. As far as it was concerned, the board believed the Americans held all the trump
cards, and, while arbitration was desirable, it might well be a
case of accepting what was offered.[54] Hutin refused to share
this line of thought. Prior to his departure for France, in
May 1901, he told Walker that he would set no fixed figure
until he had consulted with his colleagues in Paris. Even
so, he was fairly certain that any offer from the U.S. government would have to contain a guarantee of profit-sharing
for the Compagnie Nouvelle as soon as the canal was open
to traffic.[55]

Bunau-Varilla chose this moment to reenter the fray, and

it is hard to resist the conclusion that his unofficial meddling
was other than mischievous. During the first four months of
1901 he had travelled extensively in the east and mid-west
of the U.S.A. addressing groups of businessmen on the superiority of Panama.[56] He also published, at his own expense,
a pamphlet, *Nicaragua or Panama?*, a copy of which was
forwarded to Walker by a mutual friend, John Bigelow.[57]
Following a stormy meeting with Senator Morgan, Bunau-
Varilla returned to France to pen the first of his "Trois appels à la France pour sauver l'oeuvre de Panama" which
was published in a number of Parisian dailies on April 25.
In it he chided the Compagnie Nouvelle for its continuing
failure to rouse the nation's enthusiasm, and he demanded
that it make an effort to rekindle the patriotic fire which
de Lesseps had first lit and fanned, despite his faults. To
sell out to a foreign country, even one as friendly as the
United States, would be "a miserable, poverty-stricken solution that one has recourse to only when one has looked
for the noble one, the French answer."[58] He was convinced
that the canal could be completed within the given time if
his plan were followed – and for only five hundred million
francs. The bulk of the capital could still be raised from
French investors, great and small. He had already written to
Henri Germain at the Crédit Lyonnais pledging two million
francs of his own fortune; and to President Loubet urging
him to lend the prestige of his own office to this great work
of rejuvenation.[59]

Fervently patriotic though this might be, it was acutely
embarrassing to Hutin at such a delicate stage in the proceedings. He was further aggrieved by Cromwell's persistent
demand that the board should decide on a sum "in keeping with the views of the (International Technical) Commission which would have a very favorable influence on the
forthcoming report." Walker had indicated to him in private

that Hutin's profit-sharing proposal would be unacceptable to McKinley, but he was willing to delay release of the full I.C.C. report if the Director-General would reconsider his position.[60] Hutin's response to this suggestion was a brief six line letter to Cromwell thanking him for past services and terminating his appointment as of June 30.[61]

The dismissal was sudden and dramatic but not as surprising as might appear at first glance. Fundamentally, it involved a clash of personalities. Hutin may have felt that the ship did not have room for two captains and that affairs in the United States could, in future, be transacted adequately by him, alone. This was certainly the only reason to appear in the minutes where the decision was made.[62] Furthermore, if Hutin had to be absent from Washington for the entire summer of 1901, there was no telling what schemes might be hatched by the ambitious lawyer in concert with Martinez Silva. That might lead to a repetition of the crisis that had overtaken the Company in December 1899. A third contributing factor may have been Cromwell's somewhat extravagant expenditures in his employer's name. While no details were divulged in the minutes of the meeting, it was decided there that only $57,066.24 of an unspecified claim would be recognized as legitimate. A reading of the terse, two-line acknowledgement of his services leaves the impression that a serious breach had occurred.[63]

Hutin devoted the remainder of his stay in Paris to obtaining an appraisal of the Company's total worth. An independent assessor, Etienne, was brought in, and his two part report was ready by September 30. The first section included an evaluation of property on the Isthmus which was put at five hundred and sixty-five million francs.[64] The second ventured to suggest a figure of compensation that might reasonably be expected in lieu of a share in the profits of the canal when fully operational. Etienne recognized the difficulty of trying to compute a reasonable amount but felt that it ought to be based on a percentage of the initial sum paid by the Americans for the property linked to the annual rate of shipping tonnage passing through the canal.[65]

Hutin considered the estimate too low and he presented one of his own which at 1,273,000,000 francs was almost double the 'official' figure.[66] His action served to widen the breach between him and the board still further. Marius Bô and his fellow directors were more than ever convinced that he, in common with Bunau-Varilla, was indulging in wishful thinking. The reality of the situation, they held, had escaped both of them. The Compagnie Nouvelle had capital enough to enable it to continue working at the existing level of intensity for a further eighteen months to two years. Thereafter there would have to be a drastic reduction of activity – unless some unexpected expense caused bankruptcy to strike earlier.[67] Press reaction, too, was all for jettisoning the canal. Not untypical was an editorial in *L'Information* expressing the view that it was only a matter of time before American imperialism swallowed up everything on the Isthmus. This conviction was based partly on a threat to U.S. investment in the region that might result from the escalation of a border quarrel that had flared up anew between Venezuela and Colombia over the former's aid to Colombian rebels. It was doubtful, continued the editorial, whether French ownership of excavations and the railroad track would deter the Americans from occupying the strategic fifty mile-wide site between Panama and Colon, vital as it was for their trade and military requirements.[68] Thus, it was with heavy heart that Hutin returned to Washington early in October to present the Company's tentative offer to the Walker Commission.

The assassination of President McKinley on September 6 and the succession of Theodore Roosevelt meant a more vigorous canal policy could be expected from the White

House.[69] With this in mind, Bô urged on Hutin the necessity of reaching a swift and conclusive agreement. The dangers of temporising were enormous, not just because Roosevelt would come straight to the point, but also because of the new tack Colombia might follow. If it thought that negotiations were going to be prolonged, it might revoke the concession forthwith with the excuse that there was insufficient activity on site, lack of capital and little incentive to continue the work that others could take up. Bô prophesied that, having annulled the New Company's concession, the Colombians could then proceed to parley, exclusively, with the Americans and not be obliged to pay the French a single centime in compensation. The sting was left to the end of the letter:

> Allow us to mention, in conclusion, that your communications, other than your telegrams, appear to us to be far too brief; your letters do not contain any indication of the kind of program you propose carrying out during negotiations with the result that your mandate is vague and uncertain. The board is so distressed that several of your colleagues have talked of resigning. Believe me, it behoves you to give take this situation into account, to realize how grave it is and to bestir yourself to bring it to a conclusion.[70]

And so, like Napoleon's legions at Waterloo, without fear and without hope, the Director-General prepared to do battle with a specially convened session of the Isthmian Canal Commission. He did make one concession at the start. Compensation for loss of profit might be made either by an annuity or by a capital sum, to be included in the transfer price. He stressed that these were merely suggestions, open to modification. This expression of the Company's views should be regarded as nothing more than a basis on which future bargaining could take place.[71]

There followed more intimate conversations between Walker and Hutin of which no written record appears to exist. They ended on October 16, but a letter written by Walker, two days later, reproached Hutin for his continuing reluctance to state a definite price. If he was thinking of the one contained in the Etienne report, the Commission would certainly have to describe it as excessive, notably on the value it put on the excavations and the purchase price of the P.R.C. shares. On the question of profit- sharing, he was equally pessimistic. His government would have to assume all the risks attendant upon the building and operating of the canal, as well as its losses during the early years until capital was recovered from tolls. He was therefore inclined to believe that any offer made from his side would have to be regarded as inclusive.[72] Hutin's response came only two days before the full report of the I.C.C. was made public. While he adhered, as strongly as ever, to the principle of arbitration, he was willing to surrender all claims for profit-sharing. He trusted that this act of conciliation on his part would be appreciated when other factors came to be considered.[73] Hay was similarly notified of his 'concession'.[74] The I.C.C. report made no mention of this offer which was, in any case, a last resort. Its attitude to the French corporation was influenced mainly by the price it had put on its holdings. It was true, said the report, that the figure of 565,500,000 francs or $109,141,500 might be subject to downward revision; but it had taken the Commissioners the best part of two years of careful calculation to arrive at their own estimate of forty million dollars (or approximately two hundred million francs).[75] To have to re-evaluate would necessitate the creation of a sub-committee whose work might take as long again, and the President was awaiting a prompt, clear-cut decision. To cut a canal to its specifications through Nicaragua, the I.C.C. reckoned, would cost $189,864,062; that through Panama would be $144,233,358. But when the French estimate was taken into account, this would raise the cost of Panama to more than sixty-three million above that for Nicaragua. The Commission conceded that there were certain marked physical advantages in favor of Panama, as it had outlined in its preliminary report; but the price sought by the Compagnie Nouvelle was so unreasonable that it must opt for the alternative.[76]

As one might expect, Hutin had to bear the brunt of opprobium for this failure to win Walker's approval. Bunau-Varilla was one of the first into the attack with a lengthy letter in *Le Matin*. The ex-engineer had changed his stance since April, and had become converted to the idea of an American canal, although still considering it a regrettable alternative. He castigated not only Hutin but the entire board for its sphinx-like posture when faced with repeated requests for a definite price. He alleged, without any foundation for the statement, that the Americans would have been willing to pay two hundred and ninety million francs (fifty-eight million dollars) if a firm price had been stated immediately following publication of the I.C.C.'s preliminary report. This figure represented the approximate saving of the Panama route over the Nicaraguan. Instead, the Company had clung to its posture of "Guess if you can, choose if you dare!" with fatal results.[77] Several French journals joined in the chorus of lamentation. *Le Compte* in calling Hutin's figures "exaggerated", blamed the abysmal performance in Washington on a lack of expert and influential advice.[78] On the eve of his departure from Washington, Hutin received what he would afterwards describe to Lemarquis as "a terror-stricken letter" from Marius Bô roundly condemning his conduct when the board and the stockholders were of a mind to sell out according to the Walker estimate of what the concern was worth. As Hutin tendered his resignation, he commented on how sad it was to see these signs of abject surrender to "interests that are out to plunder."[79]

Morgan and his friends, naturally enough, were ecstatic. The day following release of the I.C.C. report saw Hay sign protocols with the diplomatic representatives of Costa Rica and Nicaragua as a preliminary to a canal treaty. Even better news came on December 16 when the British Foreign Office waived its previous objections to the Hay-Pauncefote Treaty amendments made by the U.S. Senate. On February 22, 1902, the second version of this treaty became law.[80] There was no visible obstacle in the way of an American canal stretching from Greytown to Brito across Nicaragua.

Thus ended one of the sorriest years in the brief and troubled history of the Compagnie Nouvelle du Canal de Panama. With the new century barely a year old, it was without a director-general, and it lacked experienced directors faced the bleak prospect of owning what had already been referred to as a muddy, unfinished ditch in a strife-ridden country – with not a rival purchaser in sight, or likely to appear.

Notes

1. *The Panama Canal: a study in international diplomacy* by Harmodio Arias (London, 1911), despite its title, is a disappointingly superficial work but useful for its source material. The Hay-Pauncefote Treaty and its antecedents are exhaustively treated in A.E. Campbell, *Great Britain and the United States, 1895-1903* (London, 1960). The genesis of Theodore Roosevelt's canal philosophy may be charted in *Letters from Theodore Roosevelt to Anna Roosevelt Cowles* (Anna Roosevelt Cowles, ed.) (New York, 1924).

2. Navarre's appointment took effect on January 5.

3. 56 Cong., 1 Sess., *Committee on Interoceanic Canals. Report of Hearings in regard to Bill (H.R. 2538)*, May 11, 1900.

4. A.N. 7 AQ 34 contains scribbled notes in pencil in the handwriting of Gautron and Lemarquis. A letter from Charles de Lesseps, dated January 22, expresses the hope that Hutin would be consulted in all cases of appointments.

5. Badois had been in charge of dredging operations at Suez.

6. February 17, 1900. In addition to Bô who placed Brolemann, Francis Monvoisin was the new representative of the Credit Industriel et Commercial; Albert Martin came from the boardroom of the Comptoir National d'Escompte; and Baron Lassus Saint-Genies deputized for Le Begue of the Société Générale. The others were Terrier, president of the Compagnie Générale des Travaux Publics; Bourgeois, a former tax inspector; Couvreux of the Compagnie du Port de Bizerte; Forota returned army comptroller; Gueydan, an import-export merchant; Rischmann, another tax official; and Hutin from the previous board. Samper also continued to represent the Colombian government.

7. One writer claimed that he had arrived only 12 minutes late to discover the entire board had been elected.

8. A.N. 7 AQ 34, Navarre to Lemarquis, February 5, 1900.

9. *Ibid.*, "Entente conclue par l'intermediaire de M. Navarre," February 10, 1900.

10. A.N. 7 AQ 35, Mancini to Hutin, August 10, 1898.

11. N.A. RG 185/1/1, Nelin to Hutin, March 13, 1899.

12. Miner, *op. cit.*, p. 58, footnotes 51 and 52.

13. A.N. 7 AQ 35, Mancini to Hutin, October 13, 1899.

14. *Ibid.*, Mancini to Hutin, December 25, 1899.

15. *Ibid.*, Mancini to Hutin, January 10, 1900.

16. This was corroborated by Carlos Calderon in a letter to *El Correo Nacional* on January 14, 1903.

17. A.N. 7 AQ 35, Mancini heard about these moves from an unnamed source. He communicated the information to Paris on February 18.

18. *Ibid.*, Mancini to Bô, March 3, 1900.

19. *Ibid.*, Lampre to Mancini, March 10, 1900.

20. *Ibid.*

21. *Ibid.*, Calderon to Esguerra (copy) March ?, 1900.

22. *Ibid.*, Esguerra to Choron, March 31, 1900.

23. *Ibid.*, Mancini to Hutin, March 15, 1900.

24. *Ibid.*, Bô to Esguerra, April 4, 1900.

25. The text of the agreement, hereafter designated the Calderon-Mancini settlement is in A.N. 7 AQ 31.

26. The original is not in the Company's archives. An English translation is in *Sen. Doc.* No. 41, 59 Cong., 2 Sess., pp. 1244-45.

27. A.N. 7 AQ 35, Restrepo to Conseil d'Administration. The Liberal junta dated from October 1899. It was joined by Uribe-Uribe in November, and was supplied with arms by the Venezuelan president, Castro.

28. In a letter to *Le Matin*, May 1, 1900.

29. Miner, *op. cit.*, p. 60.

30. Campbell, *op. cit.*, pp. 48-84.

31. The letter of instructions, dated June 21, 1899, is quoted *in extenso* in Miner, *op. cit.*, pp. 95-96.

32. *Sen. Doc.* No. 474, Cong., 2 Sess. *Diplomatic History of the Panama Canal*, pp. 289-91.

33. Roosevelt to Hay, February 18, 1900, quoted in William Roscoe Hayer, *Life and Letters of John Hay*, 2 vols. (Boston, 1915), II, pp. 339-40.

34. Roosevelt to Admiral William Cowles, February 26, 1900, in Anna Roosevelt Cowles, *op. cit.*, pp. 236-37.

35. A.N. 7 AQ 34, Cromwell to Lemarquis, January 18, 1900.

36. *Ibid.*, Cromwell to Navarre, January 25, 1900.

37. A.N. 7 AQ 38, Walker to Hutin, April 10, 1900.

38. *Ibid.*, Sullivan and Cromwell to McKinley, April 30, 1900.

39. *Sen. Reports*, 56 Cong., 1 Sess., No. 1337, p. 9.

40. The 1896 motion had spoken of "...the Nicaraguan canal... built, owned and operated by the United States." That of 1900 merely stated that the party favored "...the construction, ownership, control and protection of an *Isthmian Canal* (my italics) by the Government...."

41. *Story of Panama*, p. 158. Since Bunau-Varilla was not in contact with Cromwell at this period, and the *World* was pro-Nicaraguan, it was hard to find evidence to substantiate the charge from this angle.

42. A.N. 7 AQ 42, *Arbitrage entre la Compagnie Nouvelle du Canal de Panama et MM. Sullivan et Cromwell*, October 24, 1907. The following sums were paid him during his time in the New Company's employ:

To September 1896	$ 450.00
September 1896-February 1897	5,000.00
March 1897-February 1898	10,000.00
March 1898-August 1899	15,000.00
September 1, 1899-September 30, 1899	833.75
October 1, 1899-June 30, 1901	66,443.78
February 1, 1902-May 31, 1904	23,333.35

This figure includes	
Salary	17,500.00
Supplementary salary	12,000.00
Reimbursement of expenses	36,136.08
Interest at 1% of the above	807.70
	$66,443.78

43. *Ibid.*

44. Cromwell's papers, if available, might solve the mystery.

45. B.V. Papers, Box 21. Elmer Dover, secretary of the Republican National Committee in 1900 was asked to supply written testimony during this 1907 action. He wrote: "From May 1898 to March 1904, (I was the confidential) secretary to Senator M.A. Hanna.... In January 1899, Hanna met Cromwell at a meeting of bankers. There was talk of canals and Hanna arranged that Cromwell should come and see him and bring all data on the project.... From then on, the two were constantly in touch, the Senator relying on his firm to provide him with all sorts of data. Once or twice Hanna became weary of the struggle but was persuaded by Cromwell not to withdraw." B.V. Papers, Box 21.

46. A.N. 7 AQ 38, Hutin to Walker, November 26, 1900.

47. *Sen. Doc.* No. 5, 56 Cong., 2 Sess.

48. *Ibid.*, p. 14, and pp. 43-44.

49. For a fuller discussion of the merits and demerits of these ports, see Mack, *op. cit.*, pp. 46-47, 171-172, 322-325.

50. A.N. 7 AQ 31, "Procès verbal de la réunion des comités," December 11, 1900; also Comité de Direction to Hutin, December 12, 1900.

51. *Le Comptant*, for example, argued that the French company should be prepared to accept as little as 116 million francs ($23 million).

52. *Story of Panama*, pp. 238-239.

53. A.N. 7 AQ 38, Martinez Silva to Hutin, April 29, 1901.

54. A.N. 7 AQ 31, "Réunion des Comités: procès verbal," February 15, 1901.

55. A.N. 7 AQ 38, Hutin to Walker, May 16, 1901.

56. Copies of speeches made in Chicago, Cincinnati, Boston, New Jersey and New York are in B-V. Papers, Box 16. See also Ameriger, "Ohio and the Panama Canal" in *Ohio History*, Vol. 74, No. 1, pp. 3-12.

57. B-V Papers, Box 2, Bigelow to Walker, April 13, 1901. Walker, apparently, was not impressed.

58. *Premier appel*, p. 14. The Trois appels were published collectively in book form in 1902. The page referred to here and elsewhere refers to this collection. *Le Matin* was one of the first to accept the manuscript but it was owned by Bunau-Varilla's brother, Maurice. Predictably, the same work was refused by Drumont's anti-semitic *La Libre Parole*.

59. Both letters are in Panama: la création, Appendix B.

60. *Ibid.*

61. A.N. 7 AQ 42, Hutin to Cromwell, June 19, 1901.

62. A.N. 7 AQ 31, "Réunion des Comités," August 31, 1901.

63. *Ibid.* Cromwell was still demanding recompense for expenses incurred in the formation of the abortive New Jersey concern in 1899.

64. A.N. 7 AQ 36, "Rapport de M. Etienne sur la valeur des travaux et de la concession du canal." (September, 1901). Georges Etienne was a chief inspector of roads and bridges.

PROPERTY VALUES	in frs.	in $
Shares of P.R.C. (66,863)	55,000,000	10,000,000
Buildings	9,000,000	1,737,000
Hospitals at Colon and Panama	4,500,000	868,000
Concession, capital and interest	24,000,000	4,632,000
Excavation (both companies)	455,000,000	80,095,000
Maps, plans, charts, etc.	18,000,000	3,474,000
	565,500,000	109,141,000

65. The proposed indemnification for loss of profits was calculated as follows:

Annual Tonnage (in mill.)	Additional Income (frs./ton)
5	0
6	0
7	0.50
8	1.00
9 - 11	1.50
11 - 16	2.00
16 - 19	2.50
20 +	3.00

66. *Ibid.* Hutin and Choron's rival estimate was presented on October 4, 1901. The major discrepancy lay in the value it placed on the buildings and excavations. It was entitled, "etude concernant l'estimation de la valeur a attribuer a l'approt de la Compagnie francaise dans l'oeuvre du canal en cas de transfert de notre concession au gouvernement americain."

67. A.N. 7 AQ 38, Bô to Hutin, July 6, 1901.

68. Issue August 23, 1901.

69. McKinley survived for a week. Roosevelt became president on September 14.

70. A.N. 7 AQ 38, Bô to Hutin, October 23, 1901.

71. *Ibid.*, Walker to Hutin, October 4, 1901.

72. *Ibid.*, Walker to Hutin, October 18, 1901. Walker made it clear that he could not recommend any price to the president.

73. *Ibid.*, Hutin to Walker, November 14, 1901.

74. *Ibid.*, Hutin to Hay, November 22, 1901.

75. *Sen. Doc.* No. 222, 58 Cong., 1 Sess. Vol. 1, pp. 174-75. The I.C.C. valued the excavations at $27,474,033, the P.R.C. shares (at par) at $6,850,000, and maps and plans, etc. at $2,000,000. A further 10% of this total was allowed for buildings, hospitals and 'contingencies'. It considered that much of the excavation done at the Atlantic side could not be utilized because the proposed American route would follow a different entrance.

76. *Ibid.*, p. 175. These gross estimates did not include payments to the respective countries granting the concessions.

77. The letter first appeared on November 29 and was afterwards part of the *Troisième appel* (*op. cit.*).

78. Issue of December 12, 1901.

79. A.N. 7 AQ 38, Hutin to Lemarquis, November 29, 1901.

80. Referred to hereafter as the Second Hay-Pauncefote Treaty.

Chapter 7

Colombian Opposition[1]

When the board of the Compagnie Nouvelle assembled on December 16, 1901, it was with the grim determination to jettison Hutin and his policy of cautious inactivity which had paralysed negotiations with the United States.[2] Their intention was to offer their assets for sale, unconditionally, "taking, as a base, not the figures which the Company had set for evaluation but the calculations that the Isthmian Canal Commission regarded as definitive."[3] This decision, and another to appoint Lampré in Hutin's place at the bargaining table with "full powers to get the best possible deal" were submitted to the liquidator, Gautron, for approval.[4] He was distinctly cool. As far as he could gather, the directors were now disavowing an estimate which they had earlier accepted from a committee of their own choosing for no good reason other than the Isthmian Canal Commission's refusal to consider it tenable.[5] Lampré, who was an unknown quantity both to Gautron and Lemarquis was being given full authority to speak on behalf of all parties with a stake in the future of the New Company. His conclusion, that there existed "a grave disaccord" between the parties, revived chill-

ing memories of the conflict three years before which had led
to the disappearance of Bonnardel and the first board.[6] On
this occasion, however, level heads prevailed and a special
consultative committee was immediately set up to discuss
and make recommendations on the division of proceeds in
the event of a sale to the U.S. government. Five lawyers,
two from each side with an independent chairman, revised
Article 52 of the original statutes where the allocation had
been based on the premise that a French canal would be
built. In the light of the possible American purchase, it was
agreed that the percentage going to the liquidation would be
higher since it would not now receive anything in the way
of a share of revenue from tolls. The new agreement called
for it to take the first twenty million francs, the Company
the next five million, with the balance being split 60/40 as
before, after deductions for expenses. The net result was to
increase the share of the liquidation from 60% to just over
62.5%.[7] Even before this decision was reached, Gautron and
Lemarquis had accepted that a single spokesman for all sides
really did offer the only chance for success in America.[8] This
unanimity was timely. The annual stockholders' meeting, on
December 21 was a rowdy affair where some demanded that
Hutin answer personally for his failure, and others found
the board members collectively guilty of handing the initiative to Morgan and the Nicaraguan lobby.[9] Bunau-Varilla
made one of the few constructive suggestions from the floor
in urging that only the immediate dispatch of a telegram
to Admiral Walker could avert the triumph of Hepburn's
bill, due to be debated on January 7. In his zeal for further
action, he placed a full page announcement in twenty-eight
Parisian newspapers demanding that

> ... action is wanted, and it is wanted immediately:
> *the duty of the board is firmly indicated by the facts*

(his italics). If it does not succeed between now
and the seventh of January, its responsibility will
be made clear in the eyes of the people and of the
law.[10]

Pressure may also have been exerted on Marius Bô by Germain subsequent to Bunau-Varilla's appeal to the latter.
But, even before then, a cable reached Jules Boeufve, the
French consul in Washington, dated January 4, with instructions to communicate to the U.S. government the Company's
readiness to sell "in consideration of the sum of forty million
dollars for the property and rights evalued by the Isthmian
(Canal) Commission ... without awaiting Lampré."[11] Additional messages later in the same week included in the offer
all maps, charts and plans pertaining to the project; and it
set March 4, 1903 as the expiry date for acceptance.[12]

Having taken this momentous step of fixing a price in line
with Walker's idea of its worth, the New Company still had
three formidable hurdles – the partiality of Congress for the
other route, the explicit prohibition against sale to a foreign
government, and Colombia's suspicion of America's designs
if and when she came to choose. The first of these seemed
insurmountable when news was received that the House of
Representatives had given Hepburn's measure almost unanimous approval on January 9,[13] after rejecting an amendment to leave the selection of a location to the President.
Roosevelt had, however, already decided to reconvene the
I.C.C. in the light of the French offer, and Lampré encour-
agingly told the board not to lose hope.[14] He bravely held
his own before Morgan's interrogation during the course of
further hearings by the Senate. The mood of the moment
may be gauged by Morgan's reply to Lampré's observation
that forty million dollars was the absolute minimum his employers would accept. "I wouldn't give 37 1/2 cents for the

whole deal," replied the Senator. "If we could have the canal for nothing, I wouldn't take it. I don't want to speak of its financial worth, but I wouldn't buy it on principle."[15] Nevertheless, Lampré reported that work was still progressing on the Isthmus which was more than could be said of the other place. The consequence was that the I.C.C. filed a brief, supplementary report on January 18, advising that Panama should be considered if other circumstances permitted, "now that the estimates of the two routes have been nearly equalized."[16]

This was heartening news, better than the board had dared hope for only two weeks before, and it showed that money, not any inherent advantage possessed by the Nicaraguan route had been the stumbling block. But there was a long way to go and further victories would require much more effort both in Washington and in Bogota. Lampré had been thrust into the breach in dire emergency; but there was a limit to what he could achieve, given his tenuous grasp of the language and relative ignorance of the political scene. To win over Congress required the skills of a talented lobbyist. Therefore, it was not surprising when Cromwell was reappointed legal advisor on January 27. This came about through agencies of Bunau-Varilla and Hanna, the Senator with whom Cromwell had been constantly in touch since his dismissal. Bunau-Varilla pleaded that the New York lawyer be forgiven past sins because of his knowledge of the French undertaking which far surpassed that of any other American, and, in this he had the support of the financier, J. Edward Simmons who was Hanna's banker and president of the Panama Railroad Company.[17] Also, Hanna must have been fairly confident that his friend would be reinstated because the two of them made arrangements on January 18 to see John Coit Spooner, a past master of piloting controversial legislation through Congress.[18] Five days later Bunau-

Varilla cabled his wife in Paris:

> Urgent, phone Dollot who must tell Terrier that
> I think it indispensable that Cromwell be reap-
> pointed to his former position as legal counsel and
> do it by cable: then add that he accepts proposi-
> tion that his past and future services will be de-
> termined unilaterally by the board of the Second
> Company. Also advise Maurice.[19]

The letter of reappointment was duly sent to Cromwell with
more than a veiled reference to his past behavior, and it lends
substance to Morgan's oft-repeated charge that he had, indeed, used New Company monies for political purposes, in
1900, during the Republican National Convention.[20]

In the meantime, Hanna, Spooner and Cromwell had been
busy framing an amendment to the Hepburn bill. It proposed that the President should purchase the property and
rights of the French company for not more than forty million
dollars, and that the U.S. should obtain a canal zone in the
department of Panama at least six miles wide – in perpetuity
– from the Colombian government. Should it prove impossible to achieve this within a reasonable time and upon reasonable terms, Roosevelt would then negotiate with Nicaragua
and Costa Rica for the other route.[21] Having laid the ground-
work, the trio made further preparations to defeat the other
side's proposal. Spooner conscientiously lobbied for support
among fellow Republicans. Hanna insisted that the Walker
Commission members be recalled to give further testimony
before the Senate Committee on Interoceanic Canals (and
the questions this time were no less loaded than those put
to Lampré when he had faced Morgan).[22] Cromwell did his
part by resorting to the tactic which had served him well before. He had individuals testify to the superiority of Panama
in sworn affadavits and he presented the Senate committee

with an expensively bound volume of the New Company's performance since incorporation to convince the uncommitted members.

Those efforts were set at naught when, as the partisans of Nicaragua learnt to their delight, news came that Colombia was likely to refuse permission for the transfer of the concession. The repercussions of this refusal will be examined shortly: the immediate result was to cause the Senate committee to reject the Spooner 'amendment' by seven votes to five and recommend the alternative, after all.

Providence came to the rescue of the Compagnie Nouvelle in a most unexpected manner. On May 8, Mount Pelée on the island of Martinique erupted destroying the city of Saint Pierre and killing all but one of its forty thousand inhabitants. Although Martinique is several hundred miles distant from the Central American mainland, the event provided Bunau-Varilla with a timely opportunity. He had long condemned the Nicaraguan route for its susceptibility to earthquakes and volcanic disturbances, having elaborated on this point in a pamphlet, *Nicaragua or Panama?* Now he sent a letter to Roosevelt and each senator drawing their collective attention to "the essential characteristics of the Nicaraguan Isthmus," and underlining the fact that, "before the explosion of Krakatoa near Java, the world's record for seismic disturbances was held by Nicaragua, owing to the explosion of Coreguina in 1835."[23]

Volcanoes continued to attract attention to the problem in the weeks that followed, culminating in a graphic account in the *New York Sun* of May 28 of how Mount Momotombo had erupted on March 24, destroying a wharf on the projected canal line through Nicaragua. Predictably enough, President Jose Zelaya was quick to his nation's defence with a brusque denial of the report; and the issue at once became a political football. The *Washington Evening Star* published a cartoon on June 6 in which Hanna was shown painting imaginary volcanoes on the map of Central America, guided by a comical Frenchman.[24] Morgan read a dispatch in the Senate chamber in which the American consul in Managua affirmed that there were no active volcanoes in the vicinity. Hanna countered by asking whether too much faith ought to be placed on the testimony of the diplomat in question. After all, he was a stockholder in the Maritime Canal Company.[25] Then, in what he rightly claims was a fit of inspiration, Bunau-Varilla remembered that the Nicaraguan government had issued a series of stamps only the previous year depicting Mount Momotombo in full eruption. After scouring Washington's philatelic establishments, he gathered together ninety such stamps, enough to send each senator an example. These arrived in their mail on June 16, just three days before the crucial vote on the Spooner amendment was scheduled.[26]

It would be grossly misleading and an exaggeration to attribute the eventual victory of Panama to Bunau-Varilla's stratagem alone. Ever since the adverse decision of the Senate Committee on Interoceanic Canals had been made public, Hanna, Cromwell and Spooner had been working feverishly with the dissenting minority. Their efforts led to the appearance of a 'minority report' on May 31 containing a lot of technical data in favor of Panama. It also contained the statement that the majority of senators would have endorsed the route all along, had it not been for difficulties between the New Company and Colombia which could still be resolved to the benefit of all parties.[27] Even Bunau-Varilla did not rely entirely on the impact of the incriminating postage stamps. He travelled to New York to supervise the printing of another pamphlet, *Comparative Characteristics of Nicaragua and Panama* which contained a number of well-rehearsed arguments and was copiously illustrated with diagrams whose technical simplicity even a politician could grasp.[28]

Morgan opened the debate on Hepburn's long-delayed legislation in the Senate on June 4 with a wide-ranging attack on Panama and its proponents.[29] Hanna began his reply the following day but, after speaking for an hour and a half, was too exhausted to continue. He was in poor health and would be forced to leave politics the following year. Before he resumed, on the sixth, every senator had been given a copy of the *Comparative Characteristics* pamphlet.[30] Many contemporary accounts agree that Hanna's was one of the most eloquent discourses ever delivered before Congress, and that what was to follow was bound to be anticlimactic.[31] If Morgan's polemics are discounted, it is true that much earnest and informed debate took place in the next twelve days; but the tide was turning inexorably against Nicaragua. Cromwell was active in the Senate antechambers and hotel smoking rooms within the shadow of Capital Hill securing the adhesion of legislators; and it took Bunau-Varilla's stamp collection and writings to tip the balance.[32] On the afternoon of June 19, Morgan saw his support trickle away through three consecutive motions. The first, in favor of the minority report, was carried by forty-two votes to thirty-four. The second, proposing to limit to six months the period during which the government could negotiate with Colombia was defeated by forty-four to thirty-one. When the Spooner amendment came to be decided, sixty-seven were in favor, and only six opposed.[33]

A voice from the past joined in the rejoicing. Charles de Lesseps, long in disgrace, cabled his congratulations to Bunau-Varilla:

Extremely moved by the dispatch of the valiant apostle of French thought, creator of Suez....[34]

Yet the jubilation had to be tempered by the knowledge that the will of the House of Representatives still ran contrary to that of the upper chamber. In order to resolve that problem, a committee of six was established composed of Hanna, Kittredge and Morgan, all Senators, and of Representatives Hepburn and Fletcher. After five days of discussion, the House delegates agreed, by a majority, to recommend acceptance of the resolutions.[35]

This change of attitude is not as astonishing as first appears. The decision was arrived at only after weighing the consequences carefully. Public opinion was anxious to see a start made on a canal. Rejection of the Spooner legislation would cause unacceptable delay. Just as significant, however, was the conviction among the pro-Nicaraguan faction that Colombian intransigence would yet wreck all hope of a satisfactory settlement over Panama, and so allow their scheme to triumph after all. At this stage, such a prophecy seemed all too likely to come true.

*　　　*　　　*

In his very first communication to the New Company after his reappointment, Cromwell had expressed concern that no new effort had been made to persuade the Bogota authorities to sign an entente with the United States prior to the sale offer.[36] There had, indeed, been no progress in that direction since Hutin's few, inconclusive and convoluted talks with Martinez Silva in the summer of 1901. The telegram, quoting a definite price which the board had sent to Walker jolted Colombia out of its lackadaisical attitude and forced it to think in terms of compensation, from both foreign nations involved. Mancini reported that, incredible as it might seem, the talk in the capital was of twenty million dollars from the Americans alone. This, Mancini had been told in an aside, was the difference between construction costs for Panama and Nicaragua. The I.C.C. had put this at fifty-eight million. If the Compagnie Nouvelle were to receive forty million, it was only fair that Colombia should pocket the difference, with an extra two million thrown in as compensation for the loss of monies from the Panama Railroad Company. There was also, said Mancini, the unspoken conviction that once the deal had been completed, Panama would disappear within the American orbit as surely as had Cuba and the Philippines.[37]

Martinez Silva had spent an idle and frustrating time in Washington since Hutin's departure and knew nothing of this projected demand. Naturally enough, Cromwell took good care not to enlighten him when the two met on January 28. Instead, with the help of Mutis Duran, a former governor of Panama, he convinced the Colombian envoy of the pressing need for a draft treaty between his government and the U.S. in order to scotch the hostile allegations of Morgan and friends. It took only a matter of days to produce a draft: a canal zone ten kilometers wide which would be leased to the United States for a hundred years at an annual rent of six hundred thousand dollars, the lease to be renewable for another century on payment of an additional three per cent per annum. The New Company was to be allowed to surrender its concession with no penalty to it.[38]

This extraordinary piece of action by the Colombian envoy in Washington was doomed in advance. When Marroquin received details of what Silva had done, he called in not his fellow cabinet members, but jurists and leaders of the opposition. Not only did they condemn the projected agreement clause by clause, but there was near unanimity on a motion that the French would have to pay dearly if they hoped to sell out to a foreign government. The figure of twenty million was applied to them as well, the justification being that if the present occupants of the Isthmus had no intention of completing the canal, Bogota could play for time until October 1910 when they would see the concession expire and the rights revert to Colombia.[39] Mancini hinted darkly that these were not novel sentiments, to be sure, but they were now harder than ever to refute since Marroquin was still facing rebellion and saw in his nationalistic posture a means of rousing some support. He might have added that the coup of 1900 which had elevated Marroquin to his position had originated, in part, because of discontent with lavish concessions to foreign firms which the Conservatives had dispensed of yore. The final session of this impromptu meeting in Bogota ended on February 20 with a recommendation that no treaty whatever be concluded with the United States and that the New Company be required to fulfill its contractual obligations, or suffer the consequence. In forwarding this worst of all possible news to Paris, Mancini opined that all the Company could do was to form a link with some U.S. concern which would, itself, be backed by the American government. Any other solution would be "fraught with consequences".[40]

Then occurred another of those amazing twists in the history of the Panama Canal. Surprisingly, considering his weak political position, Marroquin disregarded the advice. Perhaps he may have felt that an excess of chauvinism had blinded his fellow politicians to the financial advantages offered by the change in the New Company's position and that what was required was someone who could extort more money both from it and the American government. If the U.S.A. went elsewhere to build, Colombia would end up in exactly the same position as its tenant. As a result, Silva was accused of having exceeded his mandate and was replaced by an old, political rival, Jose Vincent Concha.[41] Concha was a respected statesman whose loyalty to the regime was never in doubt; but he was quite unsuited for the task he was about to undertake. He had never travelled beyond the borders of his own country, and his grasp of English was minimal. His arrival in New York, on February 27, coincided with a telegram Marroquin had sent to Paris advising the board not to act hastily when the special stockholders' meeting convened on the 28th to consider the sale.[42] If it approved the sale, it would be violating Articles 21 and 22 of the Salgar-Wyse agreement. Colombia would be within her rights in seizing all the property on the Isthmus. It was a warning that Bô and his directors could not ignore. Consequently, those who gathered at the Hotel Continental in Paris had to content themselves with a vote of confidence in the board and a *carte blanche* to proceed as it thought fit.[43]

Colombian tactics are open to criticism on a number of grounds. The air of complacency in face of the threat posed by Nicaragua was wholly unjustified, given the advanced stage of legislation in the U.S. Congress. On March 17, for example, Concha received a cable from Marroquin containing such phrases as "...the Panama Canal will be built in any case...we ought not to allow ourselves to be hurried by threats...."[44] Marroquin's committee was deceiving itself if it thought the Compagnie Nouvelle would do other than sell to the United States; it certainly had no intention of trying to carry on until 1910. In the highly unlikely event that both the U.S. and Colombia were willing to wait until that date, the P.R.C. would still be under French control and, according to its charter, would have to be consulted. Not least, there was a conflict of views in the United States itself. Some saw its projected presence in Panama as another imperialist venture, following the Cuban example. By the same token, there were Colombians who abhorred the idea of delivering up Panama to the *Yanquis*.

Cromwell hoped to dispel some illusions when he met Concha for the first time on March 2. The Colombian envoy confessed that he knew nothing of what Marroquin had said to the New Company's board, and he cabled Bogota for information.[45] In the interim, Cromwell, with the assistance of Silva and Mutis Duran – whose roles doubtless went beyond those of mere interpreters – drew up a statement in Spanish. This he addressed to himself in his capacity of legal counsel to the New Company. Concha was persuaded to agree to its contents on March 7. It qualified Marroquin's utterance to the board by confirming the propriety of all moves the New Company had hitherto made, and it affirmed that the Colombian government would not be opposed to the sale in principle. On the contrary, it would do all it could to facilitate the changeover.[46]

Cromwell's next move was to prepare a new agreement that would weaken the hand of the pro-Nicaraguan lobby and strengthen the position of the Roosevelt administration which, as Hay had revealed, was not well disposed towards the French concern but was hamstrung by the lack of a draft treaty.[47] Over and above this end, the Brooklyn lawyer was plotting an even more ingenious scheme. His mind had been "whetted on the grindstone of corporate cunning" as one newsman wrote,[48] and his design was nurtured by a grim determination that his client should not be forced to surrender any of its assets to the South Americans. Once Colombia and the United States had made some sort of pact, the French should be in a position to repudiate any Colombian claim for indemnification. Let the fight be between two governments with the Company on the sidelines. The U.S.A. would use her immense strength to work on the Company's behalf. It was for this reason that he cabled Bô on March 21 warning him not to make any offer to Colombia. "I have succeeded using other means" the message concluded.[49]

For the remainder of the month, therefore, Silva was under constant pressure to commit his government to a new entente. Cromwell later recounted how, "... little by little and

day by day I was able to convince him to take a more reasonable view of matters."⁵⁰ Bunau-Varilla was also on hand to
reinforce the relentless grip warning the hapless Colombian
envoy of how he must avoid listening to voices from home
which would steer his policy towards the abyss. His nation
ought to reduce its financial demands on the Americans, just
as the Company had had to lower its sights. Nicaragua had
asked Roosevelt for seven and a half million dollars: he ought
to be thinking of around twelve and a half million "to show
your government's generosity fairly and squarely."⁵¹ Another
gambit was a letter from Bunau-Varilla to the editor of the
Panama *Star and Herald,* the biggest newspaper on the Isthmus, asking him to publish some kind of appeal representative of forward-looking opinion in the province. This would
warn Bogota that any demand in excess of twelve and a half
million dollars would signify the triumph of Nicaragua.⁵²
Panama City and Colon were under threat of rebel attack at
that moment, and the governor forbade publication.⁵³ This
did not prevent Duque, the *Star and Herald* editor from carrying out another of Bunau-Varilla's suggestions of sending
copies of the editorial to his friends and "all those who did
not want to see Panama extinguished." Among the recipi-
ents were Pablo Arosemena, Tomas Arias, Francisco Boyd
and Jose Obaldia, all of whom were destined to become involved in the revolution that would see the emergence of an
independent Panamanian republic eighteen months later.

Bunau-Varilla sent a copy of his letter to Concha who was
stung to reply that:

> The business you speak of is not only an affair of
> money but principally an affair of vital interests
> which cannot be discussed simply on a commer-
> cial level. I deplore, therefore, that you sent the
> telegram whose copy you forwarded to me since it

deals with the least important aspect of the matter
and gives an erroneous impression....[54]

Bunau-Varilla hastened to concur but he tactfully suggested
that it was on this minor point of money ("point subal-
terne") that the entire future of the Panama Canal might
founder.[55] Cromwell was also on hand, of course, and the
incessant labors of the two were rewarded on March 30.
Concha capitulated and signed a draft agreement which was
brought to Hay with indecent haste twenty-four hours later.
It called for the United States government to make an initial payment of seven million dollars and nothing else for
fourteen years, by which time the canal ought to be ready
for traffic. Thereafter, the Americans would pay an annual
sum, to be decided by negotiation between the two sovereign
states. As before, the Compagnie Nouvelle was not called
upon to contribute anything, beyond its property to the U.S.
It was a great triumph for Cromwell and Bunau-Varilla to
have saved their client from foreclosure and from having to
surrender any of the principal coming from the prospective
buyer.

The extent to which Concha's independent course of action diverged from Colombian thoughts on the matter was
made clear when the diplomat opened long-delayed instructions on April 26, by which time he had signed a very slightly
amended version of the protocol with Hay.[56] His orders called
for a financial contribution from the French as a prerequisite to any negotiation with Washington. Aghast at what he
had done, Concha offered to resign. He was refused, probably because there was no immediate replacement available;
but it was clear to Marroquin that he had been outthought
and outmaneuvered by the New Company's agents.

With the passing of the Spooner amendment, the focal
point in canal affairs reverts to Paris. Cromwell felt the sit-

uation in Washington was sufficiently stable to allow him to spend the late summer months in the French capital. It was here that he had lengthy conversations with Waldeck Rousseau who had been hired to advise the Company. Besides the Colombian problem, there was the question of stockholder ratification of the U.S. offer and the powers invested in the New Company by the French courts to dispose of its property in a manner not originally anticipated.[57] The United States Attorney-General, Philander C. Knox had sent Cromwell a ten point memorandum on August 6 requesting very specific answers. His apprehensions stemmed from an understandable ignorance of French commercial legal practice, and its application to the American situation (which Morgan and his faction insisted was invalid).[58] Knox came to Paris in September and worked with Cromwell on the legal technicalities in premises which had thoughtfully been provided by the engineering department of the Company. On his return to the U.S., he was able to reassure Roosevelt that French lawyers had given the Company a clean bill of health, and that there was no skeleton in the closet, as had been the case with its predecessor.[59]

It was at this point that unilateral action, first by Congress and then by the U.S. navy, threatened to undo all the laboriously achieved accomplishments of the previous spring. In July, Hay presented Concha with a list of seventeen amendments which the Senate wanted to see inserted in the April agreement. These were designed mainly to strengthen American military control over the projected Canal Zone. For example, Article XXIII, if changed to suit the Senate, would give the U.S. the right to land troops as it saw fit, whereas the original clause had limited their use to those occasions when Colombia itself could not control the situation and made a request for assistance. Then, in September, the U.S. fleet acted as if the amendments had been accepted. When rebel general Benjamin Herrera advanced on Panama City, Commander Thomas C. McLean of the U.S.S. *Cincinnati* landed forces to guard the P.R.C. track, and notified regular troops of the government and insurgents alike that he would decide who might use it and for what purposes. Protests from Bogota caused his replacement, Rear-Admiral Silas Cook, to relent somewhat in favor of the government troops; but for Concha this was Yankee imperialism at its worst, and a foretaste of what might be expected. He regretted more than ever what he had signed in April, and determined to cease all further efforts to accommodate the Americans or the French. For weeks he remained *in communicado*.[60] Eventually, in surly mood, he agreed to see Cromwell where he raised the ominous topic of an indemnity from the canal company and its subsidiary.[61] Next, he called on Hay. The Secretary of State, sensing his mood of anger and despair, was at pains to assure him that the administration would agree to retain the original text of Article XXIII provided that Concha made concessions on other points. These included the Colombian demand for a separate financial understanding with the Company and the P.R.C. which he, Hay, termed "wholly inadmissable."[62] Concha was non-commital. The spectacle of American intervention on the Isthmus in September still haunted him. Cromwell was on hand to suggest that the U.S. be given control of the Canal Zone for a hundred years with the right to renew it in perpetuity. The Secretary of State seconded this and said that this was all he was prepared to discuss. Cromwell reported the Secretary of State's attitude as "firm, almost aggressive."[63]

It was not far enough for the Colombian envoy. Recognizing Cromwell's hand behind every move, he defended his position in this way:

Limited as is the time during which the companies
will enjoy the usufruct from the properties, it is
clear that if these have a great price, it pertains to
Colombia, and there is no reason or motive for it
being paid to the companies, or that its owner shall
cede it gratuitously. Already, Colombia has exercised an act of exceptional liberality in extending
the period for construction of the works, the only
effect of which has been that the canal company
is now in a position to recover part of its capital which, without this circumstance, would have
passed to Colombia within a few months.[64]

The tragic position in which Concha found himself is partly
revealed by this extract. There were two separate issues –
Colombian sovereignty, and the indemnity which the French
might have to pay. They ought to have been kept apart and
dealt with in turn. Thanks to Cromwell's intrigues, they
became so firmly entwined that, if Colombia capitulated on
the one, she automatically did so on the other. For Concha, some measure of control on the Isthmus was the more
important, and it was in danger of being violated with no
compensatory guarantee for his nation. If it was inevitable
that the Stars and Stripes should fly there, then the Americans must be forced to pay sweetly for the privilege.[65]

By contrast, the motives of Marroquin and his cabinet
were less elevated. For them U.S. intervention, for all its
humiliating aspects, had actually prevented a rebel victory
in the area. Acquiescence in canal diplomacy was a price
they might be willing to pay if they could be sure of continued support from that quarter. If the treaty proved to
be unsatisfactory, they were willing to leave the thankless
task of amending it to their congress. This interpretation
was substantiated by a report Hay received from his consul

in Bogota, Charles Hart. The new Minister of Foreign Affairs, Felipe Paul, had assured Hart that "...if Minister (i.e. Concha) refuses to sign treaty, Secretary of Legation is to take charge and to sign."[66] This was a reference to Tomas Herran, a long-time confidant of Cromwell, and it was the final ignominy as far as Concha was concerned. With a minimum of ceremony, he left the embassy in Herran's control and sailed for home in the first week of December. Cromwell was surprised by this development but found it "extremely encouraging" and he foresaw "better results."[67]

This might well have been the case had not Colombian politics followed their usual devious and unpredictable course. Lago, the Minister of Finance, expressed an attitude that was diametrically opposed to that of his cabinet colleagues. On December 24 he cabled Paris asking that Mancini be empowered to act in forthcoming talks to determine the indemnity which the New Company would definitely be asked to pay.[68] Bô was naturally shocked, having just read Cromwell's cheerful forecast. But there was another reason for his pessimism. Time was running out, since the original offer to the United States was due to expire in three months. Hay gently pointed out that perhaps the time had come for Cromwell and his client to bow to defeat and give Marroquin and his friends some share of the forty million dollars that would be forthcoming from the U.S. Treasury. Otherwise, the deadlock would never be broken. Even his administration was faced with a deadline of sorts, in that section 4 of the Spooner legislation stipulated American control of the territory "within a reasonable time."[69]

There then occurred another of Colombia's unfathomable delays. On January 13, 1903 Hay showed Cromwell the text of another message from Hart. This revealed that on Lago's urging, Marroquin could be expected to take a harder line.[70] For some reason, perhaps faulty communication, Herran did not obtain the full text until the 25th, by which time he had committed himself and his country to yet another agreement. Marroquin may conceivably been encouraged by the collapse of the latest revolt to adopt a firmer line; but the underlying reasons are not important. What mattered was that the failure of this directive to arrive in time resulted in his government being presented with a third *fait accompli.*

The Hay-Herran entente, like its predecessors, was also the fruit of co-operation between a Colombian diplomat and a New Company representative. The main difference was that this one was completed under the threat of an ultimatum from the U.S. State Department to the effect that the time provided for negotiations had just about expired.[71] This one was similar to the Hay-Concha agreement, but increased the initial payment to ten million dollars. The one hundred year lease was to be indefinitely renewable at the option of the United States. On the delicate question of law and order, provision was made for joint courts and concerted action in the event of civil disobedience.[72]

Because of a crowded agenda, Congress would not be able to ratify it until March 4, at the earliest. Hay therefore asked the New Company to extend its offer beyond that date.[73] Cromwell was determined that no such thing would happen since it would require more consultations with Lemarquis and Gautron. Not only that; there was no assurance that Colombia would sit idly by while the shareholders gave their assent. On the contrary, she might well seize the opportunity to indulge in the officious meddling which had paralysed the general meeting in the previous February. But it was necessary, above all, to avoid another of those seemingly interminable wrangles between the liquidation and the mandataire on the one hand and the board on the other. As recently as July 5, 1902, a bondholder had obtained a temporary injunction opposing the sale and had asked Lemarquis

to aid in the intervention (although the latter had refused).[74]
Instead, Cromwell managed to convince Hay and Knox that
their government ought to proceed with the purchase. The
only proviso would be ratification of the Hay-Herran agreement by both nations.[75] This ingenious proposal placed the
U.S. in exactly the same position as it had been on the mor-
row of the Concha entente. Not only was it true, noted
Cromwell, with obvious satisfaction

> ...that *we do not have to give title with consent,
> we do not have to make the effort to obtain it,* (his
> italics)... this measure assures the happy success of
> our efforts for now, the government of the United
> States is obliged to defend us to the end and to
> collaborate with us in the face of any eventuality.[76]

When the Hay-Herran agreement came to be debated in
the Senate on March 5, Morgan fought it clause by clause,
proposing no fewer than sixty-two changes. He described
it as a compact with "...a crowd of French jail-birds, clev-
erly advised by a New York railroad wrecker...and a de-
praved, priest-ridden people whose constitutional government (is) a myth."[77] Even such stalwarts of Panama as
Hanna and Spooner had misgivings over the degree of control that Colombia would continue to exercise in the proposed Canal Zone. But Cromwell was adamant that the
measure would go through unchanged; and, in addition to
his own ceaseless lobbying, he persuaded Herran to write to
the senators warning them that the slightest revision would
cause its rejection by Bogota.[78] On March 17, both men had
the satisfaction of seeing the unaltered agreement pass by
seventy-three votes to five. The onus now lay squarely on
the Colombian legislators.

The atmosphere in Bogota was tense following news of the
Senate vote. Beaupré, Hart's replacement, wrote on April 15

that the past two months had seen public sentiment change "from approbation to suspicion and from suspicion to decided opposition."[79] There was a general feeling that the Americans had exploited the nation's weakness, debilitated as matters were by revolution. Its most valuable possession was being taken for "a paltry sum".[80] Beyond this, party divisions were making themselves felt, and they were to become increasingly fractious as the months passed. Liberal and Historical sentiment within the Colombian Congress was largely along the lines of an unacceptable loss of sovereignty in the Isthmus. They held as meaningless the clause guaranteeing a continued Colombian presence there because the lease to the foreigner was to be perpetual. The Conservatives, on the other hand, tended to feel that the American presence there and elsewhere in Central America and the Caribbean was an unalterable fact of life. The determining factor should be – indeed, could only be – the best price they could obtain. If it was not forthcoming from Washington, then it ought to come from the canal company in Paris.

This was the approach Marroquin favored, despite his party's view to the contrary, and so the demand for a contribution from the Compagnie Nouvelle was revived before the Bogota congress met to debate the agreement officially. This time, however, more subtlety was used. Mancini was told that his employer

> ... must contribute in order to create a favorable opinion in the congress and, ultimately, its adoption by that congress, by giving fifty million francs for permission which it must have to be able to transfer its rights and those of the Panama Railroad Company to a foreign government.[81]

This was not to be construed as a threat, but surely the French saw it was in their best interests to co-operate. It was now possible to see how the cunning Cromwell had planned to thwart this contingency. The protocol which he had induced Hay to sign was about to be invoked in the New Company's defence. Marroquin was to be warned that his envoy's signature obliged his administration to abide by its terms, irrespective of whether the canal and railroad companies paid indemnities. This same, lengthy list of instructions to Beaupré also made it clear that the United States would refuse to complete the transaction if either of the two private companies referred to were forced to relinquish any assets:

> If the (New) Company were to accede to the demands of Colombia, the President would be unable to consummate the proposed purchase from it, for it would have surrendered a material part of the property for which he is authorized to make payment.... Among the rights and privileges, one of the most important is the right of acquiring the rights, privileges and concessions of the New Panama Canal Company, secured by Article I of the Treaty; and, if these rights, privileges and concessions were to be cancelled, it would fundamentally change the terms of purchase.[82]

The logic of this statement does not bear close scrutiny, Marroquin was interested in an indemnity from the French. If he managed to obtain one, the loss would be the Company's alone. The hand of the New York lawyer is apparent in every sentence. Even more extraordinary than Hay's defence of a foreign interest was Cromwell's submission of the contents of this diplomatic dispatch to the board of directors for their prior approval. Although *prima facie* evidence that he forwarded the message is missing in the Company's archives, there is no reason to doubt his own testimony that he did act in this way.[83] The State Department never denied it, either, and most experts on the history of canal diplomacy are agreed that Hay was too much under his spell at this time.[84]

Ignoring the rising tide of anti-American sentiment in the Colombian capital, Hay pressed ahead with further orders to Beaupré whose content served to inflame native opinion to an even greater pitch. Besides the baseless assertion that "... canal negotiations were initiated by Colombia and were energetically pressed upon this government for several years...", there was a sinister threat, all the greater for not being precisely defined:

> If Colombia would now reject the treaty, or unduly delay its ratification, the friendly understanding between the two countries would be so seriously compromised that *action might be taken by Congress next winter which every friend of Colombia would regret* (my italics)[85]

Though Cromwell claimed that he was the original author of this note, as well, it says something for his native sagacity that he was coming to realize the possible dangers inherent in an approach of this sort. In an effort to redress the balance, he produced an alternative scheme, designed to meet the one objection still within the compass of French action. Just before debate began in Bogota on the treaty, he requested and received Bô's approval to an offer. If the Hay-Herran Treaty was passed, the Compagnie Nouvelle would guarantee that Colombia's share in the forty million dollars coming to the former would be at least equal to the par value of her share holdings in the Company. This had been a condition of the Concha and Silva agreements. Colombia stood to receive 8.5% of the profit, after expenses. However, the 'sentence arbitrale' of February 11, 1902 had reduced the Company's share to just under 38% of the total (from 40% originally). With deductions for costs of transfer, taxes and etc. there was a possibility Colombia might receive less than one hundred francs a share.[86]

The offer came too late to influence the outcome. From the moment debate opened, on July 2, it was obvious that Marroquin was fighting a rearguard action. A committee was struck to discuss details of the agreement, and was chaired by Perez y Soto, a Yankee-hater of the first water. Some indication of his attitude may be gleaned from a letter he wrote to *El Correo Nacional* two months previously:

> The Herran Treaty will be rejected and rejected by a unanimous vote of both chambers. That is what I hope, since there will not be a single representative of the nation who will believe the voice of the people who have had the brazenness to recommend this shameful compact. The insult which Herran has cast upon the name of Colombia will never be expunged. The gallows would be small punishment for a criminal of this class.[87]

Soto's committee advised nine amendments, including, predictably enough, a contribution from the canal and railroad companies as well as complete Colombian jurisdiction over the Canal Zone. On August 12 debate ended, with twenty-four of the twenty-nine senators voting against the treaty as it stood.[88] A supplementary resolution established another committee to draft a more advantageous settlement while a third, under the chairmanship of Guillermo Quintero Calderon, the new president of the Colombian senate, was directed to examine the concession which had been negotiated by his namesake with Mancini in 1900. This, it will be recalled, had extended the concession to October 31, 1910; but it had been accepted by Sanclemente in an emergency decree, without reference to congress. There was, in consequence, a case for challenging the constitutionality of his action; and if the challenge were successful, the charter given the French would expire in October 1904, just a year away when 'confiscation by stagnation' would occur.[89] The possibilities were intriguing. Not only would Colombia obtain her ten million dollars (or more!) from the Americans, she would have to wait for no more than a year to inherit all the French excavation and the money due to the French from the same source. There was, of the problem of the P.R.C. to consider. It would still possess its veto on construction across or immediately adjacent to its route, while the Colombian government would have to return the five million francs paid by Mancini for the concession. But, as Mancini himself noted, this would be small outlay for such a large return: and it was doubtful if the railroad could survive or even resist pressure from all sides to capitulate.[90] Calderon was careful to confine his committee's findings to the level of observations rather than binding recommendations, and left the decision to congress.

Even that was more than enough for President Roosevelt. He was later to rationalize his apprehension at the possible outcome in this way:

> If we had sat supine, this would doubtless have meant that France would have interfered to protect the company, and we should then have had on the Isthmus not the company but France; and the gravest international complications might have ensued.[91]

One must seriously question the plausibility of this line of reasoning. Perhaps enough has been said to show that the French government had never cherished much affection for the second Panama Canal Company, and that its assistance had been minimal. During the second half of 1903 when the situation was reaching its head, the Third Republic had more than enough in Europe and North Africa to occupy its attention. A crisis was looming in Morocco, the Russian alliance had not lived up to expectations, and relations with England, following the Fashoda Incident were not yet cordial. For those reasons it is inconceivable that France would have remotely considered shouldering another international obligation – especially in an area where American influence was supreme. The Maximilian fiasco was still a living memory for senior politicians, and the Hay-Pauncefote Treaty had confirmed Uncle Sam's paramountcy, even over England.

In any case, these considerations had little relevance for certain determined and powerful men in Washington, Paris and Panama City. For them, the American president's attitude was a signal for decisive action. If Colombia would not cede the Canal Zone forthwith, it would have to be taken from her.

Notes

1. The bulk of Cromwell's correspondence with the Paris office during this period was by telegram. With very few exceptions, only French copies of the originals remain in the archives. Rather than re-translate and risk straying even farther from the original version, I have, on occasion, quoted the French. Bunau-Varilla's part in the triumph of the Spooner amendment is dealt with in Ameringer's "The Panama Canal lobby of Philippe Bunau-Varilla and William Nelson Cromwell" in *American Historical Review*, Vol. LXVIII, April 1963, pp. 346-63, but it seems to the writer that Bunau-Varilla's contribution is slightly overestimated. Roosevelt's *An Autobiography* (London, 1913) though even more opinionated than most of the *genre*, is useful for revealing presidential attitudes.

2. Hutin knew exactly what to expect. While still in Washington, he had written to Lemarquis: "Mais, au fonds, je crains moindre le danger ici qu'à Paris." A.N. 7 AQ 38, November 29, 1901.

3. A.N. 7 AQ 34, Conseil d'Administration: Procès verbal.

4. *Ibid.*, Conseil d'Administration to Gautron, December 17, 1901.

5. The reference was to the Etienne Report, of course.

6. A.N. 7 AQ 34, Gautron to Monvoisin, December 19, 1901.

7. A.N. 7 AQ 35, "Sentence arbitrale en vue du partage éventuel entre la Compagnie et la liquidation du produite de la vente du Canal de Panama aux Etats-Unis," February 11, 1902.

8. *Ibid.*, "Compromis entre la Compagnie Nouvelle et la liquidation," December 24, 1901.

9. *Le Comptant*, issue of December 23, reported that the police had to be called to restore order.

10. The notice appeared on December 27. It is reproduced, in part, in *Panama, la création*, p. 275.

11. A.N. 7 AQ 37, Bô to Boeufve, January 4, 1902. Lampré was in mid-Atlantic at this point.

12. A.N. 7 AQ 38, "Conseil d'Administration to Walker, January 9 and 11, 1902. March 4, 1903 was the closing date of the Congressional session.

13. *Congressional Record*, 57 Cong., 1 Sess., January 9, 1902, pp. 557-58. The 'Canon amendment' with this recommendation, was defeated by 206 votes to 41. Hepburn's bill passed by 308 to 2.

14. A.N. 7 AQ 38, Lampré to Bô, January 10, 1902.

15. *Hearings of the Sub-committee on Interoceanic Canals*, 57 Cong., 1 Sess., January 11, 1902.

16. *Sen. Doc.* No. 123, 57 Cong., 1 Sess., p. 10.

17. Hanna, nevertheless, felt that Cromwell was not really committed. According to Bunau-Varilla, the lawyer had told Hanna that he regarded Panama as nothing but a publicity stunt (B-V Papers, Bunau-Varilla to Paul Gontard, a New Company lawyer, December 12, 1907 – in Box 13).

18. B-V Papers, Box 21, Cromwell to Spooner, January 21, 1902.

19. *Ibid.*, Box 4, Bunau-Varilla to 'Bunovarilla' (his cable address in Paris), January 23, 1902.

20. *Ibid.*, Box 11, January 26, 1902. Cromwell thanked Bunau-Varilla by letter on the 27th, adding: "I returned from Washington Friday, filled with deep concern. Not an hour is to be lost

and I will prepare to act at once." *Story of Panama* reprints the letter *in extenso* (pp. 168-69). It includes the warning: "...it is must be clearly understood that in no case could we have recourse to methods as dangerous as they are unlawful which consist of gifts or promises of whatsoever nature they may be...."

21. *Congressional Record*, 57 Cong., 1 Sess., p. 1048.

22. *Deposition of members of the Isthmian Canal Commission before the Senate Committee on Interoceanic Canals*, 57 Cong., 1 Sess. (*Sen. Doc. No.* 783), February 5, 1902.

23. B-V Papers, Box 4, Bunau-Varilla to Roosevelt, May 10, 1902.

24. The cartoon is reprinted in Duval's *Cadiz to Cathay*, p. 163.

25. *Congressional Record*, 57 Cong., 1 Sess., p. 6269.

26. *Panama, la création*, pp. 323-25.

27. *Isthmian Canals: Views of the Minority of the Committee*, 57 Cong., 1 Sess., Sen. Doc. No. 783, pt. 2.

28. These are reproduced in full between pages 299 and 311 of *Panama, la création*.

29. *Congressional Record*, 57 Cong., 1 Sess., p. 6277 *et seq.*

30. *Supra.*

31. See, for example, Herbert Croly, *Marcus Alonzo Hanna: his Life and Work* (New York, 1912) p. 384 which contains quotations by Senators Platt and Frye on how attitudes had changed in the chamber as a result. Also, Miner, *op. cit.*, p. 152, footnote 6 for editorial opinion of the day.

32. Ameringer, "The Panama Canal Lobby", pp. 361-62.

33. *Congressional Record*, 57 Cong., 1 Sess., pp. 7072-94.

34. B-V Papers, Box 5, Charles de Lesseps to Bunau-Varilla, June 21, 1902.

35. *Story of Panama*, p. 264. The House vote was 260 to 8 in favor.

36. A.N. 7 AQ 38, Cromwell to Bô, March 22, 1902.

37. *Ibid.*, Mancini to Bô, January 30, 1902.

38. *Ibid.*, Cromwell to Bô, March 22, 1902.

39. A.N. 7 AQ 35, Mancini to Bô, February 17, 1902.

40. *Ibid.*

41. *Story of Panama*, p. 252. He had been a founding member of the Historical party.

42. A.N. 7 AQ 36, Uribe to Conseil d'Administration, February 27, 1902.

43. *Le Petit Parisien*, March 1, 1902.

44. The full text is in Miner, *op. cit.*, p. 137.

45. A.N. 7 AQ 38, Cromwell to Bô, March 22, 1902.

46. *Story of Panama*, pp. 253-54. Boyard had invited Bunau-Varilla's participation because of his fluency in Spanish. See also B-V Papers, Box 4, Boyard to Bunau-Varilla, February 25, 1902.

47. A.N. 7 AQ 38, Lampré to Bô, March 5, 1902.

48. Description by Henry Hall of the New York *Sun*.

49. A.N. 7 AQ 38, Cromwell to Bô, March 21, 1902.

50. B-V Papers, Box 4, Bunau-Varilla to Concha, March 22, 1902.

51. *Ibid.*

52. *Ibid.* This was sent on March 26.

53. N.A. RG 185/1/1, Royer to Bô, March 29, 1902.

54. B-V Papers, Box 4, Concha to Bunau-Varilla, March 27, 1902.

55. *Ibid.*, Bunau-Varilla to Concha, March 27, 1902.

56. The diplomatic bags had been dispatched on March 17 but had been delayed by faulty communications for which the rebels were partly responsible. See Mack, *op. cit.*, pp. 437-39.

57. A.N. 7 AQ 36, Knox to Cromwell. The Company referred these to its lawyers on September 1 ("Consultation – MM. Limbourg, du Buit, Devin, Gontard et Thieblin". On ratification by stockholders Cromwell asked Gontard: "Will conveyance be legally sufficient if made by the New Company...ratified by a majority...at a meeting legally called, held and concurred in by the liquidator and *mandataire*? I should warn you that the policy of American law is against the inventory sale by a solvent business corporation itself of all its property. It is against the policy of American law to defeat the purpose for which it was organized, except as an incident to proceedings for dissolution of the corporation itself, in which case, the rights of creditors can

be adequately protected and the assets distributed according to the priorities and rights of the parties. As the New Company is solvent and has not failed, it is claimed that conveyance can only be made through dissolution of the company and through liquidators appointed for that purpose. Can such a sale be made?") (B-V Papers, Box 21, Cromwell to Gontard, August 14, 1902.)

58. *Ibid.*

59. *Official Opinions of the Attorney-Generals,* Vol. XXIV (1902), pp. 148, 504-30. Also, A.N. 7 AQ 36, "Memoire sur les conditions jurisdique qui rendent possible et regulière au point de vue de la loi française la cession projetée par la Compagnie Nouvelle du Canal de Panama" (undated), pp. 1-40.

60. A.N. 7 AQ 38, Cromwell to Bô, October 19, 1902.

61. *Ibid.,* Cromwell to Bô, October 31, 1902.

62. *Diplomatic History of the Panama Canal,* pp. 260-63. Also, A.N. 7 AQ 38, Cromwell to Bô, November 7, 1902.

63. A.N. 7 AQ 38, November 22, 1902.

64. *Diplomatic History of the Panama Canal,* pp.263-64.

65. He may have been influenced by America's extremely healthy financial state as revealed in M.E.J. Gage's *Annual Financial Report to Congress for 1901* (Washington, 1902) which revealed that the national debt had been reduced from $1,046,049,020 to $954,027,150 in the year commencing November 1, 1901. In the same period there had been a trading surplus of $664,592,826.

66. *State Department: Dispatches from Colombia,* Vol. 58, Hart to Hay, November 22, 1902.

67. A.N. 7 AQ 38, Cromwell to Bô, December 1, 1902.

68. *Ibid.,* Cromwell to Bô, January 10, 1903.

69. *Ibid.,* Cromwell to Bô, January 11, 1903.

70. *Ibid.,* Cromwell to Bô, January 15, 1903.

71. *Ibid.,* Cromwell to Bô, January 23, 1903.

72. The complete text is in *Sen. Doc.* No. 474, 63 Cong., 2 Sess., pp. 277-78. Provisions regarding the New Company were identical to those in previous agreements.

73. *Story of Panama*, p. 275. The request was made on February 5 and again on the 7th.

74. *Gazette des Tribunaux*, July 5, 1902. Also, A.N. 7 AQ 35, "Affaire Donnadieu."

75. A.N. 7 AQ 38, Cromwell to Knox, March 3, 1903.

76. *Ibid.*, Cromwell to Bô, February 18, 1903.

77. Quoted in Miner, *op. cit.*, pp. 197-98.

78. *Story of Panama*, p. 274. Also, A.N. 7 AQ 38, Cromwell to Bô, March 12, 1903.

79. *State Department: Dispatches from Colombia*, Vol. 59, Beaupré to Hay, April 15, 1903. Hart had been recalled following personal, financial problems.

80. *Ibid.*

81. A.N. 7 AQ 35, Mancini to Bô, April 24, 1903.

82. *State Department: Dispatches to Colombia*, Vol. 19, Hay to Beaupré, April 28, 1903.

83. Made during the Rainey Hearings.

84. See, for example, Tyler Dennett's *John Hay* (New York, 1933), pp. 375-76; Mack, *op. cit.*, pp. 446-47; Miner, *op. cit.*, p. 281.

85. *State Department: Dispatches to Colombia*, Vol. 19, Hay to Beaupré, June 9, 1903.

86. A.N. 7 AQ 38, Cromwell to Bô, June 28, 1903. This had been a condition of both the Concha and Silva ententes. Colombia stood to receive 8.5% of the New Company's allocation. However, the 'Sentence Arbitrale' of February 11, 1902 had reduced the Company's share to a little under 38% of the total. With reductions for expenses, taxes, costs of transfer and incidentals, there was a possibility that Colombia might receive less than 100 francs per share.

87. Issue of May 11, 1903.

88. *Ibid.*, issue of August 16, 1903.

89. The phrase is Bunau-Varilla's.

90. A.N. 7 AQ 35, Mancini to Cromwell, October 16, 1903.

91. Roosevelt, *op. cit.*, p. 565.

Chapter 8

Revolution on the Isthmus[1]

The roots of Panamanian separatism go deep into the nineteenth century. In the two decades following independence from Spain in 1821, Panama's attachment to New Granada was more nominal that real. Indeed, for a brief period in the 1840's Panama and the neighboring province of Veragua had formed an independent entity while New Granada was being wracked by revolution. Even after reunion, there were frequent threats of secession occasioned by the geographical isolation of the federal capital, stagnation of trade, and the intrigues of local politicians which an apathetic central authority did little to counteract. The reforms introduced by President Nunez in the early 1880's proved to be a mixed blessing. While they ended a half century of neglect, they subjected the department more closely to his ill-considered economic policies. Reference has already been made to a law of 1886 which forced businessmen to deal in an inconvertible currency which large and repeated issues of paper money had rendered almost valueless in international trading. For the last fifteen years of the century expenditure consistently exceeded revenue as one administration after another found it impossible to balance budgets. Panama defaulted on her foreign debt, as did Colombia itself, with the result that foreign investment fell to a low ebb.

To a growing list of grievances common to both the department and the nation, Panamanians added a few specific to their own situation. It was, for instance, the only department where silver was available as legal tender, thanks to the needs of the canal company and the P.R.C. for a negotiable currency. By 1903, depreciation of the piastre had caused it to sink to one-thirtieth of its 1885 value. The discrepancy between the real value of the currency unit and its paper one was aggravated in a number of ways. The Bogota government levied a tax that was three times higher in Panama than elsewhere on each head of cattle slaughtered. Basic necessities such as salt, candles, matches and tobacco were available more cheaply from neighboring states such as Nicaragua and Guatemala; but Panama, for all her links with the outside world, was forced to buy from monopolists who had paid the Bogota government for the privilege of manufacture and distribution. "One of the benefits we derive from Bogota!" wrote Carlos Constantino Arosemena bitterly. He, one of the founding members of the independence movement, also charged that the department had received only one-tenth of the annuity paid by the railway company, and that, throughout negotiations with the United States, "...never a word was said about how much Panama was to receive for needed improvements...."[2] Another writing at the same time, bluntly asserted that Colombia was, "a halter round the neck of Panama," and that if, through the former's obstinacy and myopia the rival canal route came to be chosen, his province would relapse into its former comatose, impoverished position.[3]

The secessionist movement originated with Jose Augustin Arango, a senator and agent for the P.R.C. He had boycotted debate on the Hay-Herran Treaty because he was convinced that the outcome was a foregone conclusion. At first, only his family and immediate friends were involved in the plot. The inclusion of as many railway company officials as possible, somewhat later, was conscious policy on his part for, in so doing, he hoped that nascent Panamanian discontent could be made to complement the aims of the New Company and those of the Roosevelt administration.[4] Of course, it was inevitable that the P.R.C. directors in New York, including Cromwell, should come to be implicated. But Cromwell's position was a very special and delicate one. He was well aware of how his past indiscretions had distressed the parent company in Paris to an even greater degree than those in control of the railway in Panama itself. Therefore, his conduct during the critical months leading up to the rising become quite comprehensible.

In the last week of August 1903, another of the conspirators, Manuel Amador Guerrero, met Duque aboard the steamer *Seguranca* during a business trip to New York. Although the two men were friendly, nothing was said during the voyage from Colon, and Duque suspected that his travelling companion was going north to obtain financing for a revolt. As soon as the ship docked, his suspicions were confirmed. Amador Guerrero went immediately to the Wall Street offices of Cromwell and thence to the State Department in Washington where he was introduced to Hay. Next day, September 2, Duque received a call from Cromwell asking him to pay a visit to the lawyer's office as well. The editor of the *Panama Star and Herald* was astonished when he was asked whether he was prepared to contribute to the coffers of a revolutionary fund. If he obliged, Cromwell was willing to advance security for such a loan and would support him in his bid to become president of the breakaway state.[5]

Cromwell had seriously miscalculated. Duque was not yet in the conspiratorial ring, an exclusion he may well have resented and which possibly decided his next move. He may also have felt that the course of action proposed was too drastic and that Bogota could still be made to change its attitude on canal policy. Perhaps he was dismayed, too, by news that Hay had refused to commit his government to intervene directly with troops once the rebels had taken the first steps.[6] Whatever the reason, Duque decided to limit his role to that of commentator. He decided to inform Herran that if Colombia did not ratify the treaty soon, it would lose everything it had on the Isthmus. Herran acted immediately. He informed Bogota that both the New Company and the P.R.C. were "deeply implicated" in a separation movement.[7] On September 4 he warned the New Company that he would hold it chiefly responsible for any plot that was unearthed.[8]

Before this letter reached Paris, however, Cromwell was making haste to undo what he had just undertaken. He disowned all promises he had made to Amador Guerrero only days before, and he sent a note to the Isthmus warning the employees of both concerns that they must observe the strictest neutrality if a rising should occur.[9] The next two weeks saw the Wall Street lawyer reduced to unaccustomed impotence. He was forced to ignore the burgeoning conspiracy and to cling to the increasingly forlorn hope that Colombia would see the error of her ways before it was too late. Yet matters could not be allowed to drift. An unsuccessful rising in Panama would have fatal consequences for the Compagnie Nouvelle. In the U.S.A., 1904 was the year of the presidential election; and Roosevelt was determined to have the canal issue settled before he presented himself for renomination before the Republican National Convention. If no revolution occurred, the canal would probably never be completed.

Cromwell claims credit for the next move, although there is good reason for believing that President Roosevelt was thinking along the same lines. It was the latter who suggested to Hay that there were only two courses of action to pursue:

> (i) To take up Nicaragua (ii) In some shape or way to interfere when it becomes necessary so as to secure the Panama route without further dealing with the foolish and homicidal corruptionists in Bogota. I am not inclined to have any dealings whatever with these Bogota people.[10]

Even at this late date the American president appeared undecided. In the course of this same conversation, Hay remarked that Cromwell should not "whisper over the ruin of the (Hay-Herran) Treaty through the greed of the Colombians and the disinclination of the canal company to satisfy it."[11] Roosevelt then granted Cromwell an interview in which he listened attentively while the lawyer unfolded a scheme which he had already discussed with Hay. Briefly, it called for the U.S. government to conclude an agreement with the New Company without more ado. If the Colombians tried to interfere, the 1846 Treaty would be invoked to justify retaliatory measures.[12] The Senate would have to approve, of course, but Roosevelt had long had his way in matters of foreign policy. If, nevertheless, such approval was not forthcoming, an irrevocable decision for the Nicaragua route would be taken. On October 10, Cromwell telegraphed Bô that he had achieved:

> ...sufficient support of my plan to permit me to submit it to you. The situation demands that we

act immediately and in a decisive fashion before the Congress of the United States reconvenes.[13]

The interesting phrase here is, 'the situation demands' Cromwell knew that revolutionary plans were afoot and that these might mature before the U.S. Senate met. If successful, they would leave that body with nothing to do save accept a *fait accompli*, namely Panamanian independence. For that reason, Cromwell left for Paris on October 15 partly to allay the fears of the New Company directors and partly to dissociate himself personally from the bold stroke about to be made.

The actual coup was masterminded by the Panamanians already referred to, and, specifically, to Bunau-Varilla who arrived in the United States in September for personal reasons.[14] In visits with John Moore, a former assistant Secretary of State and with his successor, Francis Loomis, the Frenchman became convinced that a declaration of Panamanian independence would be followed immediately by an American presence in the area. Though he did not meet Cromwell, Roosevelt apparently outlined what had been discussed though he gave no assurance that a revolution would receive armed support. Still, Bunau-Varilla was convinced that he had enough of a carte blanche to assist the revolutionaries. The possibility that the Clayton-Bulwer Treaty of 1846 could be invoked was additional reassurance since that implied that Colombia's presence on the Isthmus was at the mercy of the United States. He left the White House satisfied that he had achieved "all the necessary elements for action."[15]

The financing of the uprising was to lay the Compagnie Nouvelle open to charges of collusion. It was alleged that $100,000 were made available for the initial expenses incurred by the rebels. It is true that Bunau-Varilla had

50,000 francs deposited with the Crédit Lyonnais, but he would later claim that this came from his personal fortune lodged in various French, Belgian and Dutch banks and not from the New Company. As he explained:

> The Crédit Lyonnais is an enormous banking institution with a great number of branch offices all over the country, counting its clients in tens of thousands. I am one of them. It constitutes a veritable ineptitude to establish a relation between the transfer of money I made through my banker, the Crédit Lyonnais, and the fact that M. Marius Bô was, at the same time, a director of the Crédit Lyonnais and the New Panama Company.[16]

This may be the whole truth. Certainly correspondence between Cromwell and the Company reveals no hint of complicity with Bunau-Varilla. But it must be borne in mind that Bunau-Varilla was not exactly a faceless depositor in the eyes of the Crédit Lyonnais; and it is hard to believe that Bô was ignorant of his presence in Washington during these crucial months. Like a good deal more, the incriminating evidence may have been removed from the New Company's files. The most that can be said with certainty is that Cromwell and the Company had to be wary lest they become implicated in Bunau-Varilla's nefarious activities. That does not mean that they did not wish him well. If Colombia had succeeded in quelling the rising and had discovered a French connection, she would have had no compunction in evicting the offenders unceremoniously. Cromwell contented himself with a vague endorsement of Roosevelt's "masterful policy" during his sojourn in Paris.[17]

Final plans for the rising on the Isthmus were completed in October with Bunau-Varilla and Amador Guerrero busy in Washington. The insurgents' council in Panama City was informed of developments on the 27th, and five days later the first visible action was taken. The American warship, the U.S.S. *Nashville* entered Colon harbor on November 2 ostensibly to protect American citizens who were alarmed by the presence of five hundred Colombian soldiers sent there to quell a suspected uprising. This sprang from the activities of disloyal troops commanded by General Estaban Huertas, a renegade with scant respect for the government in Bogota. To these were added the Panama City police force and the members of Duque's private fire brigade. They optimistically interpreted the presence of the U.S. vessel as proof positive of U.S. support for their cause. Columbian troops were refused transportation across the Isthmus on the orders of Frederick Shaler of the P.R.C. and next day they surrendered. That same evening, November 3, independence was proclaimed by the junta and Bunau-Varilla was named envoy extraordinary and minister plenipotentiary to the United States with full powers to negotiate a canal treaty once the concession had been purchased from the New Company.[18]

Although the Company had acted with propriety throughout the whole affair, it was accused in Bogota of being the instigator. Such, at least, was the view of a group of prominent citizens who had met to advise the Colombian president of the next move. After heated discussion in which it was suggested that the United States be forced to withdraw its ambassador, it was decided to send an official to Panama to treat with the rebels. The choice fell on General Rafael Reyes who, it will be recalled, had had some dealings with the New Company. He was given authority to accede to demands for increased autonomy from the Panamanians if he could prevent outright secession. But his mission was doomed. As Renaudin had correctly forecast: "The United States are on the Isthmus and will never give it up."[19] Reyes was not even allowed to land in Colon but had to hold talks with members of the provisional government on board a French ship anchored in the bay. These were fruitless and on November 20 he set sail for New York and Washington where he hoped for a better reception. It would appear that he intended to propose immediate ratification of the Hay-Herran Treaty if his government received the assurance of the Secretary of State that it could proceed to extinguish the independence movement without hindrance.

Bunau-Varilla was determined that this must not happen. By its contacts with the revolutionary council, the United States had given the new regime *de facto* recognition. His other objective was to obtain official recognition from France. On November 16 he informed the French ambassador in Washington, that the new Panamanian government was prepared to abide by all the contracts and obligations which it had inherited from Colombia. He made it clear that these specifically included those concerning the Compagnie Nouvelle and the concession.[20] That same morning he began to work on the draft of a canal treaty which was to be of major historic importance in that it would dictate relations between the two countries for the next half century and beyond. His decision to go far beyond the provision of the Hay-Herran agreement lay in the fact that it was indelibly marked by the past behavior of Colombia and that it contained a number of clauses whose removal would improve the chances of a revised version in the U.S. Senate.[21] The new measure, the Hay-Bunau-Varilla Treaty was signed with alarming haste only two days later, on November 18. It was, in Hay's words (and they would be remembered bitterly by subsequent generations of Panamanians), "disproportionately advantageous to (our) government." Panama was to make far more concessions than Colombia had ever offered to make. Among them were: the extension of the proposed Canal Zone from ten kilometers to ten miles in width; complete American control of the police and judiciary within; and a lease in perpetuity at no greater cost to the lessee. The New Company benefitted by the terms of Article 22 in which Panama renounced all pecuniary claims against it and the P.R.C.[22]

Developments in the next few days following the signing of the treaty were to lessen Bô's anxiety over Panama's ability to maintain her new status. Cromwell reported that relations between him and Arosemena were excellent.[23] On November 23 France officially recognised the new republic. However, amid this general rejoicing there was one great uncertainty which can be traced to an omission in the Hay-Bunau-Varilla Treaty. Article 8 held that the Republic of Panama had succeeded Colombia in obtaining all rights and privileges concerning the canal – including the contracts and their prolongations. It was vague on the matter of the fifty thousand shares which the Colombian government had been given at the time of the formation of the Compagnie Nouvelle. Bô referred this matter to Waldeck-Rousseau together with a number of related questions. These included the usefulness of Mancini's continuing presence in Bogota, the status of Manuel Samper, the Colombian government's representative on the board of the Company, and the advisability of calling an extraordinary general meeting of shareholders to consent to the new policy the board would have to make with its clients in Panama City.[24]

Waldeck-Rousseau advised a 'wait-and-see' policy until Colombia, Panama and the United States had worked out their most immediate problems. A shareholders meeting could be called but only to inform individuals of what had happened since the previous one.[25] This sage, if timorous, policy could not be followed in its entirety, as events were soon to demonstrate. On November 27 a note was received from the Panamanian government in which attention was drawn to Article IV of the Roldan-Wyse agreement. The Company was bluntly told that the shares registered in the name of Colombia must now be re-registered in that of Panama's.[26] This spurred the Colombians to action. Uribe, their chargé d'affaires in Paris, sought a court order to prevent such a transfer, "reserving all freedom of action to proceed as a consequence of any nullification of contacts concluded."[27] This was most disquieting inasmuch as the situation in Washington had taken a sudden turn for the worse. That old protagonist of Nicaragua, Morgan, expressed outrage at the Panamanian coup. He launched an attack on Bunau-Varilla in the Senate, describing him as ". . . the peripatetic spellbinder for the New Panama Canal Company," and on the administration's flagrant misuse of the Spooner amendment which

> had no reference to any Caesarean operation by which a 'Republic of Panama' might be taken alive from the womb of Colombia and be empowered by our President to seize the territory of Colombia and to assume ownership and sovereignty there under mythical covenants that some diplomats, 'wise above what is written' have invented and have declared that they run with the land.[28]

There were also grumblings in Panama itself over the manifest renunciation of sovereignty over potentially valuable territory that the fledgling nation was being called on to make. Of these two centers of opposition, Washington was certainly the more serious as far as the New Company was concerned. The U.S. Senate was due to reconvene on January 7, 1904. If the Hay-Bunau-Varilla Treaty was not ratified by the Panamanians before that date, Morgan and his friends would surely exploit this as a manifestation of native reluctance to have the United States in their midst. Bunau-Varilla de-

termined to force the issue and he sent a cable to the new
Panamanian Minister for Foreign Affairs, de la Espirella,
warning of the danger that was growing daily as a result of
the

> ... coolness shown by the Panamanian government
> to the signing of a treaty which realizes the objects
> desired by those on the Isthmus, the three essen-
> tial goals of the revolution. 1. the protection of
> the Republic by the United States. 2. the con-
> struction of a Panama canal 3. the obtaining of
> financial advantages which had been acquired by
> Columbia.[29]

The Panamanians had taken no action on this communications when, on November 28, a third development occurred which boded ill for the Company. Reyes arrived in
New York where he was welcomed by no less a figure than ex-
president Grover Cleveland. As Bunau-Varilla had feared,
Reyes told the press that his nation was willing to waive all
claims for compensation from the United States if it could
launch an attack on the delinquent province, secure in the
knowledge that no foreign power would intervene. At the
same time, Reyes hired a lawyer, Wayne MacVeagh, to lobby
senators.[30]

Only one of these difficulties was resolved immediately to
the New Company's satisfaction. The Panamanian government heeded Bunau-Varilla's warning about the dangers of
temporising and they ratified the treaty on December 2. It
is doubtful whether Bô shared Cromwell's confidence that
this act put the issue of Panamanian independence beyond
all doubt, but he was sufficiently reassured by it to reject
Samper's request that he be allowed to continue attending
board meetings.[31] Bô replied that, since November 3, the
New Company had found itself dealing with a *force ma-*

juere. It had formed no opinions and taken no sides in the recent incident on the Isthmus. If, by some chance, Colombia found itself once more in a position to exercise control there, M. Samper would find the Company more than willing to abide by all the laws and concessions which it had previously negotiated with his government.[32]

The issue of Colombia's continued presence on the board was one of paramount importance to all concerned. Samper knew that if he were replaced by a Panamanian, all financial claims his country had would be void. The United States was also uneasy over the prospect of a non-Panamanian presence in the executive of a corporation with which they would soon have to deal, especially since that person represented a government which was insistent on the illegality of the Panamanian revolution. Besides principle, there was the more mundane consideration of the 50,000 shares and their market value. Their ownership was still worth contesting and that could be done most effectively in the board-room. The New Company, for its part, was indifferent as to their eventual ownership; but it regarded as anomalous the continued presence of a delegate from a nation which was powerless to influence canal policy anywhere. Further (and this was a facet of the situation to which Cromwell had drawn Bô's attention), if Colombia were to continue to be recognised as a major shareholder, she would have the legal status necessary to attack the transfer, independent of her status as a concessionary which the revolution had, of course, invalidated.[33] Roosevelt was very anxious that the impending sale be accepted by shareholders before the U.S. Congress assembled. His administration already had its hands full defending its stance during the goings-on in Panama in November.[34]

Back in Paris, Bô fought and won a battle to keep Samper in the cold. The Tribunal Civil de la Seine handed down a decision on December 29 upholding his assertion

that Colombia had manifestly shown her inability to retain
control over the former department of Panama. Moreover,
the shares she claimed were the property of the government
which now exercised authority there, and so Colombian representation on the board might prejudice the interests of the
New Company in its dealings with Panama and the United
States of America. The shareholders' meeting took place the
next day and passed off quietly. It was decided to postpone
the vote on final acceptance of the American offer until the
U.S. Senate had voted on the Hay-Bunau-Varilla Treaty.

In Washington Reyes and his recently-appointed lobbyist,
MacVeagh, fought a despairing action by trying to convince
senators of the folly of voting for a treaty which would, in
Morgan's well-rehearsed words "benefit a crowd of French
jailbirds and their New York counsel." On January 17, the
New York *World*, a long-time opponent of the French enterprise gave front page prominence to an article headlined:
"Panama Revolution – a Stock Gambler's Plan to Make Millions!" The charge was that the November rising had been fi-
nanced by a syndicate of Parisian and New York investors of
whom Bunau-Varilla had been "the chief reliance". Its gamble had succeeded in realising four million dollars in profit
from speculation in the bonds and shares of the canal companies and the P.R.C.[35] Battle was joined on the other side
of the Atlantic by that perpetual thorn in the side of the
New Company, Thièbaud. At a press conference in the Hotel Continentale, Thièbaud castigated all concerned. He was
particularly critical of Waldeck-Rousseau who had used his
elevated position in politics to give his legalistic utterances
a quasi-political imprimatur.[36] When this had no apparent
result, Thièbaud addressed himself to Ernest Vallé who had
returned to the Justice Department. He begged him to recall
his past services to the victims of Panama and to dismiss
Lemarquis, Gautron and the board of the New Company.

Only a timely act of this sort would prevent France from suffering the indignity of

> the blow of expulsion from the New World follow-
> ing the plotting of speculators and pirates, itself
> due to the disloyalty of the financial institutions,
> the abuse of power by the legal agents appointed
> and, it must be said, to the culpable indifference
> of those in positions of power.[37]

All of these attempts to turn the clock back were in vain. The fight in the U.S. Senate was a bitter one but party discipline in Republican ranks won the day. The Hay-Bunau-Varilla Treaty was passed in unaltered form by a vote of sixty-six to fourteen, on February 23, 1904.

Colombia continued fighting to the last in French courts. It appealed the decision given against Samper and maintained that it was still the legal owner of the 50,000 shares. Knox, the U.S. Attorney General, was insistent that the shareholders must give their assent to the purchase offer immediately. If, by chance, Colombia should succeed in having the December decision against it overturned there would be "fearful complications" that would delay a start to an American built canal for years.[38] Bô countered that the large financial institutions which comprised the bulk of New Company shareholders were not wont to take risks. They would vote as he, Knox, wanted only if the United States made a promise to pay up, irrespective of any court decision in Paris. He felt that the Attorney-General's apprehensions were needless. Colombia was beaten and the appeal she was making was nothing but "a method of blackmail". It would be recognised as such by French justice. It was far more dangerous for the United States to delay making the promise he had asked for because, by her hesitation and her reticence, the U.S. was allowing the belief to spread that

Colombia might have a case of sorts.[39] This was one of the very few occasions in which the New Company's will did prevail. On March 3 Knox told Cromwell that he had decided to conclude the agreement with the Compagnie Nouvelle whatever happened in the courts in Paris, and that he would back Panama in its efforts to become the legal owners of the shares.[40]

As it happened the New Company was triumphantly vindicated on all counts.[41] Three days after a decision had been handed down against Colombia, Bô presided at a special stockholders' meeting where an unusual calm prevailed. He called for a vote of confidence in the board and for permission to conclude the dreary negotiations with the United States which had been in progress almost continuously for six years. Only four dissident votes were cast against the first resolution approving the sale and general conveyance of deeds to the United States government. The second motion – to dissolve the Compagnie Nouvelle and confer powers on its directors and the liquidator of the Compagnie Universelle – was carried with only three contrary votes.[42]

Even in these final stages the negotiations were beset by complications. On March 30 a Chicago resident, Charles Wilson, tried to obtain an injunction to prevent payment to the New Company. His assertion was that the Spooner amendment applied only to Colombia. Also, the American Constitution forbade the use of public funds for the purchase of a foreign corporation which was not owned in part by a government.[43] Cromwell sent one of his staff to Chicago to study the case and from his report concluded that it would be thrown out in court – which indeed it was. But to make absolutely certain that the forty million dollars were safe from the threat of seizure by a court, he devised a method of payment which was immune from any possible confiscation. According to French commercial law, deposits in the

Banque de France were non-distrainable. The firm of J.P. Morgan was brought in to act as special disbursing agent for the largest treasury warrant the American government had issued to that time.[44] The New Company bore the costs for this transaction which included Morgan's very modest remuneration of $35,700.

In Panama City, the formal exchange of property was concluded in the Cathedral Plaza on the morning of May 5, 1904, with a minimum of ceremony, much to the displeasure of the Panamanian government which considered the event an historic one meriting as great a fanfare as that which had greeted the coming of Ferdinand de Lesseps to the Isthmus a quarter of a century before. Renaudin presented the keys of the administration building to U.S. Army Lieutenant Mark Brooke who accepted them on behalf of William Howard Taft, the Secretary of War. A similar scene was enacted at the Company's head office in Paris on May 7. Confirmatory deeds of transfer had been signed immediately following ratification by shareholders on April 23. Now, these, together with the P.R.C. shares, were delivered into the hands of the deputy Attorneys-General, William A. Day and Charles Russell.[45]

Behind the scenes, Gautron, Lemarquis and the board were making preparations to distribute the monies to the creditors of both old and new companies. The unfortunate victims of the Panama débâcle were looking forward to a recompense which would have seemed a wishful dream only ten years ago. None of them could have imagined that the cruel hand of fate was about to strike again and that four more years would elapse before they saw a single franc.

Notes

1. In "New Light on the Panama Canal Treaty" in the *Hispanic-American Historical Review*, Vol. XLVI, February 1966, pp. 28-52, Dr. Charles Ameringer shows how Bunau-Varilla's total disregard of Panamanian nationalistic aspirations resulted in a settlement that was overwhelmingly beneficial to the New Company and the U.S.A., and not at all to the government he professed to be serving. Bunau-Varilla's defence of his conduct during the critical months from September 1903 to February 1904 is contained in his *Statement on Behalf of Historical Truth* (Paris, 1912 – privately printed).

2. B-V Papers, Box 6. Note by C.C. Arosemena, December 7, 1903.

3. Morales, *op. cit.*, p. 368.

4. Mack, *op. cit.*, p. 456.

5. By August he had been able to recruit, among others, Dr. Amador Guerrero, the P.R.C. resident surgeon in Panama City, James Shaler, its chief superintendent, Herbert G. Prescott, Shaler's assistant, and the freight agent, James A. Beers.

6. On the question of armed support from the U.S., Hay said that he would not cross that bridge until he came to it, but that if the revolutionaries were able to control Colon and Panama City at either end of the Isthmus, they could then depend on American troops to prevent the landing of Colombian soldiers who might "disturb the free and uninterrupted transit" which the Clayton-Bulwer Treaty bound his government to maintain. See Miner, *op. cit.*, p. 348. Duque had been introduced to Hay by Cromwell.

7. *Story of Panama*, p. 361, Herran to de Brigard, September 4, 1903. Duque had considerable business interests in Bogota, another factor which may have influenced his decision.

8. *Ibid.*, Hall's testimony.

9. N.A. RG 185/1/1, Cromwell to Renaudin, September 10, 1903: also B-V Papers, Box 20, Cromwell to Shaler, same date.

10. Quoted *in extenso* in Miner, *op. cit.*, p. 351.

11. Quoted in Roosevelt, *op. cit.*, p. 572.

12. By the terms of the treaty, Colombia was pledged to guarantee that "free transit from one to the other sea may not be embarrassed in any future time while this treaty exists."

13. A.N. 7 AQ 38, Cromwell to Bô.

14. His son suffered acutely from hay fever and Bigelow had suggested a complete change of climate might help. See *Panama, la création*, p. 384.

15. *Ibid.*, p. 415.

16. Bunau-Varilla, *Statement*, pp. 90-91. He adds (p. 104): "I say, and repeat, that my position towards the New Panama Canal Company has always been inimical because I strongly blamed their weak policy which has led to the loss of the Panama Canal. There was neither cordiality nor any relation between us." The error of assigning Bunau-Varilla a place with the Compagnie Nouvelle has been repeated in countless studies in Panama. It is also to be found in the *Oxford History of the United States*.

17. *Story of Panama*, p. 282, Cromwell to Roosevelt, October 31, 1903.

18. B-V Papers, Box 6, Arango *et alia* to Bunau-Varilla.

19. N.A. RG 185/1/1, Renaudin to Mancini, November 16, 1903.

20. B-V Papers, Box 6, Bunau-Varilla to Jusserand.

21. This theory is discussed at length in Ameringer, "New Light on the Panama Canal Treaty", *supra*, pp. 43-50.

22. A comparison of the two is given in DuVal's *Cadiz to Cathay*, Appendix L.

23. A.N. 7 AQ 38, Cromwell to Bô.

24. A.N. 7 AQ 35, Bô to Waldeck-Rousseau, November 24, 1903.

25. *Ibid.*, "Consultation avec M. Waldeck-Rousseau".

26. *Ibid.*, Boyd, Arosemena et Amador à Conseil d'Administration.

27. A.N. 7 AQ 38, "Opposition de Colombie", November 28, 1903.

28. *Congressional Record*, 58 Cong. 1 Sess., pp. 426-430.

29. *Panama, la création*, p. 513.

30. A.N. 7 AQ 38, Cromwell to Bô; also *New York Herald*, November 29, 1903.

31. *Ibid.*, Bô to Samper, December 7, 1903.

32. *Ibid.*

33. *Ibid.*, Cromwell to Bô, December 18 and 21, 1903.

34. *Ibid.*, Cromwell to Bô, December 21, 1903.

35. This issue would be raised again and again by Morgan and features prominently in the debates contained in *The Story of Panama*. The charge is dealt with in Appendix C.

36. Reprinted in *La Vie Financière*, January 19, 1904.

37. A.N. 7 AQ 35, Thièbaud to Vallé, February 5, 1904.

38. A.N. 7 AQ 38, Cromwell to Bô, February 28, 1904. This is one of the few telegrams where the original English version remains.

39. A.M. 7 AQ 38, Cromwell to Bô, February 29, 1904.

40. *Ibid.*, Knox to Cromwell. Two days earlier, Russell, one of the assistant Attorneys-General had told Cromwell that France should be "guided only by a desire to give satisfaction to the United States". Cromwell to Bô, March 5, 1904.

41. A.N. 7 AQ 35, "Extrait du jugement du Tribunal Civil de la Seine en date du 31 mars 1904."

42. *Ibid.*, "Assemblée Générale Extraordinaire: compte rendu de séance." Because of litigation, it was decided that all documents should be signed in advance of this meeting.

43. *Story of Panama*, pp. 288-91.

44. A.N. 7 AQ 38, "Projet de contrat entre la Compagnie Nouvelle du Canal de Panama, en liquidation, et MM. J.P. Morgan et Cié," April 28, 1904. The largest amount prior to this had been the $7,200,000 paid to the Russian government for the purchase of Alaska in 1868.

45. A.N. 7 AQ 39, *Rapport final présénte au Tribunal Civil de la Seine par M. Lemarquis*, June 30, 1908.

Chapter 9

The Last Years of the Company[1]

No sooner had the New Company announced its intention to dispose of its properties than there was press speculation as to their worth.[2] It was possible to calculate in total what the bondholders of the Compagnie Universelle and the stockholders of the Compagnie Nouvelle would receive with a fair degree of accuracy. The understanding between the liquidation and the board, concluded in February, 1902, had been specific as to the method of apportionment.[3] At the existing rate of exchange, viz. five francs and fifteen centimes to the U.S. dollar, the gross paid through the Morgan company was two hundred and six million francs. It was delivered in fourteen instalments between May 14 and June 14, 1904. The division was in the ratio of 128,600,000 francs to the liquidator and 77,400,000 to the New Company.[4]

The exact sum that holders of New Company stock could expect to receive would naturally be determined by its unexpended reserve; but financial experts were generally agreed that it would be in the region of 85,000,000 francs. This would have the result of each one hundred franc share being worth approximately one hundred and thirty francs.[5]

The position of creditors of the Compagnie Universelle was altogether more complicated. As has been noted earlier, the courts had decreed that shareholders in the defunct first company would get nothing because of the speculative nature of their investment. The only beneficiaries were to be those who held bonds pertaining to the seven issues that had been floated between 1882 and 1888. These could be further classified as, on the one hand, those who had purchased fixed-interest bonds carrying various dates, from September 1882 to March 1888, and, on the other, those who had bought or been given lottery bonds in June 1888 or at various times thereafter.[6] It will be recalled that when Brunet was appointed first liquidator, 849,249 of the 2,000,000 lottery bonds had been subscribed. He had disposed of a further 357,894 to meet running expenses and settle suits. Gautron had sold a further 120,935 in lieu of payment of debts to creditors who had refused New Company stock. At various times thereafter a few holders of ordinary bonds had transferred their holding to lottery bonds because they held out the chance of a greater return. A court-appointed attorney had worked out a *taux d'admission* in 1899, based on a complicated formula. It had to take the following points into account: (1) the issue price, rather than the par value, of each category of bond (since there was sometimes a considerable discrepancy between the two figures) (2) the number of years to maturity (3) the rate of repayment up to December 14, 1888, at which time the Compagnie Universelle had gone into receivership (4) the pro rata interest, to run from the time when the last dividend had been paid until this same date. The sum thus obtained was to be subject to a fixed rate of interest from December 14, 1888 until redemption, or until liquidation, as the case allowed. In 1900 a slight alteration had been made in the rates of admission for the 1882 and 1884 issues. This was done because some subscribers had purchased their bonds in instalments and had received interest on the par value which they had not paid in its totality by December 1888. Others had paid for their bonds in advance and profitted by receiving a slight discount.[7]

The complexities of the lottery bond issue of June 25, 1888 were greater still. Two million of these had been put on the market with a par value of three hundred and sixty francs each. They carried an interest of five per cent and were repayable in two ways: either as prize money or at 400 francs in a maximum of ninety-nine years, with redemption commencing in 1913 and terminating in 1987. The task of ensuring payment of the lottery prizes and of redemption was entrusted to a body specifically set up for the purpose. This Société Civile d'Amortissement des Obligations à Lots was to receive sixty francs per bond for the purpose of servicing the lottery fund (thirty-eight francs and thirty-two centimes) and the amortization (twenty-one francs and sixty-eight centimes). Had all two million bonds been subscribed, the capital of the Société Civile would have been one hundred and twenty million francs. However, because the issue was only a partial success, the Compagnie Universelle paid only the sum necessary to ensure prize money for the totality of the bonds and for the amortization of the bonds actually sold. This came to 94,258,512 francs when the offer closed,[8] and had increased to 103,716,390.18 by December, 1903, the end of the last complete financial year for the Société, prior to distribution of the American purchase monies. As a result, a capital sum of 16,283,609 francs 82 remained to be recovered from the liquidation if the unissued securities were to be repaid at their proper redemption value. After the collapse of the first company, Brunet and

subsequent liquidators had received court permission to issue these 'obligations restées a la souche' at market value,
without payment of interest but eligible for prizes and repayable under the same conditions as bonds in the same
series bought when first issued. The directors of the Société
Civile had invested the principal in Rentes 3% and other
guaranteed government securities,[9] with the result that the
gross amount due by the liquidation was increasing every
year. In 1889, another actuary had evolved a formula for
the sum to be remitted to the Société Civile whenever future issues of these bonds were made.[10]

By the time the New Company was ready to wind up its
affairs, 670,134 of these bonds remained to be disposed of.
Gautron was about to proceed to this task when the president of the Société Civile, Edouard Maneuvrier, brought a
technical action against the liquidation on January 22, 1904,
requiring him to set aside money from his share of the American payment sufficient to repay all the bonds and prizes *in
toto* before the Old Company's ledgers were closed for the
last time.[11] Maneuvrier's reasoning for this move was probably two fold – to obtain the maximum financial return in the
shortest possible time for the group of creditors for which his
organisation was responsible; also, he wanted to dispose a
task that would not otherwise be completed until 1987, at
least in theory. Should the liquidator be forced to conform
to this arrangement, the gravity of the situation for other
categories of bondholders could hardly be exaggerated. The
redemption value of the lottery bond issue was eight hundred million francs – or more than four times greater than
all the assets at stake in June, 1904.

Henri Thièblin, a New Company lawyer, to whom
Gautron referred this latest headache, held that Maneuvrier
was technically within his rights, according to the terms of
the original agreement he had signed with the Compagnie

Universelle. Article 5 had specified that:

> If the Société Civile cannot effect the reimburse-
> ment of all the bonds at the end of the concession
> of the canal company, the canal company which is
> bound by the prospectus to guarantee repayment
> of the issue will then take the necessary measures,
> with the Société Civile, to assure this guarantee.[12]

However, Thièblin saw an escape. The guaranteed funds of
the said society, as they then stood, were more than sufficient to meet present and future needs. Thanks to prudent
investment and management, its initial capital had increased
to 138,838,270 francs by 1904, and was producing a revenue
of 4,672,867 francs per annum. Its yearly commitments, until 1913, would not exceed 3,390,000 francs. This would
leave an excess of 1,282,867 francs, itself liable to appreciate
each year through investment. From 1913 onwards, it would
have to service prize draws amounting to only 2,200,000
francs a year leaving it with an even greater surplus. Assuming, however, that the liquidator was somehow forced to
give preferential treatment to these lottery bond holders, he
would have to determine a just recompense. This, in turn,
would necessitate the creation of a new table of admission
for the other categories since they would lose in proportion.
Lemarquis would then be forced to intercede on *their* behalf,
assuming that the courts themselves were inclined to favor
this category of creditor over others. The possible complications would be mind-boggling, and the delays in repayment
lengthy.[13]

In fact, the court adopted a reasonable attitude:

> It is impossible to determine what should be done
> except in an indeterminate way. How many years
> would a sum of money have to be left in reserve?

How long will the Société Civile d'Amortissement
be in existence? A sum would have to be set aside
until its tenure expired. Can it be sustained that
the liquidation will remain in a state of suspension,
even partially so, for an inordinately long time?[14]

Although an appeal was lodged against the decision, Gautron
was sufficiently confident of the outcome to proceed with the
first distribution of assets. Notices requesting all creditors
to produce their necessary documentation appeared in the
Journal Officiel on June 1, 1904, and subsequently in a large
number of city and provincial newspapers. Bondholders
were given six months, commencing on June 15, in which to
forward their claims.[15] When the expiry date of December 15
was reached, 226,721 had been received. These represented
a monetary demand of 1,779,374,495 francs 35, which, on
inspection, was fractionally reduced to 1,779,229,205 francs
80. Verification of these claims required a staff of forty-three,
and the results filled forty-eight 600 page ledgers. Each day's
entries were diligently checked by Gautron. Now seventy-six
years old, he was in indifferent health, and this exhausting
procedure may well have hastened his death just over a year
later. He complained to Lemarquis of excessive fatigue in
several letters to the mandataire.

In preparing to dispose of the 670,134 lottery bonds,
Gautron was well aware of the pitfalls inherent in their
method of issue. It was impossible to divide their number
fairly among the multitude of creditors, and yet, as Lemarquis observed, to unload such a quantity of securities

on a relatively restricted market and in a time period which cannot be too long brings with it a risk
of depreciation in the above-mentioned securities
and a depreciation of their value which could have
disastrous consequences for the liquidation.[16]

Gautron, too, was concerned that speculation be avoided, but he wanted a reasonable price and still allow the many creditors the opportunity of investing in these controversial securities.[17] He therefore made arrangements with a consortium of finance houses, including the three *pénalitaire* banks for their issue.[18] They undertook to advertise the offer and sell it through their branches at one hundred francs per bond. For this they were to receive a total of one million four hundred thousand francs, of which two hundred thousand had to be devoted to advertising and publicity. The original agreement was also intended to give them the right to purchase all the unclaimed bonds after the issue closed to the public (which it would do on April 8, 1905). Bondholders were to be permitted to subscribe in the ratio of one lottery bond for each 2,655 francs of credit outstanding – with fractions ignored. Creditors with smaller claims, i.e. less than 2,655 francs would still have the right to purchase one bond, the value of which would be deducted from the first dividend of ten per cent. Those with claims of less than one hundred francs would be paid exclusively in cash.

The arrangements for this offer epitomize the contrast between the laxness and prodigality of the original company and the vigilance exercised by the mandataire. When Gautron submitted a draft copy of the contract with the banks for the perusal, Lemarquis objected most forcefully that a limit was being placed on the bondholders, and pointed to the unwarranted benefits that might arise to the financial institutions if the issue were very popular. He instanced a case where someone with 26,550 francs in credits outstanding was limited to ten bonds though he might be eager to buy more. Assuming this individual received ten per cent of his original investment, he would get one thousand francs worth in bonds and the surplus, i.e. 1,655, in cash. But this latter sum represented sixteen bonds (in fact, fractionally more) – which he might well have preferred. Over ninety thousand were in this situation where their individual claims exceeded 2,655 francs. Lemarquis argued that it would have been more equitable to have allowed them to subscribe in the proportions they found convenient – provided that the smallest creditors' interests were adequately safeguarded. He recalled the discreditable circumstances in which the *syndicats de garantie* had been allowed to operate in de Lesseps's heyday; and he expressed "serious doubts on the extent of the risks run by these Syndicates of Guarantee as well as the opportunity for remuneration which they were to get."[19] In plain words, there must be none of the 'heads the banks win, tails the investors lose scandal' this time.

By way of rebuttal, the banks pointed out that the investment was an attractive one, and they would labor diligently to dispose of all the bonds. In deference to the mandataire's wishes, though, they agreed to place the unsold bonds at the disposal of those creditors who might wish to buy more of them. They would become available two weeks after the offer closed, and their allocation would be in proportion to the amount of credit each subscriber was worth.[20] Lemarquis still had misgivings over the rate of commission being paid to the syndicate of banks, and he regretted the short duration of the time available to applicants to exercise their second option after the first had expired. But he confessed that he could envisage no better solution that would also allow the proceeds from the issue to be distributed with similar speed. If, however, any bondholder felt his interests were being compromised, or if anyone could suggest a fairer or speedier solution, he was willing to listen.[21] Since none was forthcoming, the existing arrangement was submitted to the Tribunal Civil de la Seine and approved by it on March 15.

The issue was a solid rather than a spectacular success, resulting in the initial sale of 551,012 bonds. The balance was then offered, in accordance with the pre-arranged agreement; and, on this occasion, demand exceeded supply by approximately four to one.[22] Gautron, now with all distributable assets made a first payment of ten per cent on June 2. The Compagnie Nouvelle had already repaid the par value of its stock on July 15, 1904. Because of his share in that concern, the liquidator had another sixteen million francs added to his holdings.[23] It only required a further distribution of monies from the New Company for a second, and final, dividend to be paid and the affairs of the Compagnie Universelle could be wound up and Gautron's long task would be over. However, the new company was experiencing difficulties with the fiscal authorities. The result was a crisis of such dimensions that the simple task of paying this final dividend was to be delayed for a further three years, until 1908. To the cynical eye, both canal companies were to end their days as they had begun them, amid a welter of legal argument and parliamentary controversy.

The situation had its origins in a court action which the Colombian government had instituted on January 7, 1904. It will be recalled that it was then claiming ownership of the fifty thousand shares it had been allocated in 1894, as well as seeking to prevent transfer of the concession. In its defence, Colombia's counsel had cited various articles in the contracts of 1878, 1890 and 1900. When the court delivered its opinion, on March 31, the receiver of the Deuxième Bureau des Actes Judiciaries asked the New Company to produce the original copies of those agreements. The intention was to submit them to the Administration de l'Enregistrement, the 'fisc', for payment of the requisite duty. To the complete surprise and horror of the directors, it was declared that the sum being claimed was 13,600,000 francs.[24] The Enregistrement had arrived at its figure by classifying the contract which Wyse had signed in March 1878 as a public works contract. As such, it was eligible to be taxed at 1,2% of the value of the work to be undertaken, commencing in 1881; and, to this figure was added a tax of one per cent of the revised settlements of 1890, 1893 and 1900. The first contract was valued at 1,050,000,000 francs, giving a claim of 13,125,000. The remaining contracts were said to be worth an additional 335,272 francs making a total of 13,480,272 to which was added a further 100,000 for delays in payment.[25] As a rival claimant to the disputed shares, Panama, no less than Colombia, was affected since whatever the New Company had to pay the French treasury would be deducted, in proportion, from their share of the concession money. The same held true for the liquidation with its 159,000 shares.

At this stage, however, the Compagnie Nouvelle had no intention of complying. On July 22, 1904, it brought a counter-suit against the fisc, claiming that it could not be a party to contracts which had been negotiated prior to its existence. Furthermore, it contended, it had not executed the ultimate object stated in those contracts, viz. the completion and operation of an Isthmian Canal.[26] Not only did this rejoinder fail to achieve its purpose, but it had the added consequence of involving the governments of Panama and Colombia more deeply. Unable to judge which country ought to be charged as party to these contracts, the Enrigstrement decided to serve writs on them both.[27] Possession of the disputed securities now became a less attractive proposition for the Panamanians; and the junta therefore informed the Compagnie Nouvelle that it was renouncing its claim to them. Cromwell had been acting as legal counsel for the new republic since the summer of 1904, and the renunciation was on his recommendation.[28] This enabled Bô to inform the Colombian chargé d'affaires in Paris that his company was now prepared to re-register them in the name of his government.[29]

Throughout the whole of 1905 dispute continued to rage over the fisc's assessment with both sides plying the courts and the Ministry of Finance with lengthy briefs containing allegations and counter-charges.[30] The Company held to its original contention that it had not been a party to the Salgar-Wyse agreement. It likewise continued to claim that, by disposing of its holdings to the United States government, it had failed to exercise the rights and privileges granted by the said contract, and all the others that followed. Even if one were to accept the Enregistrement's contention that it had functioned until 1904 under the terms of those concession treaties, it was still not liable to pay duties. The Company's rationale was that one sovereign state could not levy a tax – for that is what it amounted to – on another state. It followed that a person, or institution, entering into a contract with the said state enjoyed the same immunity. When a convention between an individual and a foreign government was approved by the latter, it ceased to have an existence of its own and became an integral part of the law of the host country.

Furthermore, the act which had legally established the New Panama Canal Company in June 1894 had referred solely to the concessionary agreements under which it was to proceed to operate, not to the contracts which had followed them. These legal agreements were all the New Company required "sufficient only for the requirements of the contracting parties." Since the Company had worked to an entirely different plan for the canal from its predecessor, its use of the original *contract*, specifying, for example, a sea-level canal, as distinct from the *agreement*, was minimal. For that reason, there was no need for the second company to submit these redundant agreements to the Enregistrement. To stretch a point still further and admit that registration of them was required would still not render it guilty. That ought to have been done when M. Brunet made the transition from Compagnie Universelle to Compagnie Universelle-in-liquidation in 1889.[31]

The Enregistrement dismissed these arguments as spurious, and stood firm on its interpretation of the civil law. Article 23 of the Law of Frimaire, Year VII required registration of all contracts negotiated abroad by parties domiciled in France. Article 58 of the Law of April 28, 1816 held that such contracts were subject to the same levies as if they had been drafted in France. The specific legislation under which the second Panama Canal Company had been constituted did not exempt it from French commercial law. Since it was registered in France, and had been administered from Paris during its entire existence added to which the revenues it had received from its activities had been returned to France for the benefit of French citizens, so

> ... it cannot use the sovereignty of another country
> to escape payment of these taxes: two sovereignties
> cannot co-exist on the same territory.[32]

The contract which Wyse had negotiated on March 28, 1878 had not, as it were, vanished to make way for legislation which embodied its terms. If Monsieur Wyse had not signed the contract, he and the Compagnie Universelle could not have participated in the benefits which accrued from the treaty; nor could the old company have imposed any obligation on the Colombian government. If the contract had been annulled by the law passed on May 18, 1878 by the senate, one would have to assume that the previous arrangement had been cancelled. Obviously this did not happen. Its transfer to M. de Lesseps's company did not affect its character in the slightest; and so, asserted the Enregistrement

... one must conclude that the act by which it manifests itself has an existence independent of the law. It is from this act only that the Enregistrement claims tax. The same reasoning applies and leads to the understanding that the agreement of December 10, 1890 is distinct from the law of December 26 which gave it force.

The Enregistrement would repeat what it had enunciated on previous occasions – that it was not claiming registration of a law but of the contracts which the law rendered definitive. The act which had constituted the New Company was made as a consequence of the contracts which had preceded the laws of concession.[33] In 1894, the liquidator had surrendered his rights and responsibilities. Whatever changes the recipient of these rights had made in the original contract, the fact remained that they were based, indeed, could only follow from, previous undertakings. It could quote precedents to substantiate its demand, dating back to the Second Empire.

All the fiscal authorities were willing to concede was that they had been remiss in allowing the transfer to occur in 1894 without submitting a claim. But, at that time, the New Company enjoyed peculiar protection against legal actions arising from the policies of its predecessor. It was doubtful whether the Tribunal Civil de la Seine would have permitted the diminution of assets which the demand would have occasioned, even for the benefit of a government agency when it had granted immunity from the demands of private creditors.[34]

The Enregistrement was triumphantly vindicated in a court decision on February 8, 1906. The only crumb of comfort for the Compagnie Nouvelle and the liquidation was a meagre one. A supplementary judgment held that the prolongation of the concession which Mancini had obtained in 1900 was never utilised, and so the amount payable was reduced by one hundred thousand francs. The 1893 agreement remained in force until October 31, 1904, by which time, of course, the French had ceased to operate on the site.[35]

This verdict was not entirely unexpected. Gautron and Lemarquis appear to have contacted a number of parliamentarians sympathetic to their cause just before the court made its announcement. They found a champion in the deputy, Ernest Flandin who raised the issue in the chamber only four days after the decision had been handed down. Flandin reminded his audience that, although the claim of the *fisc* had been levied exclusively against the Compagnie Nouvelle, it was the creditors of the Compagnie Universelle who would suffer a double blow if the former's assets were to be despoiled. First, the liquidator held some twenty-five per cent of its shares. Second, because the first company was really responsible for a considerable part of the 13,500,000 francs of duty now being claimed, the board of the New Company would undoubtedly hold it responsible for a large part of that figure. The net result would be to reduce to a pittance what monies remained to be divided among the anxious, longsuffering creditors. The government might think that it had won a victory, but it was mistaken. There was a distinct possibility that the more enraged of these creditors would petition parliament individually, or appeal to a higher court for justice. If they were successful, the government would emerge with nothing but a loss of reputation. This could be avoided if it stood firm by the spirit of the law of July 1, 1893. That, it was true, had been designed to suspend all claims against the liquidation while the New Company was struggling to be born. However, there was good reason why it should be applied in the present instance, too, and exempt the Company from the Enregistrement's demands.[36]

Gauthier de Clagny's speech in support was altogether more emotional. He spoke, he said, for the tens of thousands of small savers who had hoped for a small recompense when they saw the American money arrive in Paris. Now their hopes were to be dashed; and while he did not deny that the *fisc* had been following the strict letter of the law, "this claim by the administration of finances is revolting to our sensibilities and to the public conscience."[37]

It was, perhaps, unfortunate as well as ironic that the Prime Minister to whom these appeals were ultimately addressed was none other than Maurice Rouvier, one of the most notorious of the *Panamistes*. It will be recalled that he had made a fumbling confession in the Chamber in 1892 to complicity in the financial dealings of the Compagnie Universelle during the Boulangist episode. As a consequence, he had lived in political exile for almost a decade. Naturally, he had every reason to avoid further involvement in the affairs of Panama when faced with what could be construed as a request to interfere with the due process of the law. He expressed no sympathy for Flandin's viewpoint, and, although he promised to refer his suggestion for amnesty to the budget committee, he also warned the Chamber that the question was not as simple as the arguments that had been put forward by his honorable colleagues would lead one to think.[38]

The Budget Commission was to prove no more accommodating than the Enregistrement had been. Pierre Baudin, its *rapporteur-general*, argued that there was no justification for granting exemption to one company, so setting a precedent which hundreds of others would try to exploit. In any case, the levy being placed on the Compagnie Nouvelle was absurdly small when spread among its six thousand plus stockholders and the quarter of a million bondholders in the other concern. Its loss would impose no real hard-

ship on either category. Conversely, the adoption of the
'Flandin Law' would result in the immediate abandonment
and loss of considerable revenue for the state which it considered legitimate.[39]

The tenor of this argument brought cries of dissent, not
only from Flandin and like-minded deputies, but from several segments of the financial press. The *Revue Economique
et Financière* inveighed against the Enregistrement which,
it said, was like all the administrative bodies of the state,
"never at rest, especially when it could harass or pressure
those it thought could contribute to its coffers," It had initiated "a ridiculous action" in a despicable bid to extract
money from an unfortunate segment of the investing public by an interpretation of the law which the editorial found
"absolutely fantastic." This same journal was equally critical of the court for its refusal to raise itself "above the
narrow letter of the law" and of Rouvier who, in a fit of
"largesse electorale" had granted tax concessions to home
distillers of alcoholic spirit. That exemption had cost the
Treasury several millions, and it would benefit a section of
the community that was far less deserving of the government's philanthropy.[40] *Le Comptant* agreed with Gauthier
de Clagny that it was the moral obligation of the present
administration to conform to the spirit of the 1893 law

> whose goal was to place the chattels of the old
> company under its protection and away from the
> hands of the fisc, in a word, to safeguard the in-
> terests of the creditors of Panama and not allow
> their assets to be whittled away, bit by bit, into
> the state's coffers.

Instead, those who had already been robbed of nine tenths
of their investment by crooked deals in the past were about
to be relieved of ten percent of what was left to them, "ex-

actly the tithe of the Ancien Régime!"[41]

Not that the liquidator was willing to concede defeat just yet. With the help of Lemarquis, he resorted to a tactic which had been used to good effect by the old company. This was the organisation of a petition, similar to that presented to Alain-Targé requesting permission to float the lottery loan back in 1888. The new request, like the old, was intended to represent the collective desperation and indignation of the bondholders at the government's failure to come to their aid. A copy of the petition was included with each notice sent to the creditors on March 5. It also contained the negative verdict of the Budget Commission on Flandin's proposal.[42] By March 15, over one hundred and sixty thousand signed replies had been received. Meanwhile, Flandin was preparing a new line of approach which would shift the bulk of the responsibility for paying the *fisc* on to the shoulders of the Colombian government. He was assuming that the Enregistrement would not pursue its claim against a foreign government, even though Bogota had managed to re-establish her claim to ownership of her New Company stock.

He opened his campaign with a series of press interviews in which he expressed the view that, although Colombia should be held accountable, her position as a sovereign power would probably preclude action by the new administration (Rouvier's ministry had fallen on March 9 and had been replaced by one in which Raymond Poincaré was Minister of Finance):

> ...it is a principle of international courtesy to which there has been no exception and which the government of the Republic would certainly not wish to alter, especially vis-a-vis a small power.

For that reason, it was iniquitous that the entire burden should fall on the shoulders of those who,

> not sufficiently exploited and plundered in the past
> must now, without question, again pay millions
> in place of the true debtor.... If the coffers of
> Panama have, alas, too often served to balance
> private budgets, we cannot surely be expected to
> believe today that they are necessary to balance
> the budget of the state.[43]

But, when debate opened in the Chamber on March 20, Flandin was soon disabused of his belief in Colombian immunity. Baudin maintained that, in bringing its plea to the attention of a French court, Colombia had explicitly accepted the decisions of French justice. The law had defined what must fall within the jurisdiction of the fiscal authorities, and that had included contracts made within Colombia's borders. By persevering with her claim to the fifty thousand shares, she had underlined her acceptance of the French judicial process and would have to contribute her fair share to the Enregistrement through deduction from her portion of the concession money. Baudin also gave free rein to his thoughts when he turned to the sheaf of petitions which had been presented to the Chamber. If the New Company were granted complete exoneration, the bondholders would benefit by only two and one half francs for each five hundred francs of credit they held. The shareholders of the Compagnie Nouvelle, by contrast, would profit by as much as eight francs per hundred franc share, or sixteen times as much. The deputies should therefore beware of the consequences of misguided liberality if they were to vote for M. Flandin's motion, as it stood. Surely it was not their intention, or that of the bill's sponsor, that large institutional stockholders of the second canal company should benefit to a far greater degree than the creditors of the first? However, his Budget Commission would look more sympathetically on any amendment that would exempt only those in the last-mentioned category.[44]

Flandin accepted this suggestion as better than nothing, and framed a new piece of legislation designed to give relief only to the bondholders; but his hopes were again dashed when it was rejected by the Senate. The upper house appears to have been motivated by two considerations: first, there was the fear that the New Company might not have sufficient resources of its own left to meet the entire claim, since it had already disbursed over sixty million francs. Second, it felt that there was no justification for exonerating those creditors who, said M. Expert Bezancon, "are in a fortunate enough position, financially speaking, to bear this loss."[45] He believed that it was a ridiculous, sympathy-inducing simplification to portray all those who had invested in the de Lesseps venture as "amateur, small-time speculators."[46]

Yet again, the Panama situation demanded a compromise answer. If one accepted that there were, indeed, both poor and affluent among the investors of the old company, acceptable legislation could be drafted to take it into account. Accordingly, Flandin's third attempt to limit liability for payment to the *fisc* applied only to those who held ten bonds or less. If, and when, the liquidator was to lose some of what was coming to him as a result of the 13,500,000 being demanded, it would mean that only those who were holders of ten bonds or less would suffer no cut in their dividend; and only those with amounts superior to that would find their return reduced. The Finance Minister, Poincaré assured the Chamber that this would be more acceptable to the government than a blanket exemption, and Flandin had the satisfaction of seeing his measure pass into law with ease on April 17.

If the 'Flandin Law' relieved the bulk of creditors of the

Compagnie Universelle of a direct financial obligation, it still left them exposed to all the delays which would result from litigation still pending between the Enregistrement and the Compagnie Nouvelle. Debate on this topic continued to rage for months. Why, asked *Le Globe*, had the fiscal authorities delayed making their claim until both canal companies were no longer in operation? It supplied its own answer somewhat enigmatically:

> Certain people who are generally well informed about these matters are whispering loudly that the administration would never have demanded anything if a certain influential figure in the political sphere – let us not be too precise about him – had not reminded it of its duties and reproached it for being, on this occasion, too liberal in its dealings with the (New) Company.[47]

One can but speculate as to the identity of this supposedly powerful figure. It may have been the prime minister, Rouvier, himself, who harbored bitter memories of the first company, and saw a means of revenge by attacking its offspring. Relations between de Lesseps and Boulanger had been extremely cordial at one point, and the Republic did not forgive or forget the friends of the general.[48] On the other hand, there were many *chequards* from Andrieux's list, each of whom had ample reason to remember the indiscretions of Charles de Lesseps and his associates when they took the witness stand during the post-mortem on the ill-fated corporation. As Sir Denis Brogan has written: "He (de Lesseps) did his best to shake the faith of the French people in their rulers...."[49] Perhaps it is not too fanciful to see the hand of Poincaré behind this assault on the New Company's resources. As legal adviser to the Colombian government since 1904, he had witnessed his client's claim to the shares denied by the very concern to whom it had granted the concessions. True, Colombia had eventually managed to recover ownership of them, but it was the Republic of Panama's decision to relinquish her claim, not any sense of fairness on the New Company's part, that had allowed his client to obtain redress.

The press might fulminate, but the government remained unmoved. Expert Bezancon refuted the charge that the Enregistrement was being rapacious in its demand. Messieurs Gautron and Lemarquis he knew to be honorable and respected men; but they had allowed themselves to be unduly swayed by those who, posing as the sorry victims of Panama, wanted a reduction in what ought, rightly, to be paid for selfish reasons. There was no reason why the State should waive its right to millions of francs because of a campaign originating among financiers who were at the bottom of the agitation.[50] Gautron was now a very sick man and sought neither to deny this charge nor resolve the deadlock.[51] With his death, on September 12, 1906, it was almost an inevitability that his successor as liquidator should be Lemarquis, for who else knew the situation as well?[52]

Within days of occupying the new office, Lemarquis was working with his customary excess of energy. He initiated a series of conversations with Rischmann, the financial spokesman on the New Company's board, and with his own replacement as mandataire, Menage. All were agreed that some contribution to the Treasury was inevitable, even though the Company's appeal to the *Cour de Cassation* had not yet been heard.[53] If they were to win even a small concession, it could happen only by providing the fisc with an alternative valuation of the various concessions. This would provide a basis for negotiation in the event that a downward adjustment was still a possibility. Lemarquis and Menage were left in no doubt that a *pro rata* contribution would be demanded from the liquidation as well as from the Colombians.[54] Meanwhile, Rischmann was reassessing the original, Salgar-Wyse concession on the basis of work actually completed by the de Lesseps concern. He arrived at a figure of 1,545,051,000 francs for it, and 385,275,000 for subsequent prolongations.[55] Legal costs, which the New Company would have to bear if it admitted any liability at all would bring the actual total to be paid to the *fisc* to 2,268,109 francs 70.[56]

In the hope of obtaining a prompt decision through ministerial intervention, Lemarquis addressed himself to Poincaré. A formal note, delivered on December 1, contained the observation that M. Capatti, the Director-General of the Enregistrement, had assured the Chamber of Deputies in March that his department was eager to terminate the affair. But, as the Minister well knew, he had done nothing to implement that promise. Yet, everything hinged on the single fact of valuation. The original Wyse contract had imposed no restrictions as to the character of the work, the length of the canal, the exact route it would take, or, most importantly, how much it would cost. Subsequent estimates of the price by Bartissol, Bunau-Varilla, and others had varied widely, according to the conceptions of the authors. None of them, not even those of the semi-official Guillemain and I.T.C. Commissions had been of a nature to bind the New Company, legally. By the same logic, the Enregistrement was not firmly committed to its original figure, either: "... it has every means and right, without violating any principle, to modify its estimates by adopting a new base for its calculations...." All figures were hypothetical, given the fact that no waterway had been built. Therefore a little compromise on the part of the fisc could provide an answer to the knotty affair:

If, for example, it is resolved to look for a new formula for evaluation that it considers fair, it will
be amenable to reclaim a sum sufficiently moder-
ate to permit it to hope for a prompt solution.
The Compagnie Nouvelle will undoubtedly see, in
this reduction the possibility of an accord which
the liquidator of the old company will also seek to
facilitate.

Lemarquis appended a more personal plea in urging Poincaré to act, if only to bring an end to the mental anguish of
everyone associated with the two canal companies. Surely,
he concluded, the time had come to settle, to everyone's satisfaction this Panamanian affair which had already lasted
too long and whose prolongation "can only engender sentiments of profound lassitude."[57]

The Finance Minister was apparently impressed enough
by this letter to pressure Capatti to resume talks with the
New Company board early in 1907. No record of these
talks between Capatti and Rischmann has been found in the
archives, but they continued for the better part of the year.
As might be expected, the Enregistrement found Rischmann's estimate too low. The bone of contention was clearly
the first contract whose worth had been put at 1,050,000,000
by the government department and at only 122,000,000 by
the Company executive. It is possible that further ministerial pressure was brought to bear on Capatti, as a result of which he scaled down his demand for monies on the
1878 concession to 7,250,000 francs. This, when taken with
evaluations of the other concessions, made the revised total
7,599,076 francs 25 which legal costs inflated to 7,789,335
francs 20.[58] On December 7, Bô was in a position to inform
Lemarquis that he was ready to discuss the percentage payment due by the liquidation.[59] Colombia, rather unjustly in

the event, was neither consulted nor represented at these discussions. She was merely asked to agree to the deduction of 1,522,000 francs, after which she received the balance on her fifty thousand shares. The unduly large proportion she was forced to contribute (or had deducted) may be gauged by comparing that amount with a similar deduction from the liquidation. Although it held three times as many shares in the New Company as Colombia, it had to forfeit only 1,460,503 francs 50.[60]

*   *   *

Both canal companies were to suffer further assaults on their distributive capital before they were able to close their books. Cromwell's final service to the Compagnie Nouvelle ended in failure. On April 18, 1906, he enclosed the text of an official communication from President Roosevelt containing a flat rejection of the New Company's claim for compensation. This matter, too, had dragged on for years, and it constituted a request for indemnification for work done on the site from the time the Isthmian Canal Commission had made its inspection, in 1901, and reached an opinion on the worth of the enterprise until May, 1904 when the U.S.A. had taken over.[61] The President added nothing to the long-standing contention that the purchase price of forty million dollars had taken this additional work into account, and that no additional monies would be forthcoming.[62]

There soon followed another letter from Cromwell containing his fee for "the unique and invaluable services" he had rendered to the Compagnie Nouvelle. These he put at $832,449.38, or 4,287,113 francs.[63] It was an enormous claim, even by Wall Street's generous standards, and it far eclipsed the $200,000 he had received in 1892 for his successful surgery on the ailing steel corporation of Decker and Howell – itself a record. The board inevitably contested the amount, maintaining that he was not entitled to more than

the honorarium of $10,000 per annum which it had decided
on unilaterally when he was reappointed in January, 1902.
It did, however, admit out-of-pocket expenses, but put these
at a modest $13,1867.94.

Cromwell had calculated his fee on the basis of 2% of the
purchase price the Americans had paid the Company. The
Company, in rebuttal, said that the sale had actually been
negotiated first by Hutin and then by Lampré during the
period when he had not been in their employ. Therefore,
on the basis that he had worked for the firm from February
1, 1902 until May 31, 1904, they were prepared to pay
him $23,333.33. This, together with the expenses mentioned
above, made the total remuneration $36,520.27.[64]

With its business with the Administration de l'Enregistrement still in progress, the company had no wish, at that
stage, to engage in further court proceedings. But it agreed
to Cromwell's suggestion that the matter be submitted to
arbitration. The incident attracted an undue amount of attention in the American press, not so much for itself but for
the evidence both sides submitted to a tribunal of three jurists. Cromwell's voluminous brief, containing his version of
the intrigue to advance the cause of Panama and vanquish
Nicaragua (and, latterly, Colombia) was grist to the mill
of those who deplored his nation's role in the events. The
New Company, for its part, invited testimony from Bunau-
Varilla, knowing full well that the French engineer would
be eager to publicise his role in the dramatic events. Relations between Cromwell and Bunau-Varilla had never been
warm and, since the Panamanian revolution, the latter had
expressed a hostility towards the New York lawyer on a number of occasions. He now forwarded a considerable quantity
of documentation, all of it unflattering to Cromwell.[65]

Faced with masses of contradictory testimony,[66] the distinguished jurists could only express personal opinions. In

their view, he had played a major, though not exclusive, part in the triumph of the Panama route. Moreover, while he had been warned by the Company against lavish expenditure unless the board approved it as absolutely necessary, this could not encompass unprofitable spending and was incompatible with

> the obligation put upon Messieurs Sullivan and Cromwell to maintain permanent relations with the press, political parties and government representatives; and to be able to act, without delay when unforeseen circumstances arose implied the right to set aside suitable expenses... the liberal spirit which the Company gave proof of during its first period in op ration must equally influence the arbitrators in the consideration of their control of accounts in the final period.

They denied Cromwell had a right to a direct proportion of the concession payment from the U.S. government; but they increased his honorarium to $167,000 and allowed his claim for expenses to stand. At $227,782.71 his fee was the largest that had ever been awarded to a lawyer by a French court; and it further depleted the New Company's coffers by almost one and a quarter million francs.[67]

The liquidation of the Compagnie Universelle also lost a part of its capital as a result of an unsettled legal claim dating back to Monchicourt's term in office. On December 9, 1891, two farmers, known in the case as the Schuber brothers, had brought an action in Panama for one hundred and fifty thousand piastres. They claimed the Compagnie Universelle had trespassed and damaged their property in the course of opening up a section of the canal route at Corozal. Because of complications arising from the 1893 legislation which suspended all suits against the liquidation, the case was not heard until 1896. By this time, the Schuber brothers had scaled their claim down to one hundred and thirty four thousand piastres, but had been joined by the surviving members of the Icaza family. Icaza was also a landowner in the same area who had lost property said to be worth 41,225 piastres when it was sequestered in 1886. The 1893 law was regarded as inapplicable in these cases since they were matters outside France and were being heard in a foreign court. Colombian justice worked with painful slowness, and it was not until 1898 that decisions were handed down in favor of both parties.

These judgments were not to be executed for some time. The reason for this lay in a technicality in French law which stipulated that verdicts in civil suits concerning trespass against concerns registered in France could not be enforced until examined in a French court.[68] By this time, discussions for the sale were well underway, and Gautron had made no haste to comply. He appears to have been acting on what was, at the time, a reasonable assumption – that the United States would soon be in possession of the territory and the headache would be theirs. It was in a much better position to pay, anyway. The American authorities, though, had no such intention. In November 1903, Admiral Walker advised Cromwell of the administration's attitude and suggested that Gautron be told to lay aside enough to settle both claims.[69]

Hearings were resumed in 1904, but were frequently suspended. It was alleged by the liquidator that Icaza's lawyers were doing everything in their power to delay a decision, in the hope that the American governor of the Canal Zone, Charles Magoon, would intervene and impose an arbitrary amount.[70] In fact, it was not until March, 1906 that a verdict was delivered – in favor of the plaintiffs. The damages awarded, coupled with legal costs, deprived the liquidation of a further 335,495 francs 35.[71]

This, and the major settlement with the Enregistrement, removed the last hurdle in the way of final liquidation of both companies. Lemarquis's promise to contribute a fixed sum to help meet the *fisc's* claim enabled the New Company to proceed to a second payment. On February 3, 1908, it was announced that a distribution of 20 francs 36 would be made on nominative shares, and 19 francs 41 on bearer shares. A third, and final dividend was possible on June 14, after the necessary deductions had been made to meet all remaining expenses. This totalled 8 francs 23 per share. Therefore, those who had invested in the Compagnie Nouvelle at the time of its formation received a return of just over 128 francs per 100 franc share – this being the equivalent of an annual return of 3% for the ten active years of its existence.[72]

Lemarquis was also able to pay a second, and final dividend, to the creditors of the old company. The 'Flandin Law' was applied and exempted 197,650 individuals holding ten bonds or less from any reduction in their credit. Final payment began on December 1, 1908, according to a strict schedule where each issue of bonds was dealt with in chronological order.[73] As a result, those protected by the law received 1 franc 0195 per hundred francs of allowable credit making a total dividend of 11 francs 01%. Those from whom deductions were made to meet the *fisc's* claim, the so-called *créanciers non-dégreves*, obtained a second payment of 0.8749 francs per 100 francs of credit for an equivalent dividend of 10 francs 87%.[74] When all categories of bondholders had been paid, Lemarquis performed his last service for the canal company by closing its accounts permanently.

*   *   *

Once a number of administrative difficulties had been overcome, United States army engineers worked steadily towards completing their own plan for the Panama Canal.

They saw their efforts rewarded on August 15, 1914 when the first official transit took place.[75] They had long since acknowledged their debt of gratitude to their French predecessors. Though able to utilise less than forty per cent of the excavations they inherited, mostly in the section between Gamboa and Miraflores, they fell heir to considerable quantities of equipment and property. On the thirty-three thousand acres which the two companies had occupied, there were fifteen hundred houses for workers and administrative staff and over two thousand storehouses of all sizes. Contrary to some dismal reports that were first circulated about the inadequacy of the machinery, much of it was in regular use until 1912. In brief, there seems little doubt that the U.S.A. obtained its concession at a bargain price. The *Isthmian Canal Commission Handbook* for 1913 put its value at $42,800,000, and this did not include the 'contingencies' for which the original I.C.C. had made an allowance of ten per cent.

But if the Americans were fortunate in their acquisition of this massive public works project for less than it was worth, they also inherited a fund of bitterness which no amount of money could assuage. A generation of Colombians could never forget that their nation had been deprived of property in a particularly underhanded manner. The twenty-five million dollars given to the Republic by the United States government in 1922, as a sort of belated indemnity for the loss of the Isthmus was regarded by the more charitable as an expression of Wilsonian guilt and penance, and by the cynics as a bribe to allow American oil interests to prospect in a land where their name as a bad word.

Panama, for its part, became rapidly disillusioned when it saw how few were the benefits that accrued to its population. The Canal Zone, from the outset was an insulated extension of the American mainland, aseptic, prosperous,

alien and heavily fortified against foreigners – and the Panamanians often felt they were included in that definition. As
Dr. Ameringer put it, "... most Panamanians share the view
that he (Bunau-Varilla) mortgaged the happiness of their
country for eternity."[76]

Notes

1. The only study of the final act of liquidation of the two canal
   companies is a brief study in Appendix A of Pierre Loewel, *Le
   Canal de Panama: étude historique et financière* (Paris, 1913).

2. See, for example, *Le Droit*, February 22, 1902.

3. See Chapter 7, p.

4. A.N. 7 AQ 38, Versements efectuées par le gouvernement
   américain sur le prix de cession du canal (unsigned), May 14,
   1904.

5. *Le Comptant*, issue of February 3, 1903, estimated its assets at
   7,000,000 francs.

6. See Chapter 2, pp.

7. A.N. 7 AQ 42, *Rapport final (aux créanciers de la Compagnie Universelle du Canal Interocéanique, en liquidation, par M.
   Georges-Emile Lemarquis,)* November 27, 1908. Table of admission for credit:

Bond Issue	Date	Subscription price	Amount admitted
5%	Sept. '82	437.50	811.11
3%	Oct. '83	285.00	544.33
4%	Sept. '84	333.00	618.37
6%	Aug. '85	450.00	1002.78
6%	Jul. '87	440.00	932.90
6%	Mar. '88	460.00	702.63
5%	Jun. '88	300.00	532.17

8. By July 1, 1888 only 812,662 had been sold. The company
   therefore paid the Société 76,640,000 (i.e. 2,000,000 x 38.32) +
   17,618,512 (i.e. 812,662 x 21.68) = 94,258,512.

9. It also held bonds in the Midi and bone railways.

10. A.N. 7 AQ 39, "Note sur le valeur des bons a lots de la Compagnie de Panama" (unsigned and undated). The formula was:

$$x = \frac{21.68 \ (1 + 0.0075)n \ C}{83}$$

where x is sum due per bond
n is number of trimesters
since June 25, 1888
C is current rate of Rentes 3%
83 was rate of Rentes on June 25, 1888

For example, lottery bonds issued by Gautron on December 31, 1898 cost him 36.47 francs on the calculation

$$x = \frac{21.68 \ (1 + 0.0075) \ 42 \times 102}{83}$$

11. A.N. 7 AQ 40, Société Civile d'Amortissement des Obligations à Lots. Assemblée Générale, 17è réunion, Rapport general, March 31, 1905.

12. *Ibid.*, "Contrat entre la Société Civile d'Amortissement des Obligations a Lots et la Compagnie Universelle", June, 1888.

13. *Ibid.*, "Consultation – M. Thieblin", February 21, 1904.

14. *Ibid.*, "Note" (undated, but annotated by Lemarquis.)

15. A.N. 7 AQ 42, Rapport final, p. 19.

16. A.N. 7 AQ 39, *Avis aux créaciers, February 17, 1905.*

17. Ibid., *Avis aux créaciers, March 2, 1905. In this second communication, Lemarquis was at pains to show that the investment was a worthwhile one.*

18. *The others were the Banque de Paris et Pays Bas, the Banque de l'Union Parisienne and the Crédit Algerien. The separate contracts are in A.N. 7 AQ 39.*

19. *A.N. 7 AQ 39, Lemarquis to Gautron, February 16, 1905.*

20. Ibid., *Lemarquis to Gautron, February 16, 1905.*

21. Ibid., *Avis aux créanciers, March 2, 1905.*

22. Ibid., *"Resultat de l'émission de 670,000 bons à lots arreté le 8 avril 1905." Three thousand were reserved for overseas clients unable to comply with the two week deadline.*

23. Le Comptant *on June 9, 1908 gave a summary of the stages of distribution. The serious lack of documentation on this aspect of New Company affairs is discussed in Appendix C.*

24. *A.N. 7 AQ 42, "Reclamation de l'Enregistrement", March 31, 1904.*

25. Ibid.

26. *A.N. 7 AQ 40, "Assignation de l'Administration de l'Enregistre ment devant la deuxième chambre du Tribunal Civil de la Seine."*

27. Ibid., *"Contrainte décerné par l'Enregistrement contre le gouvernement de la Colombie" (copy), August 3, 1904. An identical summons was served on the Panamanian government on October 10.*

28. Hearings before the Committee on Interoceanic Canals of the U.S. Senate, *59 Cong., 2 Sess., Sen Doc. No. 141, Vol. 2, p. 1116 (testimony of Cromwell).*

29. *A.N. 7 AQ 35, Bô to Rougeot, January 30, 1905.*

30. *These are contained in A.N. 7 AQ 41 and often run to more than 70 pages of closely reasoned argument.*

31. Ibid., Mémoire en response pour la Compagnie Nouvelle du Canal de Panama contre M. le Directeur-Général de l'Enregistrement des Domaines et du Timbres au Ministère des Finances, *May 29, 1905.*

32. Ibid., Mémoire en replique pour M. le Directeur-General de l'Enregistrement contre la Compagnie Nouvelle du Canal de Panama en l'étude de M. Dubourg, avoué, *November 17, 1905.*

33. Ibid., *Mémoire pour M. le Directeur-General de l'Enregistrement au Ministère des Finances,* February 14, 1905, p. 48 *et seq.*

34. *Ibid.,* pp. 7-8.

35. *Ibid., Tribunal Civil de la Seine. Deuxième Chambre: audience du 8 février, 1906. Jugement: la Compagnie Nouvelle du Canal de Panama, en liquidation contre l'Administration de l'Enregistre ment.*

36. *Journal Officiel,* Chambre des Députés, 1906, 8è législature, February 12, 1906.

37. *Ibid.*

38. *Ibid.*, see also Chapter 2, pp.

39. *Le Comptant*, March 13, 1906.

40. Issue of March 10, 1906. Rouvier held the portfolio of Finance Minister until June 19, 1905. The reference to the *bouilleurs de cru* was a little unfortunate in that their cause, too, had been championed by Flandin.

41. Issue of March 13, 1906.

42. A.N. 7 AQ 40, *Circulaire de la Compagnie Universelle, en liquidation, par MM.* Gautron et Lemarquis.

43. *Le Comptant*, March 20, 1906.

44. *Journal Officiel*, March 20, 1906.

45. In a statement in *Le Comptant*, May 15, 1906.

46. Expert-Bezancon's charge was not without foundation. At prevailing wage rates of the 1880's, a 500 franc bond would have cost the average worker in the provinces almost his entire annual wage. See Paul Combe, *Niveau de vie et progrès technique en France, 1860-1939* (Paris, 1956), p. 617, table 7.

47. Issue of May 10, 1906.

48. The general had bought lottery bonds in 1888 and de Lesseps gave a dinner in his honor on the eve of the famous Paris election of January 27, 1889 which some regard as the apotheosis of the Boulangist movement. A London *Times* correspondent described the investor's attitude in this quotation: "M. Floquet is in power; yet, while sympathising, he either cannot or will not help us. Parliamentarianism is unable or unwilling to assist us. Our interest is, therefore, to promote a dictatorship."

49. *Op. cit.*, p. 282.

50. *Supra*, p. 269, footnote 2.

51. The only official piece of correspondence he appears to have written during the summer was a request to the court to destroy registers, receipts and other miscellaneous pieces of correspondence. See A.N. 7 AQ 43, Gautron to M. le Président de la Tribunal Civil, June 11, 1906.

52. *Rapport final*, p. 22.

53. The lawyers, Morillot and Boivin-Champeaux had told Bô that, in their opinion, it had no chance of success. A.N. 7 AQ 41, "Note envoyée à M. Menage" (unsigned), October 30, 1906.

54. *Ibid.*, Rischmann and Bô to Lemarquis, December 21, 1906.

55. These figures were based on the same percentages as the Enregistrement had used in 1904.

56. The legal costs were estimated at 337,783.45 francs.

57. A.N. 7 AQ 41, Lemarquis to Poincaré, December 1, 1906.

58. The Wyse contract was revealed anew at 580,000,000 by the fisc, and subsequent ones were said to be worth 27,921,000 collectively.

59. A.N. 7 AQ 41, Bô to Lemarquis.

60. *Ibid.*, "Transaction sur procès" (unsigned), May 9, 1908.

61. See Chapter 4 pp.

62. A.N. 7 AQ 38, Cromwell to Bô, April 18, 1906.

63. *Story of Panama*, p. 141. A breakdown reveals the following:
    For additional expenses incurred, 1896-1901 . . . . 60,782.71
    Honorarium (2% of 40,000,000) 800,000.00
    Services rendered, 1902-06 . . . . 25,000.00
    Less payments made by the New Company . . . . -53,333.33
    832,449.38

64. A.N. 7 AQ 42, Arbitrage entre la Compagnie Nouvelle du Canal de Panama et MM. Sullivan et Cromwell, October 24, 1907.

65. B.V. Papers, Box 13, Marie to Bunau-Varilla, December 10, and Bunau-Varilla to Gontard, December 12, 1907. The letter with evidence is 34 pages long.

66. *Ibid.* Box 21 contains copies of letters in Cromwell's support from several prominent U.S. senators.

67. A.N. 7 AQ 41, "Sentence arbitrale rendu par MM. Henri Barboux, Georges Devin et Alexandre Ribot entre Messrs Sullivan et Cromwell, d'une part, et, d'autre part, la Compagnie Nouvelle de Canal de Panama, December 23, 1907."

68. Ibid., Rapport présenté au Tribunal Civil de la Seine par M. J.-P. Gautron, November 26, 1900.

69. *Ibid., Rapport par M. Lemarquis aux M. le Président et Juges composant le Tribunal de la Seine,* October 1, 1907.

70. A.N. 7 AQ 38, Renaudin to Gautron, June 14, 1904. There were also complaints that the Company's counsel was too lethargic in its defence.

71. *Hearings before the Committee on Interoceanic Canals,* Vol. II, p. 1117. The judges were Mutis Duran, Gudger, formerly U.S. Consul-General in Panama and Collins of the Illinois Supreme Court. Legal expenses came to 36,137 francs 45.

72. *Rapport final,* p. 23. Bearer shares were proportionately less, at 127.64.

73. *Ibid.,* Avis final aux obligataires de la Compagnie Universelle, en liquidation, November 27, 1908.

74. Details of percentages paid to each category of stockholder appear in Appendix B (ii).

75. Contrary to popular belief that the P.R.C. steamship *Ancon* made the first transit, the honor actually goes to the tug *Mariner* which towed a string of barges from Christobal to Balboa on May 19, 1914, three months before the official opening.

76. *New Light on the Panama Canal Treaties,* p. 52.

CONCLUSION

Commenting on a dinner given in honor of Bunau-Varilla in Paris in June, 1906, the journalist, Ernest Judet, remarked that it would be instructive to learn the identities of those present. What nature of person, he wondered, would fete the man responsible for the worst defeat the Third Republic and suffered since the Fashoda Incident in which French arms had to bow to British?[1] Judet was an ultra-nationalist, a polemicist whose adherence to lost causes had reached its apogee during the Dreyfus Affair when he had supported the mendacious Col. Henry to the bitter end. Although his personal opinion does not warrant serious examination, it does raise the interesting questions of the role of the New Company in Isthmian projects and of whether a Panama Canal, built and operated by the French concern could every have been a viable proposition.

In an effort to arrive at an answer that is not mere speculation, one can begin with a brief survey of the American experience. Popular narratives have tended to contrast the brisk efficiency of the military regime of Uncle Sam which assumed control of the site in 1904 with the stagnation that had characterised the final three years of the New Company's tenure there. They highlight the indisputable fact that the U.S.A. achieved in eight years what de Lesseps and those who followed him failed to accomplish in quarter of a century, and that the finished product was superior to anything conceived by French engineers. The present canal, despite its age, is still able to handle ships of up to fifty thousand tons and is regarded by experts as a marvel of engineering skill.[2]

To accept this comparison uncritically, though, is to ignore not only the far more modest means at the disposal of the French, but the very real difficulties encountered by the Americans in the period 1904-14, and beyond, difficulties which were overcome only because the nation had unlimited resources to ensure completion whatever the cost. Mack states quite bluntly: "The first year of American canal administration was a year of bungling, bickering and incompetence."[3] There were conflicts of authority between the new Isthmian Canal Commission and the technicians on the spot. Government bureaucracy was exhibited at its worst as requisitions for supplies lay unanswered in Washington for months at a time. As late as February 1906, the board of consultant engineers had failed to reach a consensus on whether to recommend a canal with locks or a return to the de Lesseps idea of a sea level waterway. In exasperation, Roosevelt took the matter out of its hands and referred it to another commission. Its recommendation, favoring a plan for a lock canal actually overrode majority opinion among the engineers on it.

The President was also forced to find three chief engineers in as many years. The first, John Findley Wallace, resigned in 1905, and John Frank Stevens did the same in 1907. Reference was made earlier to the far-from-acceptable health record during those early years. The death rate from all causes, per thousand employees, remained at, or slightly above, the New Company average and did not begin to decline until 1908. There was, in fact, something of a panic in 1906 when yellow fever swept the Isthmus. Landslides of the type which had plagued the French continued to pose serious problems not only during construction but long after the canal had been completed. One, in 1913, dumped two million cubic yards of earth into the Cucaracha Cut, thereby delaying the opening for at least three months. On September 15, 1915, both banks of the notorious Culebra Cut subsided without warning, forcing closure of the canal to all but the smallest ships for seven months. Lesser cave-ins occurred in 1920 and 1922. These disasters inevitably caused an escalation in costs far beyond the original estimates. The first Isthmian Canal Commission had reckoned that the canal could be built, exclusive of the purchase of property or indemnity to Colombia, for $144,233,358. By January 1906 this had risen to $175,929,720, and this figure did not include administrative costs, sanitation, defence or interest on borrowed capital. By the time the S.S. Ancon made her inaugural voyage through the canal, the total had almost doubled, to $335,200,900.[4]

The 1914-18 War dealt canal finances another unexpected blow. On the one hand there had to be increased expenditure on defence installations, lest German sea raiders attempted to disrupt this major sea route, especially after U.S. entry into the War in 1917. On the other, there was a general decline in international trade, to which must be added the disruption in shipping caused by the German submarine campaign. This had the effect of reducing the number of vessels using the canal which, in turn, made for a disappointing income in revenue from tolls. Marlio has estimated that it was not until 1923 that a profit began to be shown (which he defines as a surplus of revenue over expenses such as running costs and annual interest on borrowed capital).[5] As late as 1941, practically on the eve of America's entry into the Second World War, the overall balance sheet still showed a deficit.[6]

Of course, it must be borne in mind that the United States has always conceived of the Panama Canal in terms of strategic necessity as much as in those of economic worth. Financial profit has never been an overriding consideration. In fact, the toll rates in force for several decades were lower than those decreed by President Taft in 1912.[7] For the French, on the other hand, the operation would have had to be commercially viable from the outset, and, like Suez, it would have been expected to yield an acceptable return for it shareholders. Given the sad reputation of Panama, it is surely inconceivable to imagine that French investors would have supported it for so long, with no prospect of return in the immediate future. In any case, the issue of a transisthmian canal built and managed by a foreign, i.e. non-U.S., corporation became a hypothetical one as soon as the United States government decided that a speedier and more convenient sea link between East and West coasts than that afforded by Cape Horn was a strategic necessity. Had it failed to obtain rights in Panama, there is no doubt it would have turned to Nicaragua leaving the Compagnie Nouvelle in possession of an exceedingly costly and non-disposable white elephant. For despite all that adverse publicity disseminated by Cromwell and Bunau-Varilla in their feud with Morgan's rival conception, one fact remains – Nicaragua did not suffer from insuperable disadvantages. In might have taken the Americans an additional five or six years to build there because the canal would have been longer, but they could have done it, and at a price not significantly greater than for Panama, as a glance at I.C.C. estimates reveals. Indeed, in one respect, a Nicaraguan canal would have been superior in that it would have provided a shorter passage between the Pacific west coast and the Atlantic and Gulf ports.

It was Cromwell, the *enfant terrible* of the New Company,

who saw the dangers that Nicaragua posed sooner and more clearly than anyone else associated with the French concern. This is not to disparage Bunau-Varilla's role which was clearly of major importance especially in the latter stages of negotiations among the U.S., Colombia and the French. But is must be emphasised that the veteran engineer was still agitating for a canal under New Company control as late as 1901. By then, three years had elapsed since the American government had shown an interest in the Company's concession. Not only was Cromwell convinced that his countrymen were intent on building a canal, he knew that they, and they alone, had the wherewithal to finish the task. Hence his curious ploy to organise a company in New Jersey in 1899. This was designed to circumvent the technicality in the various concession treaties by which the French were effectively restrained from selling out to a foreign power. The fate of that particular project did not deter him in the least. When he returned to direct the campaign in January 1902, he continued to work on the premise that his employer could not complete a canal under any condition; and this included withdrawal of the American offer.

There is no denying that he manipulated successive Colombian ministers to Washington for his purposes. It is true that he never expressed outright contempt for their capabilities in the manner of Roosevelt; but he used first Silva and then Concha and latterly Herran to conclude agreements whose concealed intent was to safeguard the French and the monies coming to them. When the Colombians baulked at ratifying treaties which they considered unsatisfactory, Cromwell achieved his supreme triumph by enlisting the support of the Roosevelt administration to defend the interests of his foreign client. Colombia was understandably bewildered and dismayed by such intervention when she was trying to reach an understanding with her own concessionary. Her politicians could see no good reason why Washington should concern itself with problems which the Compagnie Nouvelle alone should have to solve. It would not make the slightest difference to the United States whatever proportion of the forty million dollars was surrendered by it. As matters stood in 1903, it was felt reasonable to assume that the Americans would desire good relations with the Republic as a prerequisite to a canal treaty. Instead, the Colombians were forced to witness the amputation of Panama. What made the experience doubly bitter was the fact that it was achieved not by the disgruntled local population alone but with the overt support of the U.S. naval and military as well as the connivance of a paid and unpaid agent of the Compagnie Nouvelle. In this respect, Colombia was one of the first Latin American states to feel the impact of 'big stick' diplomacy.[8]

Cromwell's part in the events leading to the Panamanian revolution was not in the least damaging to his career. His appetite for intrigue had merely been whetted, and he was soon serving his government in another capacity. The Roosevelt administration was anxious to obtain complete control of the Panama Railroad Company and its subsidiary steamship line, and so he was asked by William Howard Taft to track down the balance of their shares that had not been bought by de Lesseps or transferred to the New Company. Later still, he recommended one of his most promising lawyers, John Foster Dulles, to the State Department as a suitable agent for investigating possible subversion in and around the Canal Zone on the eve of the United States' entry into the First World War. But it was in the 'Twenties and 'Thirties that Cromwell applied the lessons of November 1903 with a vengeance. One of his major clients during this period was the United Fruit Company of Boston. The policy of this corporation was to expand in Central and South

America, secure in the knowledge that its privileged position in the economy of the host country would be maintained by the unspoken but real threat of intervention against subversive elements in the U.S.A.

The comparative weakness of the landowning aristocracy in the republic chosen usually decided matters. If it had little popular support and was militarily weak, it looked to the *frutera* and its friends in high places to help it maintain its grip. It was in this way that the United Fruit Company often became a state within a state. By the time Cromwell died, in 1940, it was able to call upon the assistance of the State Department whenever it felt seriously threatened.

Bunau-Varilla's activities in the cause of the Compagnie Nouvelle are more difficult to evaluate. He was its constant critic, and his repeated call for a Panama Canal completed by the French, alone, was both naive and embarrassing. He was full of schemes, providing a plan for the Americans in the early years of their occupation by which a canal with locks could eventually be changed into one at sea level. He was far more effective for the New Company as a diplomat once he had come to accept the inevitability of U.S. ownership. He played a significant role in the fight to have the Spooner amendment accepted by Congress, though here, as elsewhere, his contribution was not as overwhelmingly decisive as he later implied. His best chance to serve the interests of the Company came in September 1903. At that point Cromwell was despairing at ever finding a solution to the impasse which Colombia's rejection of the Hay-Herran Treaty had occasioned. Bunau-Varilla became the link between Panamanian revolutionaries, the Company and the White House, and convinced all three that separation of Panama province was a possibility if his plans were allowed to mature.

If the stockholders of the second company have cause to

be grateful to these two, the creditors of the first are no less in the debt of Gautron and Lemarquis. When they received their commission from the court, there was every reason to suppose that the future held nothing for any of those who had been misguided enough to invest in the de Lesseps fiasco. Monchicourt's efforts to launch a successor had failed, partly because the seamy side of Panama had been exposed at that very moment, deterring prominent financiers like Christophle and Hiélard from obtaining capital, and partly because he had flinched from attacking the powerful beneficiaries of the debacle. The advent of new liquidator and the creation of a mandataire, both tenacious in their pursuit of the *pénalitaires*, gave the legion of bondholders a glimmer of hope. Once the New Company was launched, trouble was far from over. There were several occasions on which the two might have been tempted to capitulate as the sensible way out. In 1899, Bonnardel and his friends seemed determined to sell out at any price. Again, in 1901, Hutin's failure to commit himself to a definite price for the concession and the property provided them with ample reason to put an end to their anxieties. The dispassionate observer would not have judged them ill had they distributed the pathetically few assets then remaining, and allowed the rival concept to triumph. The Enregistrement's formidable claim, coming when total victory seemed to have been won provides yet another instance where resignation to a formidable opponent would have been the less painful course. That they choose to contest and fight for a fair deal is a tribute to their concern for the tens of thousands of investors entrusted to their care. And, despite what hostile parliamentarians might say in the Chamber, there were many among them who were poor, defenceless and dependent on a champion of their cause.

Panama is not a particularly admirable episode in the history of the Third French Republic. It is peopled by the idealist, the ignorant and the villainous. Yet, in the final act of the drama, it did well to produce two men who served the cause of justice well.

Notes

1. In an editorial in *L'Eclair* entitle "La Faillité de Panama."

2. The American canal differs from the New Company's conception in a number of ways. The entrance is at Limon Bay, not Colon, and the ascent from the Atlantic side begins at Gatun. An artificial lake has been formed there and the canal continues at this level through the Gaillard (Culebra) Cut to locks at Pedro Miguel. There, and further on, at Miraflores, the descent is made to the Pacific. All locks are in pairs to allow two-way traffic. As with the French conception, pumps are used to fill the lock chambers: the principle used is that of gravity. Towing locomotives, called mules, pull the ships through these locks.

3. *Op. cit.*, p. 487. Also, David McCullough, *The Path Between the Seas* (New York, 1977), Chap. 16.

4. The bond issue authorised by Congress to cover all costs except payment to the New Company, the Panamamian government and defence and interest charges comprise this amount.

5. Profit and loss on canal operation, 1914-24:

Year	Profit	Loss
1914		11,087,787.36
1915		10,767,097.92
1916		15,360,262.07
1917		11,871,173.98
1918		10,433,292.84
1919		10,628,103.27
1920		8,303,667.47
1921		7,895,927.47
1922		7,141,118.89

1923   210,756.26
1924   6,278,619.88

Source: Louis Marlio, *La véritable histoire de Panama*, p. 85.

6. Mack, op. cit., provides the following summary:

Revenue from tolls	492,532,337.56
Civil revenues	5,804,001.13
Business profits	18,214,738.78
	516,551,117.47
Net expenses	235,452,623.31
Net revenue	281,098,494.16
Interest on capital 3%	316,937,151.32
Deficit	35,838,657.16

(Figures in U.S. dollars)

7. The present rates (1912 equivalents in brackets) are: for laden vessels, 90 cents per ton ($1.20); for unladen 72 cents per ton (72); for warships and other vessels, 50 cents per ton (50 per displacement ton). The difference in money values is very significant, of course.

8. For a contemporary verdict, see *Panama Canal Treaties*, testimony of Abraham F. Lowenthal before Foreign Relations Committee, 1977 where he opined: "United States relations with Panama, and especially the status of the Canal Zone itself, have long symbolised, for many in Latin America, all that was regrettable about some aspects of the so-called "special relationship" with the United States." The Carter-Torrijos Treaty of October 14, 1977 seeks to redress the balance, not only by granting the Republic of Panama complete control of the Canal by the year 2000, but by increasing substantially, the annual payment to the Panamanian government. The new formula takes into account the rise in the U.S. cost of living.

APPENDICES

A. (1) Proposed route of the New Company's canal

   (2) The Panama Canal route with completed canal (1914)

B. (1) Final balance sheet of the Compagnie Universelle

   (2) Credit payments made to bondholders of the Compagnie Universelle

C.   A note on the distribution of New Company assets.

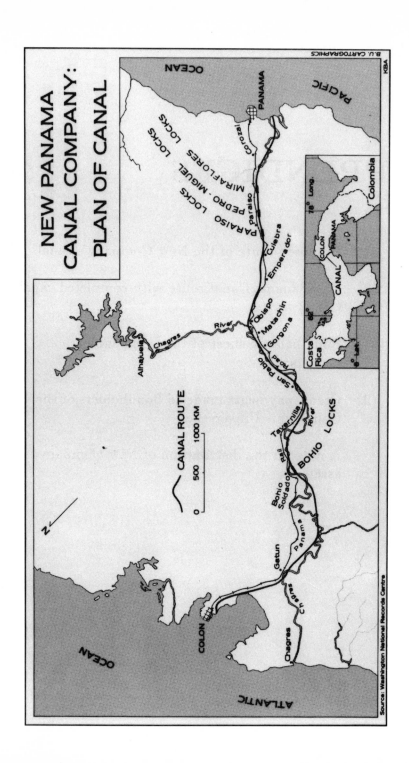

NEW PANAMA
CANAL COMPANY:
PLAN OF CANAL

CANAL ROUTE

0   500   1000 KM

OCEAN

PANAMA

PACIFIC

Corozal

Paraiso
PEDRO - MIGUEL LOCKS
MIRAFLORES LOCKS
PARAISO LOCKS

Culebra

Emperador

Obispo
Matachin
Gorgona

San Pablo Road

Chagres River

Alhajuela

Tavernilla

BOHIO LOCKS

Bohio
Soldado Rio

Panama

Gatun

Chagres

Chagres

COLON

ATLANTIC

OCEAN

Colombia

78° Long.

COLON

PANAMA

CANAL

Costa
Rica

PANAMA

B.U. CARTOGRAPHICS

KBA

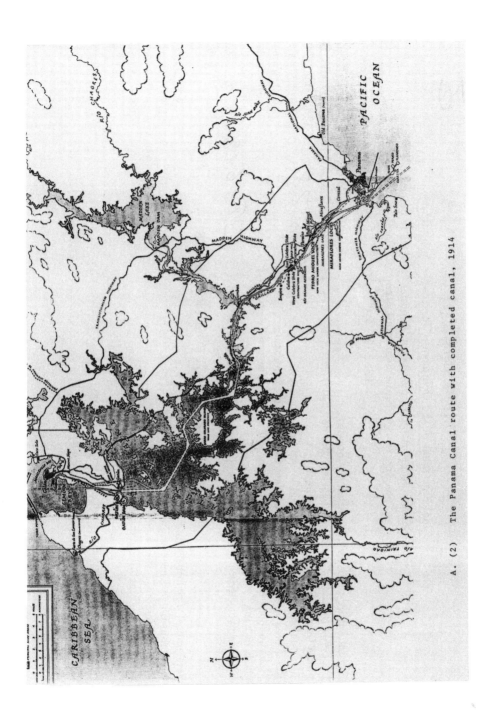

A. (2)   The Panama Canal route with completed canal, 1914

APPENDIX B (1)

Final Statement of the Compagnie Universelle, in liquidation

(Source: Rapport final presente au Tribunal Civil de la Seine,
par M. Georges-Emile Lemarquis, June 30, 1908)

ASSETS

Revenue from prize money on lottery bonds	4,329,180.10
Proceeds from sale of unissued lottery bonds (1905)	67,013,400.00
Share from U.S. concession payment	128,600,000.00
Accumulated interest on disposable capital	3,014,574.65
Recovered in legal actions after New Company incorporation	519,973.84
Miscellaneous sums received, including sale of Cie, Universelle property	55,774.29
Cash in bank	868,814.05
Dividends cashed on New Company stock	20,500,063.40
	224,901,780.33

LIABILITIES & BONDHOLDERS' ASSETS

Settlement of Schubert and Icaza claims	335,495.35
Contribution to Enregistrement	1,499,490.83
Paid to Societe Civile for bond issue of 1905	27,139,384.50
Miscellaneous, including salaries, rent and legal costs	2,434,880.86
	31,409,251.54
First distribution (paid in cash and lottery bonds)	177,925,589.16
Second distribution (paid entirely in cash)	15,566,939.63
	224,901,780.33

APPENDIX B (2)

Credit payments to bondholders

Date & type of bond offered	Par value	Subscription Price	Number Subscribed	Company's Receipts	% of offer subscribed	Amount admitted for credit	First Dis-tribution	Second*	Total credit* received per bond
Sept. '82 5% ord.	500	437.50	250,000	109,375,000	100% +	811.11	81.11	8.27	98.38
Oct. '83 3% ord.	500	285.00	651,439	171,000,000	100% +	544.33	54.43	5.54	59.97
Sept. '84 4% ord.	500	333.00	318,245	105,975,585	82.2%	618.37	61.83	6.30	68.13
Aug. '86 6% ord.	1,000	450.00	458,802	206,460,900	91.8%	1002.78	100.27	10.23	110.50
July '87 6% ord.	1,000	440.00	258,887	113,910,280	51.8%	932.90	93.29	9.51	102.80
Mar. '88 3% ord.	1.000	460.00 including 70.28 amortization	89,890	35,031,931	25.7%	702.63	70.26	7.17	77.43
June '88	400	360.00 including 60.00 prize /amort.	812,662 as of 30 June 1888	243,798,600	40.6%	532.17	53.21	5.42	58.63

* Only to those benefiting from Flandin Law exemption.

APPENDIX C

A note on the distribution of the New Company's assets after 1904 sale of concession to the United States

One of the most serious of all the gaps in documentation relating to the Compagnie Nouvelle is that of a detailed financial statement covering the years from 1904 to 1908. The few statistics which follow have had to be culled from various newspapers and journals of the period and give a very incomplete picture.

Immediately after receipt of its share of the American government payment of 77,400,000 francs, in May 1904, the gross assets of the Company stood at 92,483,039 francs. From this, a number of deductions had to be made during the next four years. These may be summarised as follows:

Commission to J.-P. Morgan & Co.	183,855.00
Settlement of Sullivan & Cromwell action	1,173,808.95
Contribution to l'Enregistrement	4,806,831.50
Salaries	632,683.59
General administrative expenses	1,543,714.55
	8,340,165.59

There remained 84,142,873 francs 41 to be distributed among the holders of 650,000 shares. The question of the identities of those who actually surrendered the stock certificates remains a mystery. The shares had originally been registered so that transactions in them could be traced, in order to discourage speculation. But, by May 1904, they had become bearer stock, and the Crédit Lyonnais, for example, disposed of its holding of 40,000 for 5,000,000 francs in that same year (see Bouvier, *Les Bonnardels*, p. 203, footnote 5). As was noted, in Chapter 9, there were alleged irregularities in the New York *World* as early as January of 1904. It was charged that brokers in Paris and New York had bought stock and bonds in the respective canal companies, following rejection of the Hay-Herran Treaty. They had seen their clients deliberately connive at revolution in Panama. They had done this because they were determined that there would be no siphoning off of monies by the Colombian government, and they had calculated to a nicety what they would receive.

These allegations were regarded, at the time, as merely another gambit by the anti-Panama faction. Then, in 1906, the redoubtable Senator Morgan raised them anew during hearings of a Senate committee on interoceanic canals at which Cromwell had been testifying. To Morgan's insinuations that fraud had been committed, Cromwell retorted that he knew nothing of how the assets had been distributed, and that it need not trouble the Senate. A further two years elapsed before a third attempt was made to find an answer, this time on the eve of an American presidential election. On October 3, 1908, one month before polling was due to take place, Joseph Pulitzer, the 'muck raking' editor of the anti-Panama *World*, tried to involve the Republican candidate, William Howard Taft, in the affair. Pulitzer alleged that Cromwell, Bunau-Varilla and some of their friends had formed a syndicate in 1903, just prior to the Panamanian uprising. Among those indiced to join with Charles P. Taft, a brother of the presidential nominee, and Douglas Robinson, Roosevelt's son-in-law. Its purpose was to buy securities in both French canal companies during a period when Colombia's attitude had caused the stock to slump in value. The November revolution (in which the syndicate had naturally had a hand) resulted in a sharp upsurge in their price. By this means, a profit of many millions had been obtained.

Both Cromwell and Bunau-Varilla vehemently denied the

charge. However, Roosevelt went further and tried to discover the answer to the riddle of who had benefited from the forty million dollars. He was no more successful in his quest than the *World* which, having the same idea, had sent an investigator to Paris to unearth the elusive proof. Through Charlton, a law officer with the Bureau of Insular Affairs and Rogers, general counsel for the I.C.C., Roosevelt learnt that the stockholders' lists of the Compagnie Nouvelle had not been surrendered in 1904, with the other archival material. Rogers' letter concluded:

> Nor, in my opinion, did any obligation rest with the government of the United States, or upon its representatives, to follow the application of the fund paid as purchase money to the French owners of property and rights in the Panama Canal Companies, otherwise than was agreed in the document which is a matter of public record (i.e. the article of conveyance).
>
> Therefore, the fact being that the documents mentioned, both in the letter of the President to you, in your letter to me, and in rumors current in the public press, not now being in the hands of the Isthmian Canal Commission, so far as records show at the present time, or when I made my examination in May 1905, and such documents not being necessary to a complete conveyance,... no inference critical of the action of the United States can be predicated upon their absence; and if the same are in existence at all, they must be in the hands which would properly have held them, namely in the records in possession of the liquidator of the old French canal company, and the offices of the new French canal company.[1]

The information the *World* obtained from its Parisian source was no more illuminating:

> There is nothing to show the names of the owners of the stock at the time of liquidation of the (New) Company, and who actually received the money, or the proportions in which it was paid. The liquidation of the New Company finally closed its doors on June 30 last, and the offices of the liquidator were shut. No one is there to give the slightest information concerning it, although questions are still arising necessitating information.[2]

This did not deter Roosevelt; and he prepared to bring a libel action against Pulitzer and his paper, making the U.S. government the plaintiff. The *World*, for its part, sent agents to Bogota, Paris and Panama in renewed efforts to find substantiating evidence. It appears that nothing novel or revealing came to light. However, in the event, the indictment was rejected, and the libel – if indeed it was such – went unpunished.

It is, in view of the fact that such modest gains were made, even after the triumph of the pro-Panama factions, highly unlikely that financiers of the calibre supposedly involved would have been attracted to such speculative stock. Even so, the verdict on whether revolution and speculation were linked must be the Scots one of 'not proven'.

Bibliography

MANUSCRIPT SOURCES

France: Paris.

Archives Nationales, 7 AQ 1 – 45.

————. F30 394 – 96.

United States of America: Washington, D.C.

Library of Congress. Bunau-Varilla Papers.

————. U.S. Department of State: Dispatches from Columbia, Vols. 58-60: Dispatches from Panama, Vol. 1: Instructions to Colombia, Vol. 19: Instructions to Panama, Vol. 1.

National Archives. Cartographical Records of the Panama Canal.

Federal Records Center Number One (Suitland, Maryland). Record Group 185/1, French records. 185/37, Records of the Panama Railroad Company.

Canal Zone: Balboa Heights.

Canal Zone Library CZL 2.

PRINTED SOURCES

France: Paris.

Bibliothèque Nationale. Rapports sur les études de la Commission Internationale d'Exploration de l'Ishtme américain, par MM. Lucien N.-B. Wyse. Armand Reclus et P. Sosa, 1879.

————. Le Canal de Panama. L'Isthme américain. Explorations, négoçiations, état des travaux, par M. Lucien N.-B. Wyse, 1886.

————. Commission d'enquête de 1892. Rapport général de M. Vallé, et rapports partiels de MM. Dupuy-Dutemps, de Villebois-Mareuil, Gauthier de Clagny, Bory, Bertrand, Vallé et Guillemet.

————. des Députés: 5e législature, session de 1893. No. 2921. Rapport fait au nom de la commission d'enquête chargée de faire la lumière sur les allégations portées a la Tribune, à l'occasion des affaires de Panama. Rapport général par M. Ernest Vallé. Annexe No. 1 au rapport général: dépositions. Annexe No. 2 au rapport général: rapport de M. Flory, rapport de M. Rousseau: annexe au rapport de M. Flory. 1893.

————. Commission d'enquête de 1897. Tome 1. Rapport général de M. Vallé et rapports spéciaux de MM. Guillemet, Bienvenu, Martin, de Ramel, Viviani, Samary, de la Noue, de Casablanca, Claport. Tome II. Rapport de M. Rouanet sur les dossiers du Panama (scelles Imbert; instructions Franqueville, etc.), No. 2942. 1898.

————. Chambre des Députés: 6e législature, session de 1898. No. 2992. Rapport général fair au nom de la commission d'enquête sur les affaires de Panama par M. E. Vallé, député. 1898.

United States of America: Washington, D.C.

Library of Congress Congressional Record, 54 Cong., 2 Sess. to 63 Cong., 1 Sess..

————. Diplomatic History of the Panama Canal. Sen. Doc. No. 474 (1914), 63 Cong., 2 Sess..

————. 54 Cong., 1 Sess., House Doc. No. 279.

————. 55 Cong., 3 Sess., Sen. Doc. No. 26.

————. 56 Cong., 1 Sess., Sen. Doc. No. 50.

————. 56 Cong., 1 Sess., Sen. Doc. No. 161.

. 56 Cong., 1 Sess., Sen. Doc. No. 237.

. 56 Cong., 1 Sess., Sen. Doc. No. 188.

————. 56 Cong., 1 Sess., Sen. Doc. No. 268.

————. Cong., 1 Sess., Sen. Doc. No. 114.

————. 56 Cong., 1 Sess., House Report No. 351 (Hepburn Report).

———. 56 Cong., 2 Sess., Sen. Doc. No. 5 (I.C.C. Preliminary Report)

———. 57 Cong., 1 Sess., Sen. Doc. No. 54 (I.C.C. Report, 1899-1901 – reproduced with maps as

———. Sen. Doc. No. 222, 58 Cong., 2 Sess.).

———. 57 Cong., 1 Sess., Sen. Doc. No. 123 (I.C.C. supplementary report).

———. 57 Cong., 1 Sess., Sen. Report. Doc. No. 1.

———. 57 Cong., 1 Sess., Sen. Report. Doc. No. 783.

———. 59 Cong., 1 Sess., Sen. Doc. No. 457.

. 59 Cong., 1 Sess., Sen. Doc. No. 474.

. Senate Committee on Interoceanic Canals. Hearings on Bill (H. 3110), 11 January – 10 March 1902.

———. 60 Cong., 2 Sess., Sen. Doc. No. 589.

———. House of Representatives Committee on Foreign Affairs. Hearings on the Rainey Resolution. The Story of Panama.

———. Isthmian Canal Commission: Official Handbook of the Panama Canal (2nd., 3rd., and 4th. editions).

———. Justice Department. Official Opinions of the Attorney-Generals of the United States: Panama Canal Title. 1902.

———. Richardson, James D. A compilation of the Messages and Papers of the Presidents, 1789-1908. New York, 1909.

———. State Department. Interoceanic Canal Congress held at Paris, May 1879. Instructions to Rear Admiral Daniel Ammen and civil engineers A.G. Menocal & etc., U.S. Navy delegates on the part of the United States, and reports of the proceedings of the Congress, 1879.

BOOKS AND PAMPHLETS

Abbot, Willis John. *Panama and the canal.* The story of its achievement, its problems, and its prospects. New York, 1914.

Arias, Harmodio. *The Panama Canal: a study in international law and diplomacy.* London, 1911.

Bishop, Joseph Bucklin. *The Panama Gateway.* New York, 1913.

Bouvier, Jean. *Les deux scandales de Panama.* Paris, 19

Bressolles, Paul. *Liquidation de la compagnie de Panama: commentaire theorique et practique de la loi du 1er juillet 1893.* Paris, 1894.

Brogan, D.W. *The Development of Modern France, 1870-1939.* London, 1940.

Bryce, James. *South America. Observations and Impressions.* New York and London, 1912.

Bunau-Varilla, Philippe. *Panama. Le passé – le présent – l'avenir.* Paris, 1892.

————. *Panama. Le trafic.* Paris, 1892.

————. *Nicaragua or Panama?* New York, 1902.

————. *Trois appels à la France pour sauver l'oeuvre de Panama.* Paris, 1906.

————. *Statement on behalf of Historical truth.* Washington, 1912.

————. *Panama, la création, la déstruction, la resurrection.* Paris, 1913.

————. *De Panama à Verdun. Mes combats pour la France.* Paris, 1937.

Cameron, Rondo E. *France and the Economic Development of Europe, 1800-1914.* Princeton, 1961.

Campbell, A.E. *Great Britain and the United States, 1895-1903.* London, 1960.

Chidsey, Donald Bar. *The Panama Canal.* New York, 1970.

Combe, Paul. *Niveau de vie et progrès technique en France, 1860-1939.* Paris, 1956.

Cornish, Vaughan. *The Panama Canal and its Makers.* London, 1909.

Courau, Robert. *Ferdinand de Lesseps.* Paris, 1932.

Croly, Herbert. *Marcus Alonzo Hanna. His Life and Work.* New York, 1912.

Cowles, Anna Roosevelt (ed.). *Letters from Theodore Roosevelt to Anna Roosevelt Cowles, 1870-1918.* New York and London, 1924.

Dansette, Adrien. *Les Affaires de Panama*. Paris, 1934.

——. *Le Boulangisme, 1886-90*. Paris, 1938.

Drumont, Edouard. *La dernière bataille*. Paris, 1890.

——. *De l'ordre, de la boue, du sang*. Paris, 1896.

DuVal, Miles P. (Jnr.). *Cadiz to Cathay*. Stanford and London, 1940.

Edgar-Bonnet, G. and Lucas, Louis. *Le Canal de Panama*. Paris, 1929.

Famin, Etienne. *Mission aux Antilles*. Paris, 1896.

Floridian, L.-M. *Les coulisses du Panama*. Paris, 1891.

Goguel, F. *La politique des partis sous la IIIè République, 1871-1939*. Paris, 1946 (2 vols.).

Grodinsky, Jules. *Transcontinental Railway Strategy: 1869-93*. Philadelphia, 1962.

Haskin, Frederic J. *The Panama Canal*. New York, 1914.

Hammond, R. and Lewin, C.J. *The Panama Canal*. London, 1966.

Henao, Jesus Maria and Arrubla, Gerardo. *A History of Colombia* (trans. by J. Fred Rippy). Chapel Hill, N.C., 1938.

Herring, Hubert. *A History of Latin America*. New York, 1962.

Huberich, Charles Henry. *The trans-isthmian canal: a study in American diplomatic history, 1825-1904*. Austin, Texas, 1904.

Johnson, W.F. *Four Centuries of the Panama Canal*. New York, 1906.

Lesseps, Ferdinand de. *Souvenirs de quarante ans* (trans. by C.B. Pitman-Bridier). London, 1900.

Le Batut, Guy de. *Panama*. Paris, 1931.

Loewel, Pierre. *Le Canal de Panama: étude historique politique et financière*. Paris, 1913.

Mack, Gerstle. *The Land Divided*. New York, 1944.

Marlic, Louis. *La véritable histoire de Panama*. Paris, 1932.

McCullough, David. *The Path Between The Seas*. New York, 1977.

Miner, Dwight C. *The Fight for the Panama Route.* New York, 1940.

Nelson, Wolfred. *Mes cinq ans à Panama.* Paris, 1890.

Paponot, Felix. *Le canal de Panama. Étude rétrospective, historique et technique. Solution rationelle pour l'achèvement gradual de l'oeuvre, sans augmenter la dette.* Paris, 1890.

Pensa, Henri. *La République et le Canal.* Paris, 1906.

Pepperman, Walter Leon. *Who built the Panama Canal?* New York, 1915.

Parks, E.T. *Colombia and the United States, 1765-1934.* Durham, N.C., 1935.

Porter, Charles W. *The career of Théophile Delcassé.* Philadelphia, 1936.

Sautereau, Gustave. *Commentaires sur Panama. Notes et documents présentés à la commission d'enquête parlementaire.* Paris, 1893.

Roosevelt, Theodore. *An Autobiography.* New York, 1920.

Sibert, W.L. and Stevens, J.W. *The Construction of the Panama Canal.* New York, 1915.

Siegfried, André. *Suez, Panama et les routes maritimes.* Paris, 1940.

Simon, Maron J. *The Panama Affair.* New York, 1971.

Soulier, A. *L'instabilité ministérielle sous la Troisième République, 1871-1939.* Paris, 1939.

Thayer, William Roscoe. *The Life and Letters of John Hay.* London and New York, 1916. 2 vols.

Whitaker, A.P. *The United States and South America: the Northern Republics.* Cambridge, Mass., 1948.

Williams, Mary Wilhelmine. *Anglo-American isthmian diplomacy, 1815-1915.* Washington and London, 1916.

Wyse, Lucien N.-B. *Le rapt de Panama. L'abandon du canal aux Etats-Unis. Protestations de M. Lucien N.-B. Wyse et plaidoiries de M. Georges Guillaumin.* Toulon, 1904.

Zevaes, Alexandre Bourson. *Le scandale de Panama.* Paris, 1931.

MISCELLANEOUS

Dictionnaire des Parlementaires françaises, 1889-1940, compiled under the direction of M. Jean Jolly, archivist of the National Assembly. Vols. 1-6.

ARTICLES AND PERIODICALS

Abbot, Henry Larcom. "The best isthmian canal" in *Atlantic Monthly*, Vol. 86, No. 518, December 1900.

—————. "The new Panama canal" in *Forum*, Vol. 26, No. 3, November 1898.

—————. "The present status of the Panama Canal" in *Engineering News*, Vol. 40, No. 14, 6 October 1898.

—————. "The solution of the isthmian canal problem" in *Engineering Magazine*, Vol. 26, No. 4, January 1904.

Ameringer, Charles D. "The Panama Canal Lobby of Philippe Bunau-Varilla and William Nelson Cromwell" in *American Historical Review*, Vol. LXVIII, January 1963.

—————. "Ohio and the Panama Canal" in *Ohio History*, Vol. 74, No. 1, Winter 1965.

—————. "Philippe Bunau-Varilla: New Light on the Panama Canal Treaty" in *Hispanic American Historical Review*, Vol. XLVI, No. 1, February 1966.

—————. "Bunau-Varilla, Russia and the Panama Canal" in *Journal of Inter-American Studies and World Affairs*, Vol. XII, No. 3, July 1970.

Ammen, Daniel. "Recollections of the Panama Canal Congress" in *North American*, Vol. 156, February 1893.

Bonsal, S. "The French Republic: Panama Scandal" in *Illustrated Harper's Weekly*, Vol. 37, 7 January 1893.

Bigelow, Poultney. "Our mismanagement at Panama" in *The Independent*, Vol. 60, No. 2979, No. 4, January 1906.

Bouvier, Jean. "Une dynastie d'affaires lyonnaise aux XIXe siècle: les Bonnardels" in *Revue d'Histoire moderne et contemporaine*, Vol. 2, 1955.

Brainard, F.R. "Panama and Nicaraguan Canals" in *Scientific American*, Vol. 68, February 1893.

Bunau-Varilla, Philippe. "Nicaragua or Panama?" in *Scientific American*, Vol. 52, December 1901.

————. "La question de Panama" in *La Nouvelle Revue*, Vol. 27 (new series), 15 April 1904.

Burlingame, Roger. "The 'great' Frenchman. A new interpretation of Ferdinand de Lesseps and the Panama Scandal" in *Scribner's Magazine*, Vol. 94, No. 4, October 1933.

Burr, W.H. "The Republic of Panama" in *National Geographical Magazine*, Vol. 15, No. 2, February 1904.

Chaloner, W.H. "The Birth of the Panama Canal" in *History Today*, Vol. 9, No. 7, July 1959.

Chanel, E. "Les Etats-Unis et le traité Hay-Pauncefote" in *Revue française de l'Etranger et des Colonies et Exploration*, Vol. 26, No. 268, April 1901.

Clark, John Maurice. "The Panama Canal and the railroads" in *Commercial and Financial Chronicle* (Panama-Pacific Section), 28 November 1914.

Cornish, Vaughan. "The Panama Canal in 1908" in *Geographical Journal*, Vol. 33, No. 2, February 1909.

Cullom, Shelby Moore. "The Panama Situation" in *Independent*, Vol. 55, No. 2869, 26 November 1903.

Daggett, Stuart. "The Panama Canal and transcontinental railroad rates" in *Journal of Political Economy*, Vol. 23, No. 10, December 1915.

Dennis, William Cullen "The Panama Situation in the light of International Law" in *American Law Register*, Vol. 43 (new series), No. 5, May 1904.

Edgar-Bonnet, G. "Ferdinand de Lesseps et les Etats-Unis" in *Revue d'Histoire diplomatique*, Vol. 69, No. 4, 1956.

Ford, W.C. "Commercial Aspects of the Panama Canal" in *Harper's Magazine*, Vol. 96, April 1898.

Godkin, E.L. "Panama Corruption Fiend" in *The Nation*, Vol. 36, December 1892.

Gordy, J.F. "The ethics of the Panama case" in *Forum*, Vol. 36, No. 1.

Guyot, Y. "Où allons-nous?" in *Nineteenth Century*, Vol. 33, January 1893.

Haupt, Lewis Muhlenberg. "National influence and the isthmian canal" in *Engineering Magazine*, Vol. 15, No. 4, July 1898.

————. "Why is an isthmian canal not built?" in *North American Review*, Vol. 175, No. 548, July 1902.

Hazeltine, Mayo W. "The proposed Hay-Pauncefote treaty" in *North American Review*, Vol. 170, No. 520, November 1954.

Huberich, Charles Henry. "Le canal transatlantique" in *Revue du Droit Public*, Vol. 19, No. 2, March-April 1903.

Hyde, Charles Cheney. "The isthmian canal treaty" in *Harvard Law Review*, Vol. 15, No. 9, May 1902.

Johnson, Willis Fletcher. "Justice and equity in Panama" in *Forum*, Vol. 36, No. 1, July 1904.

Keasby, Lindley Miller. "The national canal policy" in *American Historical Association Annual Report* (1902), Vol. 1, pp. 275-88.

————. "The terms and tenor of the Clayton-Bulwer Treaty" in *American Academy of Political and Social Science Annals*, Vol. 14, No. 3, November 1899.

Lambert, E. "Panama, the story of a Colossal Bubble" in *Forum*, Vol. 15, No. 9, March 1893.

Latané, John Holladay. "The effects of the Panama Canal on our relations with Latin America" in *American Academy of Political and Social Science Annals*, Vol. 54, July 1914.

Lefebure, Paul. "A la conquête d'un isthme" in *Annales des Sciences Politiques*, Vol. 16, July and September 1901.

Le Normand, Robert G. "Panama et Nicaragua" in *Revue des Revues*, Série 3, Vol. 29, 15 June 1899.

Mahan, Alfred Thayer. "Was Panama 'A Chapter of National Dishonour'?" in *North American Review*, Vol. 196, No. 683, October 1912.

Marvaud, Angel. "Le canal de Panama et les intérêts français" in *Questions diplomatiques et Coloniales*, Vol. 38, No. 417, 1 July 1914.

Menocal, Ancieto G. "The Panama Canal" in *American Society of Civil Engineers Proceedings: Papers and Discussions*, Vol. 32, No. 2, February 1906.

Morales, Eusebio A. "The Political and Economical Situation of Colombia" in *North American Review*, Vol. 175, No. 547, June 1902.

Metford, J.C.J. "The Background to Panama" in *International Affairs*, Vol. 40, No. 2, April 1964.

Moore, John Bassett. "The inter-oceanic canal and the Hay-Pauncefote treaty" in *New York Times*, 4 March 1900.

Muhleman, Maurice L. "The Panama Canal payment" in *Journal of Political Economy*, Vol. 12, No. 4, September 1904.

Ogden, R. "Possibilities of a Panama Canal" in *The Nation*, Vol. 56, March 1893.

Perez, Raul. "A Colombian view of the Panama canal question" in *North American Review*, Vol. 177, No. 560, July 1903.

Pierson, William. "The political influence of an inter-oceanic canal, Whatley 1826-1926" in *Hispanic American Historical Review*, Vol. 6, No. 4, November 1926.

Pratt, Julius H. "American business and the Spanish-American War" in *Hispanic American Historical Review*, Vol. 14, February 1934.

Reclus, Armand. "Canal de Panama: Ses origines" in *Géographie*, Vol. 41, No. 1, January 1924.

Roosevelt, Theodore. "How the United States acquired the right to dig the Panama canal" in *Outlook*, Vol. 99, No. 6, 7 October 1911.

Speed, J.G. "The Panama Crisis in France" in *Illustrated Harper's Weekly*, Vol. 36, 2 December 1892.

Smalley, E.V. "A Panama canal scheme" in *Outlook*, Vol. 60, December 1898.

Thayer, William Roscoe. "John Hay and the Panama Republic" in *Harper's Magazine*, Vol. 131, No. 782, July 1915.

Travis, Ira D. "The attitude of the American government towards an interoceanic canal" in *Yale Review*, Vol. 9, February 1901.

Viallate, Achille. "Les Etats-Unis et le canal interocéanique. Un chapitre d'histoire diplomatique" in *Revue Générale de Droit International Public*, Année 10, No. 1, January-February 1903.

Walker, Aldace F. "The preliminary report of the Isthmian Canal Commission" in *Forum*, Vol. 31, No. 2, April 1901.

Wallace, John Findley. "Plain facts about the Panama canal" in *Engineering Magazine*, Vol. 30, No. 6, March 1906.

————. "Preliminary work on the Panama canal" in *Engineering Magazine*, Vol. 30, No. 1, October 1905.

Webster, S. "Diplomacy and the law of isthmian canals" in *Harper's Monthly*, Vol. 87, September 1893.

Wellman, Walter. "The Panama commission and its work" in *American Monthly Review of Reviews*, Vol. 29, No. 4, April 1904.

Woolsey, Theodore S. "Suez and Panama – a parallel" in *American Historical Association Annual Report*, (1902) Vol. 1.

NEWSPAPERS AND JOURNALS

<u>France</u>:

Bulletin du Canal Interocéanique

Le Comptant

Le Compte

Le Droit

L'Eclair

L'Echo de Paris

La Gazette de France

Le Globe

L'Information

Le Jour

La Libre Parole

Le Matin

Le Messager de Paris

La Patrie

Le Petit Parisien

La Revue Economique et Financière

Le Soir

Le Télégraphe

La Vie Financière

United States of America:

New York Daily Tribune

New York Sun

New York Times

New York World

Panama:

El Mercutio

Star and Herald

Colombia:

El Correo Naçional

El Porvenir

Great Britain:

The Times

Index